ROBERT

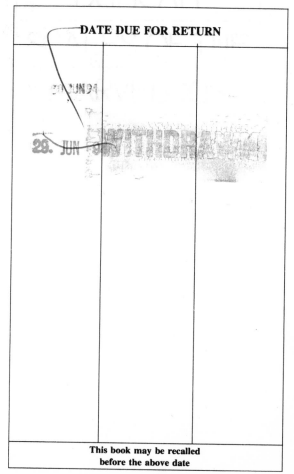

Jess Collins, "Drawing of Robert Duncan"

Robert
6 - 15 - 75

INSIGHTS

WORKING PAPERS IN CONTEMPORARY CRITICISM

ROBERT

DUNCAN

SCALES OF THE

MARVELOUS

Edited with an introduction by Robert J. Bertholf and Ian W. Reid

A NEW DIRECTIONS BOOK

Manufactured in the United States of America
First published as New Directions Paperbook 487 in 1979
Published simultaneously in Canada by George J. McLeod Ltd., Toronto

Library of Congress Cataloging in Publication Data

Main entry under title: c̄ c
Robert Duncan, scales of the marvelous.
    (A New Directions Book)
    (Insights, working papers in contemporary
criticism)
    Bibliography: p. 241
    1. Duncan, Robert Edward, 1919-   ---Addresses,
essays, lectures. 2. Poets, American--20th century--
Biography--Addresses, essays, lectures.
I. Bertholf, Robert J. II. Reid, Ian, 1943-
III. Series.
PS3507.U629Z86   811'.5'4   79-19663
ISBN 0-8112-0735-8 pbk.

New Directions Books are published for James Laughlin
by New Directions Publishing Corporation,
80 Eighth Avenue, New York 10011

CONTENTS

INTRODUCTION

Robert Duncan has declared himself a derivative poet. As such, he projects both the romantic tradition of the theology of poetry and the Poundian disciplines of the intense search for poetic forms. In aligning himself with Pound on one side and Blake on the other, both of whom, like Duncan, claim Dante as a generative center, he combines a multiplicity of poetries into an art of the collage. In announcing the freedom of the imagination, he is apart from the religious orthodoxy and the literary conformities of Eliot; and not dominated by the ego's "I" as the only voice in the poem, he has rejected the confessional of Robert Lowell and his followers. Like Blake, Whitman, and Pound, he has studied out his poetic origins and projected a new poetry where ancient wisdom interacts with the facticity of his life as a lover of words and people. He takes the imagination of the cosmos to be as immediate as the imagination of his household.

But Duncan's position as the heir to the two major literary traditions was not as distinct as it now is. There was a first Berkeley period, where he entered as a freshman in 1936. Almost immediately there was a circle of friends and writers, which established a pattern and introduced another form of a tradition, that of living and writing in a community of poets. Sanders Russell was one of his first masters; and then there were the contemporaries, Pauline Kael, Virginia Admiral and Mary Fabilli. In this early period he discovered Ezra Pound and Gertrude Stein, read D.H. Lawrence and Edith Sitwell. In 1938 Duncan went East, and then in New York City came into the literary circle around Anaïs Nin, which included Henry Miller, Kenneth Patchen and George Barker. It was a world of high literary enterprise and intense psychological probings where the fundamentals of Freud were actualities of daily experience.

In 1946 he returned to Berkeley, via Healdsburg and Treesbark. Here again there was a literary community. Jack Spicer, Robin Blaser, and most of all, Kenneth Rexroth, as the leader of the San Francisco literary scene, came into his circle. At this point he was not a fledgling poet, but an experienced and published one who had been tempered by the literary world of New York City; so the appearance of the first book, Heavenly City Earthly City (1947), was a fulfillment and not a bold beginning. In the next year he wrote "Medieval Scenes," a serial poem which was completed in each part (cf. a "serial movie") but all the parts rounding a whole **structure**. And then there was **"The Venice Poem,"** a long poem which took the analogy of the symphonic sonata as its informing structure and enacted the search and longing for human love. In this second Berkeley period Duncan edited "The Berkeley Miscellany Editions," at first to get Mary Fabili's work into print, but then to publish his book Poems 1948-49 (1949).

"Medieval Scenes" and "The Venice Poem" were written before Charles Olson and his energies of "Projective Verse" entered Duncan's world. The appearance of Olson's poetics came in as a confirmation of his derivation from Pound, and as the start of a rich poetic community that would include, among others, Robert Creeley, Denise Levertov and Paul Blackburn. But in addition to the activity of the community (often alive in long letters), in January 1951 he and Jess Collins began a domestic life together that has been a foundation of Duncan's progress as a love poet. With the domestic life came a period of great activity. The illuminated manuscript of A Book of Resemblances: Poems 1950-1953 was completed, though not published until 1966, and there was the year-long period of writing imitations of Gertrude Stein, later published, in part, in Writing Writing (1964). The poems from the years 1949-1950 were published in 1955, with Jess's collages, as Cae - sar's Gate, and the first book to be conceived as a whole book, Letters, was printed in 1958.

Duncan and Jess spent the period from March 1955 to April 1956 in Mallorca, and while there the first version of "Often I Am Permitted to Return to a Meadow" was written. This was also a period of reading Blake, Joyce, The Zohar and George MacDonald. Upon returning to the United States, Duncan went to Black Mountain College, where he taught from April 1956 through August 1956. More poems for The Opening of the Field, now conceived of as a whole book growing out of the idea of a field, were written, and the ties with Olson strengthened. When they returned to San Francisco in September 1956, Duncan took up the position of Assistant Director of The Poetry Center at San Francisco State University. He was influential in bringing poets there for readings, and in insisting on the vitality of the poem as a spoken medium. Charles Olson came to read, and to deliver lectures on Whitehead in February 1957, and others: Marianne Moore, Robert

Lowell, Denise Levertov, Randall Jarrell, Richard Wilbur, plus those already part of the poetry scene there, Jack Spicer, Allen Ginsberg, Gregory Corso, Helen Adam, Kenneth Rexroth. Duncan served The Poetry Center until June 1957. After living in the city for about a year, he and Jess moved, for the period March 1958 to March 1961, to Stinson Beach. During this period The Opening of the Field (1960) was printed, as was his play Faust Foutu (1959), under his own imprint, Enkidu Surrogate, and Selected Poems (1959).

In 1960 Duncan began his intensive study of the poet H.D., honoring an affinity going back to 1942 when he began reading the poems in Life and Letters Today that would make up The Walls Do Not Fall. When the next large collection appeared, Roots and Branches (1964), printing poems from 1959-1963, it was clear that he had entered a practice of poetry which allowed diverse poetic forms, and far from being pretentiously learned, the poems were studied, in the sense that he studied out and knew the passages of his poetic life, and how that life manifests itself in the medium of its informing subject matter. There were poems like "Apprehensions" that reworked the symphonic structure of "The Venice Poem," the continuation of the open sequence "Structures of Rime," which began in The Opening of the Field; and sets of poems--"Variations on Two Dicta of William Blake," and "The Continent" which brought forward the serial form of "Medieval Scenes" into a new realization, again assuming a musical analogue, that finally led to suites of poems, like A Seventeenth Suite (1973), and Dante (1974), taking its lead from Schumann's etudes. In this period also, partly from reviewing his early poetry for "The H.D. Book" and partly from Duncan realizing the potentialities of a form without closure, "The Passages" poems began to arrive, and appeared in the integrated context of Bending the Bow (1968) and Tribunals (1970). In prose, The Truth and Life of Myth in Poetry confirmed that Duncan was fully engaged in mythopoetic generation bringing attunement with the grand poem of the imagination's life.

The essays which follow formulate the double lines of Robert Duncan as a poet working within poetic traditions, and Robert Duncan as a member of a community of fellow poets. Denise Levertov, drawing upon their correspondence, charts the course of a deep and emotive engagement between two poets which began in the early 1950's and lapsed in the turmoil of the Vietnam war. Her testimony is matched by that of Hamilton and Mary Tyler, whose narrative of their life with Duncan gives supporting information about the writing of the early poetry, mainly the poems in The Years As Catches. Joanna and Michael McClure in a similar way talk about Duncan as a teacher of poetry and as a friend whose resources of assistance (along with Jess) reached even to help establish a household. Helen Adam also talks about him as a friend and a poet sincerely dedicated to poetry and open to the world of the mysteries. R.B. Kitaj, the distinguished artist, and Lou Harrison, the equally distinguished musician, both confirm that Duncan has busied himself with painting and music as companion activities.

The personal reminiscences complement the essays which explore the messages of the poems. Three long essays deal with the three major books. Michael Davidson introduces the poems in The Opening of the Field, points out some primary themes and sources as well as offers readings of some of the main poems. Eric Mottram traces out the multiple forms in Roots and Branches, and also gives many readings of poems. Ian Reid, in the third essay, discusses "The Passages" poems in Bending the Bow (and Tribunals and elsewhere) and shows how these poems achieve a structure without closure. With Nathaniel Mackey's essay on A Seventeenth Century Suite and Dante, the discussion reaches to the most recent books. The lines of derivation, again, come into three other essays. Jayne Walker examines Duncan's attachment to the writings of Gertrude Stein, and Don Byrd outlines Duncan's affiliation with Charles Olson and defines their shared point of origin in the poetry and the methodology of Ezra Pound. Then, Mark Johnson and Robert DeMott establish that for Duncan, Whitman is as strong a base for poetry in the American tradition as Dante is in the European tradition. It is left to Séan Golden to outline still another strain of derivation: Celtic materials come into the poems and further exemplify Duncan's sense that the poem operates in many artistic fields. The theme of love enters all these discussions. Thom Gunn, writing about the homoerotic love, clarifies how love pervades the poetry and how central it is to it. In the end, a picture of Duncan's poetry as an intricate grand collage of forms and subjects emerges that confirms his position as an articulate artist of the genuine.*

*A few of Robert Duncan's essays are tentatively scheduled to be collected and published in a single volume by New Directions in the near future. As of this writing, the book is to be titled "Fictive Certainties: Five Essays in Essential Autobiography," and will include the following pieces, with some revisions likely: "Eros," "Rites of Participation," "Occult Matters," "Man's Fulfillment in Order and Strife," and "The Truth and Life of Myth."

Abbreviations: (for full bibliographical data see selected checklist, where the individual chapters of "The H.D. book" are listed)

A/P	Audit/Poetry
BB	Bending the Bow
BR	A Book of Resemblances
CG	Caesar's Gate
D	Derivations
FD	The First Decade
I	Robert Duncan: An Interview
M	Maps
NAP	The New American Poetry
OF	The Opening of the Field
PNAP	The Poetics of the New American Poetry
RB	Roots and Branches
T	Tribunals
TLM	The Truth and Life of Myth
TOU	"Towards an Open Universe," in Poets on Poetry
YAC	The Years As Catches

IN THE BEGINNING, OR RECATCHING THE YEARS AS CATCHES
with
Robert Duncan, in the years 1942 and 1945-46

Hamilton and Mary Tyler

Most friendships which have lasted for a very long time have in the
recollection a shadowy beginning. It happens that one acquaintance among
many becomes more, and then perhaps still more important, until at last we
think of him or her as that great rarity, a lifelong friend. The origin of
our friendship with Robert had no such slow growth, but was sudden and all
on a spring day, in Berkeley and in 1942. No one can now remember what the
exact date was, or even which night of the week it may have been, but a
month or so after our marriage I came down the usual midnight street after a
shift in the shipyards to find Mary looking for me. She seemed in the best
of spirits and ran down the outside stairway which led from our apartment
above, greeting me with, "Ham! What do you think? Robert has come to live
with us!" I cocked my head back into the collar of my greasy tin-coat and
looked up the wooden stairs. There at the top in the lighted porch was a
young man I had known slightly as Symmes. He was smiling faintly while
waiting to be introduced, or explained. The remainder of that meeting has
slipped away but I think it was easy enough on all sides. Robert was a
"literary" person, with politics on my side of the fence, and he had lost
his room; because of the influx of war workers any room was hard to find.
For a lodging with us Mary had fixed a bed on the small entrance porch
where he had been standing. And so, with no more preparation than that,
began the first of two periods during which Duncan was an everyday member
of our household.

When Mary and I began recalling those times together, I mentioned that
it was remarkable for two people of strong opinions to remain friends for
thirty odd years with never a falling out. She replied, "but there was one

1

evening, just before you were ill, when we were at Duncan's house and the
two of you had a terrible argument; later he wrote you a letter of apology
which I remember."

"Strange," I replied, "there's no letter like that in the Duncan-file
and whatever it was is completely blotted out of mind." But the hands
sometime remember independently what the mind has set aside and they later
reached toward the bookshelves where the volumes of Martin Nilsson on Greek
religion had a place. These works occurred to me because by 1942 Robert
and I had independently arrived at a number of similar views, many of which
were not common currency at the time. Pacifists are always a minority dur-
ing a war but I, through a round in the Spanish Civil War, and Robert partly
from a term in the U.S. Army, were pacifists, and we had added a number of
radical political ideas in a mixture which could have no label. A more un-
usual conjunction of ideas was that we were both "pietistic atheists," al-
though neither of those words are quite right for expressing the position.

Since "piety" as a word has been reduced to tatters, I first picked
up Nilsson's Greek Piety to see if he had explored more primitive views of
the concept, but there was nothing there. Then my hand stopped at a little
paperback called Greek Folk Religion, a compilation from some lectures Nils-
son had delivered in this country. There was already a folded marker in
the book, so it opened naturally to that page, and I picked up at a para-
graph which began with, "The hearth was the center of the house cult and of
the piety of daily life." After noting how bread with a few drops of un-
mixed wine was offered on the hearth, Nilsson concluded, "Thus, the hearth
was sacred, and the daily meal was sacred. The sanctity of the meal found
expression in the rites which accompanied it."

The folded marker was still between my fingers. My next thought was
of the time Robert put his New York railway ticket in a book to mark his
place--a hasty loan was then arranged with his mother and some months later
the railroad made a refund when the ticket showed up in some volume of Mil-
ton's prose. So, I was not surprised at all when the unfolded book-marker
proved to be a letter in Robert's neat handwriting. It was dated May 10,
1962, from San Francisco where he had just heard of my illness and recovery.

Here it was then, the missing letter!

"But my other hope," he writes, "is that I might restore some con-
fidence of friendship." The argument, he states, was "a bogus issue be-
cause at heart I did agree with you, Ham, that there was a human insolence
towards humanity, a practice of hardness of heart in my talk--but accused,
self-defensive, I was ready to defend even hardness of heart, tho there was
no defense in my heart for it. What did I want--to challenge the love in
friendship to allow for my not being entirely lovable?

"Our friendship has always been grounded not only upon good times, the
company we've had since days of The Years As Catches in the food and wine,
the glow of Mozart and Milton, but it was also, is, grounded in a common
view of what humanity might mean--well, and I'd gone against that. I won't
stand by my going against it, and ask forgiveness there." No wonder the
argument had been forgotten.

Reading the letter brought back the room and the time referred to,
but as through a telescope, distantly. There was the room in the small
garden house in Berkeley, with Robert working over his poem. The lines he
refers to are:

> I brood upon these lines of Milton, words
> where there moves such a tide to feed
> my restlessness. Where shall we sometimes meet
> in this dark land no longer having
> darkness in us? And bring our tired souls home
> to linger over wine about a fire, to hear
> with equal grace a little Mozart playd
> within the gloom of an Autumnal room, to linger
> over these last rude & somber moments
> come to rest.   (YAC 37-38)

During the late spring and summer of 1942 Robert had worked on and completed
"An African Elegy" and he spent a great deal of time on "The Years As Cat-
ches," to which the quotation belongs, but he may not have finished it in
Berkeley. In truth it was very difficult to tell just when one of his more
ambitious poems was done, for he rewrote endlessly, never changing just a
single word or phrase, but each time re-sounding the whole poem and rewrit-
ing as he did so. All of us worked at the same round oak table in a small,

book-lined room which was one half of the apartment. The second room was similar, except that the central piece was a phonograph, and there was an old couch and a stuffed chair or two. The reference to Mozart in the stanza quoted is quite literal, as the prize of the record collection was the complete piano concerti of Mozart and these were played that year in all spare time. There had to be time to spare since the old 78 records were short playing and in addition we insisted on using cactus needles; these were better for the records than the steel ones, but they had to be resharpened after every side or two. The "gloom," apart from that shed by the war, came from the dark panelling, the casement windows and the books, all combining to maintain a sort of perpetual twilight indoors.

At the round oak table Duncan would work away at his poem, speaking each line as he wrote it again, but if we were all together he might recite in a stage whisper because his voice, even at that modulation, more than filled the little house. We never made suggestions as a poet is struggling with both the unwinding of his thoughts and of the sound which sheathes the skein of ideas within; the listener at first hears only the sound and then works back to reconstruct the thoughts. It was clear to us then, and I think still true, that these two poems stood well above his own earlier work and that of the other younger poets we knew, and would likely find a lasting place in the field of Anglo-American poetry. We were convinced of this even though none was published then and they would not appear even in little magazines until several years later.

Our days were about equally divided between study and pleasant nonsense, for we were all in our early twenties. The studies were on our own but often had some distant relationship to previous courses at the university. Mary had mastered the knack of getting from one end of a course to the other, but Robert and I shared a common fault--if we had read one example of Milton's prose, such as the assigned Areopagitica, why not then go on to find out what else he had to say on church and state, and then perhaps why? If that approach is multiplied by the number of important writers, past and present, it is easy to drop out of phase with requirements.

That year Milton was to the second room what Mozart was to the other-- the center piece. It was his prose rather than the poetry which held most

attention, while all of the Metaphysical poets of the seventeenth century
were also mined for ideas. Among these poets George Herbert was the one
held most highly by Duncan and it might be said that "The Years As Cat-
ches" resulted from joining Herbert's poetic vision to Milton's prose
rhetoric. Henry Vaughan and his brother Thomas were also important since
they led into the Brothers of the Rosy Cross, and Robert was already begin-
ning to analyse and struggle with the theosophical heritage from his adop-
tive mother and aunt. The mixture of Neo-Platonic and occult thought of
the seventeenth century writers was both a justification for his own herit-
age and a bridge to its re-examination. It is probably important to his
later work that Duncan, because of his theosophical home background, was
never quite within the Christian framework and for that reason his non-
belief was without the emotional charge of those who have rejected a Chris-
tian or Jewish heritage. Furthermore, we were so steeped in seventeenth
century writers that our own thought took on shadings of their values, even
though their beliefs were not accepted in any literal way. The problem
then becomes one of handling "belief" within a larger context, or perhaps
of holding this belief in a gentle suspension of disbelief.

When Duncan in "The Years As Catches" speaks of "His harmony, my
chaos" we sense a reference to Christ, but the cross is quickly lowered to
the level of earthly love:

> His clamorous bright day, see still
> that unbroken rose that broken is
> no other cross than love. (YAC 39)

Although there is an echo from the Brothers of the Rosy Cross, it is human
love at issue and the stanza closes with, "my harmony, His chaos," and we
realize that the god addressed is a Spirit-of-the-Year deity, albeit a year
within another "weary stretch of Christendom." Robert's hymn ends with a
prayer:

> Catch from the years the line of joy,
> impatient & repeated day,

The spirit of this closing has become the god-like personification of our containing reality, which might be called Being--the all encompassing "Other" against and within which the individual lives and works. Robert's work, poetry, is a struggle against this Being, which is also a void,

> where words pass thru their cells,
> where they go utterly, utterd unheard,
> into the ear of eternity. . . . ,   (YAC 30)

as he had written in an earlier poem, but poems can also come back from that void: "they return to the future as phosphorous suns. . ." (YAC 30).

If poetry has this after-glow in the void, then Literature, which is all writing taken together, must also have a luminous existence beyond individual writers, and thus a devotional attitude toward the Order of Literature is perfectly proper. One has taken vows which are strict--honesty in writing, for example, is not merely an ideal, it is an absolute. When Robert acknowledged a debt to St. John of the Cross and to Freud, on the dust jacket of Heavenly City, Earthly City, he was thinking of Freud's work as a means to honesty. While a writer must be honest he is also constantly dealing in fictions, and he often takes ways within a work which are paths independent from his more basic views. What Freud offered in his clear prose, to us then, was a simple and usable model for self-analysis. The Modern Library edition of his basic writings had appeared in 1938 in a volume which began with the "Psychopathology of Everyday Life." It was most intriguing to us, and a kind of revelation, that even typing errors were meaningful. The fact that every action, each spoken phrase, and of course, dreams, could be analyzed and made to tell a different story made a game out of ordinary living.

The game could be played against each other or on one's self, but it was even better if we could persuade some unsuspecting visitor to recount a dream. We would then listen as expectantly as students taking a quiz, each taking account of the gaffes and most of the time we were able to keep a straight face until the unsuspecting dreamer had departed. Then there would be shouts of glee, fist pounding laughter and a reworking or enlargement of the hidden story. Behind the lightheartedness of this kind of Freudian

romp there was also a serious attempt to question each phrase, every spoken
or written line, and every thought. Soon one was immediately aware of all
the secondary levels within any expressed meaning. For that reason alone
Robert could write in "An African Elegy":

> In the groves of Africa from their natural wonder
> the wildebeest, zebra, the okapi, the elephant,
> have entered the marvelous. No greater marvelous
> know I than the mind's
> natural jungle.   (YAC 33)

Toward the fall of 1942 Robert, after buying his second railway ticket,
left for New York. Not very long afterwards Mary and I also left Berkeley
for our first farm, located in Placer County in the foothills of the Sierra
Nevada. There we spent two and a half years clearing fields, planting al-
falfa, gathering in livestock, and enduring poison oak. After one segment
of the war had ended we felt free enough from draft-boards to look for a
new farm in an area more congenial to us. Our dream was the north coastal
area where the climate is mild, except for rains which make the grass grow
tall and thick. Probably Pond Farm was first called to our attention by
William Everson and his friends who were sitting out the war in the Wald-
port, Oregon, camp for conscientious objectors. For some reason word had
circulated there that Pond Farm was a cooperative for artistic people, a
thought which was scarcely the truth, but it was nevertheless a reasonable
dream. What it did have was a well-known European potter and her students,
occasional craftspeople with hopeful pupils. Beyond that there was the
owner, Jane Herr, who sincerely espoused Lawrencian views of no certain
shape.

Pond Farm was perched on a hilltop which was more suitable for crafts
students who summered there than for our herd of cows, but the fragile
arrangement was that we would feed these artisans in summer, then sell
cream to the buttermaker and eggs to the co-op for the remainder of the
year. We had hardly settled into the new life when tangible anticipations
of Robert began to arrive in the form of cartons of books from New York.
A notice and bill came from the county seat, but the cost was well worth
it as the parcels contained the latest little magazine and volumes of

unknown recent poets. Next letters began to arrive, followed by the complete library.

Robert was to make one stop, in Sacramento, before coming on to Pond Farm and while in the capital he was to stay with the aunt who was a devotee of both poetry and the occult. What should have been a simple enough family duty became more complex and before long turned into a family crisis which influenced Robert's next poems and cast a shadow for some distance into his future. The aunt held, among other posts, that of chairwoman of the Sacramento poetry club and, on finding a live poet in her hands, took the reasonable-unreasonable step of arranging for Duncan to address her club members and to read some of his poetry to them. Her next decision, and one much less reasonable, was that Robert should be fitted with a new suit and in general brought into conformity with the image of a poet as conceived by the local club members.

At some point along this dark progress Robert fell into despair, or perhaps terror, and fled. What happened next was off-stage to us, but it seems that the aunt summoned his mother and the two of them then decided that Robert was probably "insane," whatever that might have meant to them, and should be committed to some kind of an asylum for care. As a result Robert arrived at Pond Farm looking back over his shoulder in a high state of excitement, though perfectly reasonable. Mary and I wrote letters assuring his mother that we knew her son well, that he was of sound mind though a poet, and that in any case working on a farm was a far preferable solution to any she had in mind. The two women let matters stand at that and pursued him no farther, but the experience hung over Robert like a fog and it accounts for some of the chilling lines in "The End of the Year," a poem he was working on soon after. In it he writes,

> I have come
> from childhood terror, from a seizure by my mother
> bearing her curse. . . .

or again he refers to,

> that mothering shark in my childhood sea. (YAC 59)

These feelings were not altogether resolved until some twenty years

later in the concluding stanzas of "My Mother Would Be A Falconress," where
the symbolic events of this early time are seen in perspective.

> My mother would be a falconress,
> and even now, years after this,
> when the wounds I left her had surely heald,
> and the woman is dead,
> her fierce eyes closed, and if her heart
> were broken, it is stilld
>
> I would be a falcon and go free.
> I tread her wrist and wear the hood,
> talking to myself, and would draw blood.   (BB 53-54)

*

The daily round of life on a farm was not new to Robert as he had lived
and worked on James Cooney's place in Woodstock, New York, in 1939. At Pond
Farm the three of us lived in a converted chicken house which made one side
of a corral where the cattle came up to await feeding and milking. For a
"barn" we had the underside of the high end of the occupied hen house which
projected outward from a steep hillside. After the milking was finished and
the cream separated, the skim-milk was taken back to the hen house where it
was mixed with rolled barley and fed to the hens. One was constantly busy,
but never too busy, with chores of this kind and Robert fitted into them
very well, helping with both the feeding and the milking which was done by
hand.

We had moved to Pond Farm in July of 1945 and Robert probably arrived
in September. After completing the poem "Upon Watching a Storm," which he
brought from the East, Robert began working on "The End of the Year," which
was in part a nature poem where "October's revelry" is seen as "this debacle,
berried and painted." If the outside world of wild nature is a dubious show,
the inner one of farm life is reassuring: "In the early dark we move about
our chores." And afterwards, while listening to a guest read a poem, his
own meditations are,

> We have come safely
> thru a war, and we face
> another war. In the hiatus, momentary & still

> nightly shadow, the cows low and stir
> upon the hill; the generator hums;
> and we, after supper, settle down to rest. . . (YAC 60)

The picture is true enough. During the day there were hundred-pound sacks of oats and mill-feed to be hauled in and stacked, baled hay by the ton to be piled and unpiled, young stock to be fed, eggs to be gathered, and the milking; but after the last cream had trickled from the magic separator and was stored away, there was time for reading and literary talk. The generator which intrudes into that poem--there was no electricity at Pond Farm either--was a dismal engine that chugged and pounded along from dark until the owner chose to turn it off.

Many unknown visitors called or were paraded through our quarters, but old friends also showed up after the long wartime drought. One memorable evening Rexroth and others arrived for a poetry session which began with Kenneth reading a new play by lamp light--the electic generator having broken. Then the younger poets had their turn with Kenneth playing the schoolmaster. Finally, Robert read, concluding with Sitwell's "Serenade: Any Man to Any Woman." That really marked the end of the war for all of us; we were free again, writers were writing and we could be together once more.

Just after the turn of the year on Jan 7th of 1946, which was Duncan's birthday, we found the farm for which Mary and I had been looking. "Treesbank" was a place of eighty acres in a nearly perfect setting, the heart of which was an open space on a gentle slope with deep woods on both sides. Around the house, at the end of a country lane, were twenty five acres of apples and cherries while below these acres hayfields and pastures drifted into a quite valley.

We moved six hundred laying hens in crates, with Robert at the Treesbank end to take care of the eggs which after a day or two had begun to pile up fearfully. Any dirty eggs had to be polished with a sander before they could be packed. Mary and I were still bringing over the cattle in ones and twos in a trailer behind the auto and so were of no help in the egg crisis. When we pulled up to the barn to unload, Robert would be there

sander in hand, trying to catch up, but he was also deep into Dorothy
Richardson at the moment and while we were gone he would have thought of
many things to say. On our arrival there would be a rush of words, too
heavy a hand on the sander, and another squashed egg dripping to the floor.
Somehow, after a terrible week, everything was safely at the new farm and
as the time was spring with the grass lush and green, a routine began to
form again.

Mary was already carrying our daughter Brenda, who would be born on
the second of July, but she too joined in with the work of cleaning up the
old farm. The former owners had left all of their outworn machinery, gen-
erations of it, somewhere about the place. Fortunately there were any num-
ber of extra hands and at times we even had poets to spare. Not Robert
though; he stuck with the things he knew well how to do and liked doing.

My own attention became more and more fixed on the problem of tying
together the operational ends of a farm the size of Treesbank, particularly
since the price of apples fell disastrously with the end of the war boom,
and that first year it was probably only the cherries which kept things
going. Robert still had time to work at his craft and was in the middle
of another poem which was major in terms of time and thought. We could
tell which ones were intended to be major by the reciting and reworking,
and equally by the statement of some form of a polarity which was a re-
current theme. The polarity might be the Being and chaos mentioned earl-
ier, or its alternate, Harmony and chaos, or again simply light against
dark. In the concluding lines of "The End of the Year," he had shown a
twist to the light-and-dark theme by making the final light also a chaos:

> Clang! my ship, my dreamer, bursts into flame;
> appears as a blazing pyre upon the welter, the flood.
> What against Chaos then my Christ avails? (YAC 63)

The most important of the Treesbank poems, "An Apollonian Elegy," again
uses the dark/light theme with the Sun god Apollo providing the great
brightness and man a little phosphoresence, as in the single line from a
very early poem, which has already been quoted. According to the Apollon-
ian elegy,

> We live in the night broken by the sun; we are
> ourselves each suns to break the darkness, Man.
> We shine alone in an expanse of night
> that is all our time. We shine in eternity
> and our light floods back from other suns.
> Where we began is an utter beginning.
> That is the unreal that haunts our days.
> And when we are gone, death-done undone,
> where we end is an utter end, the blank
> real equality of the persisting black. (YAC 70-1)

Since the three of us no longer worked in a little room Robert could use his full voice when reading the Apollonian poem and when he came to the iterated cries of grief, "AI AI," the resonance filled the whole house, passed through the wooden gate into the barnyard and finally expended itself beyond the oat field. Apollo might have become a meaningful god in later poems if Robert had chosen to weave, interweave and rework all of the concepts related to that god who sang to the Muses. Without a beginning of that complexity the Apollo of this poem is nearly "wingd and splendid," or "lion-visaged," and it becomes clear that the god hasn't moved the poet and will remain only a decorative figure. Neo-classicism in any form had no appeal for Duncan and what he liked about the classic Greek was the view of them presented in Jane Harrison's _Prolegomena_. His real interests were increasingly with the Hellenistic rather than the Hellenic age.

Christ is in every way a typical Hellenistic god and for Duncan even his very ordinariness is a virtue; "Apollo" could never be used as a profane oath while "Christ" is commonplace. It is the fact, I think, that "Christ" is common currency of our everyday language and culture, that makes him a useful god in Duncan's poetry.

The other Treesbank poems reflect Robert's increasing discontent with the monkish life he was forced to lead in the country. He had no automobile and refused to drive in any case, so, with the exception of occasional bus trips to the cities, he was living an isolated life. By summer he had moved back to Berkeley again, but we still saw him often as he brought up friends like Jack Spicer or Mary Fabilli for visits of several days at a time and Treesbank continued to be a meeting place for poets and writers.

In the foregoing account of those times past the question of what to do with the gods, who are real, but not real in the believer's sense, has been kept in the foreground since we were both preoccupied with the nature of the gods. It is of interest that there are two unpublished poems which were written at this time and just after in which Duncan speaks rather clearly on the topic. The poems are handwritten and appear as a kind of coda in the limited edition of <u>Heavenly City</u> <u>Earthly City</u>. One is dated 1946 and the second 1947; both are without titles.

> The blessed Herbert in his love does sing
> "our life is hid with Christ in God."
> He is a faithful and single-minded lover.
> "Thou art my loveliness, my life, my light.
>   Beauty alone to mee," he writes.
>
> And I:
>
> There is not One God.
> There are many Gods. They pass away.
> There is an endless beautiful company
> in which our life is hidden. Our loveliness.

The second poem in logic might have come first, or perhaps it might not have; it is difficult to say.

> Faithless and many minded Muses--
> Each as a lovely woman or a stream
> that flows of music
> ever changing and yet constant because lovely,
> that beauty Heraklitus sang
> not of the thing but of its being.
>
> Faithless, O myriad minded.
> the sun is new each day;
> never to step twice in the same beauty
> (river of music) but other
> and yet other waters,
> each as a lovely woman,
> the dark and the gold of beauty
> replenish the constant single source.
>
> Thou art new loveliness, new life, new light.
>   Beauty alone to mee
> In which my life is hid anew in God.

A CONVERSATION WITH JOANNA AND MICHAEL McCLURE

Robert J. Bertholf

RB: What was the occasion of meeting Robert Duncan for the first time?
MM: I met Robert at The Poetry Center at San Francisco State in 1954 in his
workshop class. One of the things Robert did on the blackboard stands out
as representative of many insights he created. I'd written a double Petrar-
chan sonnet, in the style of Milton. It began: "Dead drugs, dead dogs,
have split my neighing head/in colloquies of bitter light and shade."
Robert considered it eccentricity bordering on madness that I was writing
sonnets. It took a while to assure Robert that I was going thru a period
of learning forms. His vision was beautiful. I remember him writing the
opening quatrain of that sonnet on the board, and breaking the poem down in
such a way that he would say, "look here, there's a <u>collie</u> in the colloquy,
and that's how that relates to the dog in 'Dead drugs, dead dogs. . . .'"
Robert would take several lines by a student and make that kind of inter-
relationship between words--and in multiple combinations and dimensions.
By the time he had finished it was as if the lines had become a galaxy of
interrelationships and related images.
JM: That's my first memory of Robert. Michael was living on Scott Street
then. I didn't know one could dissect a poem, just like Michael said--and
every little part fit in some way into the whole poem. Robert had so many
dimensions of a poem he could draw on when he was describing it that I
remember my eyes fell wide open in surprise. He had all those fascinating
things to say. It's the way his mind will play on any subject.
MM: When Robert began teaching the workshop he had just evolved a fully
matured system of poetics, or so it seemed. We felt the inspiration of the

14

maturation. He always knew what might be done with the line, and that was
thrilling. It was new and he enjoyed speaking of it. He hadn't absorbed
his own system; he was still flowering with the system.

RB: How did Duncan behave himself at The Poetry Center to make you get go-
ing on your own kind of poetry? This is not a question of influence, but
a matter of stimulation.

MM: Robert was an ideal Romantic poet. There has been a vital literary
tradition in San Francisco since the Second World War--and back before that.
The early, and elegant pa·t of the tradition revolves around Robert Duncan,
Kenneth Rexroth, James Broughton, Madeline Gleason, William Everson and
Philip Lamantia. There were printers in the early 1950's like David Ruff,
and painters like Ronald Bladen--all part of the anarchist tradition; the
literary and the anarchist traditions became woven together. There was a
rough and readiness to those people. Before hitchhiking was popular,
Robert would get out on the bridge and hitchhike to Berkeley to maintain
himself as a typist, instead of doing a job that would infringe upon his
mind. Jess also worked part-time in a capacity relating to chemistry.

   Robert took on the mask (or cape like a super hero's cape) of saying
he wasn't a poet of the first magnitude. He said that in order to free him-
self from the vicissitudes of belles-lettres. He was a free individual. I
remember hearing Robert read those early poems like "Song of the Borderguard."
Those are poems of a man who was free from _having_ to be himself. He _was_
being himself. I often thought that the Stein imitations (_Writing Writing_)
were some of the most intensely Duncanesque poetry he ever wrote. Robert
had no program of what he had to do, or had not to do. He was acting spon-
taneously.

RB: How much of that instruction from The Poetry Center stuck with you?

MM: Oh, 100%. I don't think he said anything that didn't stick. We all
sensed that a treasure of poetic perception was being opened, and I think
all of us allowed as much of it to remain as possible.

JM: Didn't being in that class free up your poetry?

MM: That's a very interesting point. My early verse that I wrote in high
school was pictographic, post-Williams, post-Patchen, post-Cummings--

emotive and highly graphic. Then in college most of what I wrote, and what
intrigued me the most, was formal experiments. There were also free verse
experiments that I was seldom satisfied with. I was more pleased with
pieces in the manner of Blake. Then there were the Roethke villanelles
that appeared in Poetry. Robert showed us the real possibilities of free
verse--that free verse could be an implement for thought. I needed just
such an example, and Robert was the living example.

RB: Was one of the possibilities of poetry the notion that the poem in
some way was an extension of the body?

MM: Robert never said the poem was an extension of the body, but whether
he said so or not he was making the poem an extension, in the same way the
abstract expressionists were making painting a bodily, physical amplifica-
tion. Robert didn't look at you and then to your poem and say it was a
reflection or extension. He took the poems as being literally real. You
began to see that they were literally, really you. It was incontrovertible
if you were in your poetry.

JM: Your poetry shows that; it spreads out in different ways over the page.
It really doesn't get on the axis until later. Robert still badgers you to
free it up. He is always pulling for that side.

MM: Robert was the first poet I knew who showed me that one could use poetry
as a vehicle of thought without disengaging it from feeling. It could be a
real thing. I had been looking at and listening to Dylan Thomas, but Robert
made me see that poetry like Thomas's can be a manufactured thing, to ful-
fill an image of what poetry may be. On the other hand, poetry could be a
free flow becoming itself as it manifested itself thru the poet.

RB: Was Duncan talking about the achievement of form in 1954? Was he then
making the distinction between form and convention?

MM: The word form is a semantic confusion. I suggest that the word shape
be substituted. Hopefully it could become more like what Creeley meant
when he said form is an extension of content. By shape we seem to have a
more organic idea. Form, one thinks of geology; shape, one thinks of biol-
ogy. Shape could bring the poem back to a sense of being animate, able to
turn its head from side to side. But in the class I don't remember Robert
speaking of form.

RB: Who was in the class, and how did the class members contribute to the
milieu of time.

MM: Helen Adam and Paul Dreykus, Larry Fixel, Paul Cox, Ida Hodes. Paul
Cox was a brilliant and prolific playwright and poet, who later ceased
writing. Paul Dreykus had a brief period of writing--and a published
book. Ida Hodes was in there, an old friend of Robert's. Larry Fixel is
still writing--mostly prose poetry. Helen was one of Robert's discoveries.
She was writing romantic ballads. My strong association in the class was
with Robert. But we had another considerably different association with
Robert and Jess because they were an older couple who knew the ways of San
Francisco. Joanna and I picked up much lore about living with one another
and with the city from them. When we visited them--as often we did--we ad-
mired their life style, saw how they lived with painting, and how they came
to terms with San Francisco as a city. They made the most gracious possible
arrangement with it. A lot of my friendships came from meetings at Robert's.
I met Philip Lamantia, James Broughton, and Stan Brakhage and Larry Jordan
there. About the same time I met Allen Ginsberg at a party for W. H. Auden
at Ruth Witt-Diamant's. Allen and I were looking at the rest of the people.
We began speaking together. Thru that association I met Gary Snyder and
Phil Whalen.

RB: Didn't Jonathan Williams arrive in San Francisco about that time; and,
did you attend Olson's lectures on Whitehead in 1957?

MM: Yes, I was at the lectures. The first set of them was at Robert's
apartment. We met Jonathan thru Robert. When he stayed with us on Sacra-
mento Street he was going around as "Jargonathan" with his Jargon books.
He literally made you read Creeley and Olson. In 1954 I hadn't been able
to focus on the page in regards to projective verse, and Jonathan was there
with the books in his hands insisting that you buy the book. If you couldn't
buy it he gave it to you.

There was a feeling in Robert's poetry in the early 50's that involved
the romance of the city. Perhaps San Francisco is the only city in the USA
that actually has romance. Part of the glamour is the Victorian gothic, and
the fog that swirls thru the Victorian gothic. The willingness to go to all
extremes has been characteristic of this city. I mean, extreme in the sense

of the most extreme painting such as Clyfford Still's. The most extensive
practical freedom has often existed here. The city abounded with extreme
types from worker anarchist to intellectual. It's a place where mixes can
come together in the same way the architecture and fog come together with
the Pacific Ocean to create a fairy tale quality. I don't find that in
other cities. Robert seems to personify the beauty and the various capac-
ities of this city and to let them into his poetry in the same way Jess
does with his painting.

RB: What poems are you talking about now?

MM: The poems of the period of _Letters_. In those poems Duncan had freed
romance from formal forms. The poetry was a flowing state of possibilities
that one moved thru and allowed to _move_ oneself. At a perfect moment you
took an area that manifested itself in you. And that was the poem.

RB: Were there specific poetic practices that drew you to those poems?
Did Duncan at that time put into practice things that he had been talking
about in the class?

MM: The thrill with the _Letters_ poems was the changing line lengths. The
dance, and I suppose it begins with Williams, but with Robert it's an en-
tirely different kind of dance. It becomes very changeable to suit the
particular melody that Robert must have brought from his childhood. The
romantic melodies of the 1920's are the ones turning into a kind of fairy
tale. My mother sang that kind of song to me when I was a child. Robert
experimented with it in his poems in _Letters_. Later, "The Structure of
Rime" started to come along. I didn't understand those poems at first. I
was not prepared to accept that there could be language rivulets and pools
and cataracts and so forth. I still had a young man's view of consciousness
and unconsciousness. There was a real mystery to Robert arising with part
one of "The Structure of Rime." Then he wrote a lot of other poems and came
up with part two and part three. Poems like "The Law I Love Is Major Mover"
come at this time. Sometimes Robert went back to "The Venice Poem" and
brought it out to read to us.

RB: You really had the sense that Duncan was moving into a new kind of
poetry.

MM: Yes, it's as if Robert felt that any time a boundary had clarified he
was willing to go a little further than the boundary. Increasing those

boundaries was part of Robert's approach to consciousness. One kept getting
a more and more unlimited, multiple-directioned Duncan, until you get those
classical, mellifluous, statuesque poems that are in The Opening of the Field,
like "The Law I Love Is Major Mover" and "The Dance." I am crazy about
Letters, about "An Owl Is An Only Bird of Poetry," the Stein poems and "The
Venice Poem," and those early plays—I like them all. The marvelous thing
is that I was there when it was just a little stretch of the mind to see
that they all cohere.

RB: So, you continued to see Robert and Jess, and to learn from them both.

MM: I took poems to Robert and asked his advice. The class was a divine
milieu that Robert created, and I think all the students were part of that
occasion, although the inspiration came from him. After the class was over,
and I'd learned how Robert thought and felt, it was a much simpler thing to
take a poem to Robert. He advised me about line length, or sound, or
whether I was writing my own impressions. He would also read a new poem or
an old poem, like "An Owl Is An Only Bird of Poetry" because he was discus-
sing the importance of vowels in a poem. He is not a man secretly writing
poetry in his garret. He is a very earnest man moving thru the labyrinths
and meadows of his life.

JM: We saw less of them during the 1960's, but we didn't ever stop seeing
them. I sensed they didn't approve of all that was happening in the Haight-
Ashbury, the rock-'n-roll—the things I think Robert would look askance at.
In the late 1950's they gave us help with a flat we took. We literally fell
apart—we came down with the flu. The flat had to be cleaned, we had no
money, no light fixtures, no means of making a home. They took us under
their wing.

MM: And not only that, Jess came over and helped us put in the gas and
electric fixtures, which had been taken away by the people who lived there
previously.

I went over to Robert's many times because I didn't know what the world
was taking me into. Not only was there the warmth and the literary discus-
sion for a young writer, but the warmth of any kind of discussion for a
young man.

JM: Robert could give a description of editors that was very meaningful, and then turn to Gertrude Stein's essay on editors.

MM: For all the hoariness and wisdom that is attributed to him, Robert is a rebel poet. Both Robert and Jess are almost mystically <u>independent</u> in <u>all their activities</u>. They were willing to love and hate for their own pure reasons. They were willing to love McDonald's fairy tales or the Oz books before others knew that such things existed. And they were willing to praise Gustav Moreau when Moreau was considered a nightmare—in 1954 when he was in his nadir and nobody knew there was such a painter Robert pointed to him. There was a mystically independent, deeply intelligent, capricious joy and love of sensibility in all that Robert and Jess did. And their lives manifested that. In the 1950's, when they were buying meat only a couple of times a week, to save money, they were also buying a painting by Ed Corbett. At the same time, in the 1950's they were collecting pieces of <u>art</u> nouveau.

JM: He was giving us a personal example day after day, from the books he was reading to everything he did. There was that sense of being able to form your own individual pathway, with all the human understanding that he could bring to the question. He was interested in people doing their own bit of creation of their lives. They had created something and they were showing you things, and you could make your own mark too. It was a matter of giving out human understanding.

And the sense of justice was another thing that always impressed me. They were wearing black arm bands for the Viet Nam war dead. You always had the feeling that something like that came out of a very strong feeling, and it wasn't a particular political party or a current issue that made them wear the arm bands: it was a private issue of moral value.

MM: One of the reasons Robert is so important is that he has a great understanding. He is a staunch figure in the middle of his own field of poetry. He wasn't involved in literary competition. Let me say something about that kind of competition. Literary competitions either force destruction, or removal of an individual from the field of competition, or they can bring about a larger area of a sense on larger areas of subject matter, or larger areas of sensibility. The poetry of the 1950's and 1960's expanded the possibilities of poetry. It forced into existence areas of poetry that might not have come into being. I remember we looked at the late 1950's as a kind of break thru period; we were looking for poems that were break thru poems, and many poems were.

RB: It adds up, then, that Duncan was an important stimulation for you, both in and after the workshop, both in and out of poetry.

MM: Yes, of course. When, in the workshop, he went over particular lines and words and vowels. In the poem he always allowed you to look into your own poem. That is not the kind of workshop situation that produces imitation Robert Duncans. I've seen many people coming out of workshops who wrote poetry like people teaching the workshops, or who were trying to do so unsuccessfully. But Robert was turning each individual back into himself, into his own work, so that each individual could see that his work was potentially a universe that he could inhabit--a universe like a cave where he could go on hammering out greater and greater ballrooms from the solid rock. Mainly Robert turned you back into your work, so that you could see that it was reality itself. With Jack Spicer you get an entirely different thing. Spicer left people divided whether to be like themselves or to be like Jack, and he left a lot of people divided and standing tiptoe on the barbed-wire fence of their own indecision. If Robert had something for your world it caught immediately or it didn't. If it caught, you wanted more of it. Basically it was narcissistic--Robert was feeding you yourself.

RB: What was your relationship to Jess's painting of that period?

MM: Jess's painting plainly amazed me. Jess began as a pupil of Still. We have one abstract ink painting he did by pouring ink on the paper and going over it with his fingers. There were big design patterns that he painted with house paint. One was called "The Texts of the Kants in the Tents of the Khans." When they went to Europe they gave us that painting but the tar paper it was done on disintegrated. And Jess's figurative paintings were beautiful--long skinny, male faces done in blues and yellows and greens in the most outré style so that they came very close to being abstract expressionism. And then a big clot of paint right in the middle of the faces. The backgrounds of those paintings melted from realism into imaginary, gothic sfumato. I thought of Jess's painting as being San Francisco--as Robert's poems are.

EXERCISES IN DISORDER:
DUNCAN'S IMITATIONS OF GERTRUDE STEIN

Jayne L. Walker

"The H.D. Book," Duncan's fullest exploration of his literary and spir-
itual ancestry, does not name Gertrude Stein as one of his "masters" in the
art of writing. Her absence from his roll of ancestors is striking, because
in the 1960's, when the chapters of "The H.D. Book" were being published,
Duncan was also issuing a series of volumes which demonstrate and acknowl-
edge the centrality of her work to his own writing of the previous decade.
Two major sections of Derivations: Selected Poems 1950-1956 are labeled "Im-
itations of Gertrude Stein"; and Writing Writing is unmistakably a "deriva-
tion" from Stein. In his prose commentaries of the 1950's she had a promin-
ent place on his lists of literary ancestors; from 1950 to 1956 his appren-
ticeship to Stein was more programmatic than his relationship to any other
writer. Her absence from "The H.D. Book" seems to suggest that, before 1960,
he decisively broke away from Stein's model. Indeed, Stein's work cannot be
comfortably assimilated into the lineage Duncan traces in "The H.D. Book."
His version of the modern tradition has H. D. at its center and pays homage
to Pound and Williams as preservers of a spiritual heritage. Stein was
perhaps the greatest and surely the most radical of what Frank Kermode has
called the "schismatic modernists." Cutting all ties with the literary
tradition and working in direct relationship to the modern painters, she
explored the substantial qualities of language as a medium; beginning in
1912, she tried to create verbal structures that would directly "represent"
the movements of consciousness in what William James called the "concrete
chaos" of immediate experience. Her playful texts systematically demystify
and deconstruct language as a medium for logical utterances. Duncan was

never totally committed to Stein's project. Even while imitating her style,
he was often straining against some of her theoretical and epistemological
presuppositions. After 1956 he turned to other "masters" and other modes
of writing. But his more recent work still shows traces of techniques and
theories he developed during his apprenticeship to Gertrude Stein.

Duncan's acquaintance with Stein's work began early.[1] As an under-
graduate at Berkeley, he pursued a remarkable extra-curricular education in
modern literature, under the tutelage of Robert Bartlett Hass, who was then
a graduate student writing a dissertation on Gertrude Stein. In 1937-38,
Duncan read all of The Little Review and transition, Eugene Jolas' attempt
to promote the "revolution of the word," which published Finnegans Wake,
contributions by Stein, and a series of other radically modern writings.
Hass (who with Donald Gallup published A Catalogue of the Published and Un-
published Writings of Gertrude Stein in 1941) was a knowledgeable guide for
Duncan's early enthusiastic, wide-ranging explorations of Stein's writing.
In April 1937, Hass arranged for Occident, Berkeley's literary magazine, to
publish a short piece by Gertrude Stein, "Is Dead." Coincidentally, the
same issue contained a poem by Robert E. Symmes (later Robert Duncan), en-
titled "People."

The following year, in Epitaph, his own little magazine, Duncan print-
ed his first imitation of Gertrude Stein, "Relativity, a love letter, and
relative to what; a love letter."[2] It is an adept imitation of Stein's
early portrait style, which he had been studying in Portraits and Prayers,
the first Stein volume he owned:

> Suddenly one comes to be one living and one ceases to be one
> studying to be living. Suddenly one comes to be one living
> another one outside. Always one is living another one inside
> entirely, and sincerely another one being outside. Another is
> one inside who is outside.
>   This one is entirely this one. There are many ones and
> this one is entirely and sincerely this one.

The style echoes many characteristics of Stein's early portraits: the pro-
noun "one," with its strange lack of specificity; the attenuated, present
participial verb forms; the repetition of words and syntactical patterns.
Stein's "Galeries Lafayettes" begins:

> One, one, one, one, there are many of them. These are very

> many of them. There are many of them. Each one of them is
> one. Each one is one, there are many of them.[3]

Duncan seems to have been attracted not only by the artfully patterned lan-
guage but also by the possibilities it afforded for personal concealment.
The second part of his piece imitates a later style of Stein's, "partially
punning and partially making sense": "Sense and senses for Cecily. Some of
the sensed senses. Cecily sensing and Cecily sensing and Cecily sensing."

Although Duncan did not immediately pursue his imitation of Stein any
further, her work continued to interest him throughout the 1940's. His
Stein collection contains many volumes acquired and read before 1950. But
it was not until the early 1950's that her work became central to his own
writing. In 1951 Yale published <u>Two</u> <u>and</u> <u>Other</u> <u>Early</u> <u>Portraits</u> <u>(1908-1912)</u>,
the first of a series of Stein volumes to appear in the 1950's. This text
rekindled Duncan's active interest in Stein's work. He immersed himself in
her writings, reading them aloud or listening to recordings, enjoying and
imitating the sound and rhythmic structures of her artfully patterned lan-
guage constructions. In 1953, Duncan produced two of Stein's plays in San
Francisco: <u>Please</u> <u>Do</u> <u>Not</u> <u>Suffer</u> and <u>The</u> <u>Five</u> <u>Georges</u>. His Stein imitations
continued from 1951 to 1955; the last of them, which play with Spanish words,
were written during Duncan's trip to Mallorca. Although he never abandoned
other modes of writing, he produced an enormous number of imitations of Ger-
trude Stein; they pervade all of the collections of his work from the early
1950's. <u>Writing</u> <u>Writing</u> is the central text of Duncan's Stein period. (He
wrote it for a young poet, as his own reply to Stein's <u>How</u> <u>to</u> <u>Write</u>, which
he had seen in a bookstore, couldn't afford to buy, and had not yet read.)
While the other imitations were written separately and later collected,
<u>Writing</u> <u>Writing</u> was originally conceived as a book; like some of Stein's
most interesting works, it simultaneously formulates and demonstrates its
radical poetics. None of these derivations from Stein was published until
the 1960's. <u>Letters</u> (1953-1956), a collection issued in 1958, contains none
of these direct imitations of Stein, although the volume reveals some traces
of her impact on his work. Before 1958, Duncan had already reoriented his
writing to eliminate direct signs of Gertrude Stein.

According to his own account, Duncan began his imitations of Gertrude
Stein as he "set about questioning the whole basis of an unbroken continuum

in poetic language and tried to force a new sense of interrupted movement."[4]
Already in the previous decade, Duncan had been experimenting with differ-
ent kinds of "interrupted movement" in long poems. The sectional structure
of Medieval Scenes, with its variety of verse forms, was loosely modeled on
Pound's "Hugh Selwyn Mauberley."* "The Venice Poem," more discontinuous in
its structure, owed something to the example of Stein's "A Valentine for
Sherwood Anderson."* But "The Venice Poem," with its "musical form" that
freely incorporates shifting metrical arrangements, is still unified by a
complex network of recurring themes and images. The discontinuities, the
interruptions of the discursive movement of the poem, are self-consciously
signaled: "the mirror as imitation, as poem,/STOPS, changes."

Stein's writings provided Duncan with a wide range of radical alterna-
tives to conventional poetic and linguistic structures. In her work, struc-
ture is the most directly "representational" element of the composition.
For Stein, the "realism of the composition" resides in the patterning of the
language; what it "represents" is the "realism of the composition of [her]
thoughts."[5] At the same time, she believed that these verbal structures
would reflect her sense of the historical situation:

> The only thing that is different from one time to another
> is what is seen and what is seen depends upon how everybody
> is doing everything. This makes the thing we are looking
> at very different and this makes what those who describe it
> make of it, it makes a composition, it confuses, it shows, it
> is, it looks, it likes it as it is, and this makes what is
> seen as it is seen.[6]

By 1912, what Stein was "looking at," what informed her own compositions
and those of the Cubist painters (which she was also "looking at"), was the
"twentieth century . . . a time when everything cracks, when everything is
destroyed, everything isolates itself."[7]

Stein's earlier writings also "represent" the movements of the mind,
but these compositions reflect an entirely different set of epistemological
assumptions. The style of The Making of Americans and the early portraits
portrays a mind circling in a field of abstract categories, attempting to
create a massive synthesis of human experience. Two and Other Early Por-
traits (1908-1912) records the process by which she radically changed her
epistemological position and, as a result, her mode of writing. Two begins

in the early style, as a double portrait contrasting a man whose rational, categorizing mind separates him from direct experience and a woman immersed in the flow of experience unmediated by conceptualization. As the text progresses, Stein gradually rejects her own rational, synthetic habits of thought and composition. In opposition to her previous methods of writing, she develops new verbal structures to "represent" the disorderly mass of raw sensations and perceptions that flood into the (Jamesian) consciousness, unfiltered by the "attention." The transformation of Stein's writing was not completed in Two; it continued in other transitional works, including Jenny, Helen, Hannah, Paul and Peter and G. M. P. (both of which Duncan also studied carefully in 1951)* and culminated in Tender Buttons in 1912. Stein's new verbal structures play havoc with conventional modes of ordering experience in language; in the linguistic universe of Tender Buttons, "real is, real is only, only excreate, only excreate a no since."[8] These deliberately disordered compositions embody both the "concrete chaos" of immediate perceptual experience and the external breakdown of order which Stein saw as the essential characteristic of the twentieth century.

    In 1951, Duncan found Two "totally illuminating"--for his life as well as his writing.* The polarities of order and disorder which it explores, both thematically and stylistically, delineate aesthetic choices which were of vital concern to him at that time; he directly confronts their implications in "An Essay at War" (1951-1952), his poetic response to the Korean War. The poem presents war as "a mineral perfection, clear,/unambiguous evil"; the "art" of war is:

                the responsible traind military technician's art
            without rage   planning campaigns,
            organizing, ordering, giving orders until
            the blood flows red from each page.

As an act of opposition to this fearful symmetry, he conceives the poem

            as a shatterd pitcher of rock crystal,
            its more-than-language not in the form
            but in the intrigue of lines, the shattering,
            the inability.
            tracing the veins of an imaginary conclusion,
            the faults along which the tremor runs. (D 23)

Duncan's poem, which insistently announces its refusal of a preconceived

plan, proposes to enact in its formal structure the "faults," the "flaws"
which serve as signs of human resistance to the inhuman order of the war.
One of the prose sections that break the flow of the verse announces, "You
see, what I feel is needed at this point is a nadir, a breakdown. . . .
Without a plan I was destined to come to this pass, to this foreclosing of
all promise. The poem defeated" (D 22). But the poem is not defeated; it
goes on to celebrate poetic disorder:

> We did not make sense.
> We made words dance. Dance,
> we said. What is left is the hearth.
> Dance by the light of the war. (D 22)

In fact, Duncan's poem does "make sense." The surrender of control, the
created disorder, is only partial—and part of the larger design. Like
"The Venice Poem," this one is unified by a network of themes and images,
especially the light and flames associated with the opposing but comple-
mentary principles of love and war. The "faults" in the poem's form never
indicate a loss of thematic control; they are, themselves, significant.
The poem ends by describing itself:

> the clear immutable pitcher
> flawd by our rage. No calm
> unbroken by variations of the line
> or by the rime just off beat, repeated
> tokens for the listening ear of the endeavor
> to shape war.
>
> The skull forward.
> The flesh having melted into a dew. (D 24)

The deliberate breaches of poetic convention are artful structural signs of
the "rage" that runs through the poet's "endeavor to shape war."

"An Essay at War" clearly indicates that Duncan was primed for Stein's
more radical assaults on poetic and linguistic order. He was already work-
ing with the idea that the structure of the composition should embody both
the movements of the mind and his sense of the historical situation. As a
sign of its own precarious balance between traditional poetic symmetry and
deliberate disorder, the poem starkly juxtaposes the voices of Dante and
Stein:

> *profunda*
> *e chiara sussistenza dell'alto lume*!
> *What is a nail? A nail is unison.* (D 17)

In the next few years, Duncan chose to follow Stein, experimenting with a
truly "incoherent art":

> a created theory to stand in place for, to act out in its
> conception, not its integration (its mere creation) but its
> disintegration. That the poem, the drama, or the painting
> or music go beyond its nature as a created thing toward
> reality (as imitation—that it resemble the meaningless, the
> un-considered, the extra-harmonious).[9]

This statement and others from Duncan's unpublished 1953 Laboratory Records
Notebook reveal that by imitating Stein's stylistic effects he was also
flirting with her "concept of the ultimate reality of chaos" (LRN 49), cre-
ating verbal structures which embodied, rather than simply thematized, this
reality.

Duncan's Stein imitations are not simply extensions of his search for
freer, more discontinuous poetic structures; they entail a far more radical
assault on the structures and functions of language. Abandoning the discur-
sive function of language as a means to a conclusion, they enact a surrender
to the substantial qualities of the medium, to associations of sound and
rhythm which subvert and resist rational ordering. In a discarded preface
to a series of Stein imitations, Duncan makes clear the terms of the experi-
ment:

> Time come for serious non sense of a dance to begin . . .
> but the words are already begging to dance, to give up
> their destinations. . . . As our words will. To go. We
> are no longer writing home, or portraits, or up or down,
> but, as you see, are writing writing.[10]

Stein, in Two and the other transitional works, had rejected "writing por-
traits" in favor of "writing writing." In his imitations of Stein, Duncan
turns his back on writing as self-expression, political commentary, or spir-
itual exploration. No longer a communication about or directed toward some
object or idea, writing is its own subject, object, and end—a serious play
on the surface of language. The medium is dense—almost, but never entirely,
opaque. The writer is free to follow associations of sound and rhythm into
the realm of "non sense."

Two and the other transitional pieces provided Duncan with a wide range
of verbal structures to imitate, from the repetitious, complex syntax of the
early portrait style to the concrete, nominal style of Tender Buttons.

Sometimes, as in the opening sections of Writing Writing, he used the re-
petitive syntactical patterning he learned from Stein to liberate the flow
of his language from rational control, just as she did. At other times he
mimicked Stein's patterns of language merely as verbal mannerisms, as a
stylistic medium through which to express his own ideas. But many of Dun-
can's imitations, especially in Writing Writing, echo not only the rhythmic
structures of Stein's prose but some of her major theoretical concerns as
well:

> Love is sometimes advancing and including. Love is some-
> times overcoming and not beginning. Love as a continual
> part of some writing is imagining expansion of loving to
> include beginning as continuing. (D 41)

Duncan did not need Charles Olson's "Projective Verse" essay to introduce
him to the idea of writing as a processive form anchored in the immediate
moment. Stein's texts provided a prior model for that rigorously temporal
discipline; and her essays formulate a theory of writing as continual begin-
ning, in what she called the "continuous present." Beginning with Writing
Writing, this discipline, and this liberation, of "[O]pening our mouthed
words to encompass the passage of time," has directed Duncan's poetic enter-
prise (D 46).

For Stein and Duncan, words are substantial entities, with their unique
sounds, rhythms, and weights ("The poet can barely lift these words" [D 67]).
They generate their own trains of associations. Many of Duncan's Stein im-
itations explore the free-play in the system of language: words, decon-
structed and re-formed, move through a series of linguistic transformations.
At the outer limit of this mode of writing, words break down into nonsense
syllables. In "An Arrangement," the word "locomotive" is introduced in the
first section; the second section of the poem separates and regroups the syl-
lables in a pure play of sound rhythm ("loco-coco moto mo mo/locomomo cotiv-
ecomo"), which continues for five more lines before it finally modulates into
sense: "At Lake Como we saw mountains" (D 32-33). This piece radically
foregrounds its surrender to the raw material of language; the process it-
self is central to all the imitations.

Words are slippery entities, as Stein reminds us: "I and y and a d and
a letter makes a change."[11] Language functions through a complex interplay
of similarity and differentiation. In "A Song Is a Game" Duncan plays with

this structural characteristic of the medium:

> Naked as a word
> Sound as a bird
> Ten foot high to be heard
>
> Spelling is hard
> but only the absurd renders
>   rendering absurd.
> Naked as a ward we keep
> Sound as a bard.   (D 31)

Many other pieces, following similarities of sounds, create logically absurd
catalogues. "Bail bonds,/The ties that bind you./Belly bands" is part of a
series generated by language in "Walking on Kearney Street" (D 34). In
these phonetically harmonious but logically disjunctive language construc-
tions, the "order" is purely linguistic; in any external frame of reference,
the connections seem absurd. The "meaning" of these texts, like Stein's,
lies in their enactment of this tension between coherence of sound and ap-
parent incoherence of sense; they demonstrate the arbitrariness of the "or-
der" found in the sound equivalences of the linguistic system.

Duncan was fascinated by the implications of this play of coherence
and incoherence in language. In "The Feeling of Language in Poetry," his
most sustained meditation on the problem of meaning in Writing Writing, he
uses a cloud, a "mysterious grey that does not yield meaning," as an image
of the movement of the mind through the medium of language, "a moving that
has departed from any intention" (WW,[44]). Later, in Letters, the same
image of the cloud describes the mode of writing Duncan "IMAGINED" Stein to
have created: "a cloud dispersed, a falling apartness in itself having no
other images," in contrast to the "actual procession of clouds we watch
where meanings appear and disappear" (D 119). But, as Duncan knew, the
question of meaning in Stein's writing, and in his imitations, is more com-
plicated than he sometimes liked to "imagine." He writes of the pleasure
of "Naming/no more than our affection/for naming" (D 54); but language is,
inescapably, a system of referential signs. Stein's writing after 1912
absolutely depends on the denotative function of nouns and the power of syn-
tax to create connections between them. Stein wanted to strip words of
prior emotional, literary associations and sharpen them to pure denotation,
in order to name "real" fragments of the material world and combine them

into logically disordered patterns.

For a time Duncan experimented with Stein's idea of language as rigor-
ously denotative, naming only the "actual":

> What was it that I imagined the language to be?
> Not mythy (except as there is the actual mythy
> evening, an atmosphere or preconception at best of
> the darkness of the actual night). Not visionary
> (except as the seen is real in its intensity; this
> is the scene wordwise.)
>
> But a hut of words primitive to our nature. The
> Language in its natural disarray. (D 77)

But Duncan's imitations of Stein were always a conscious experiment; he was
never completely converted to her theoretical and epistemological premises.
As early as 1953, he wrote in his Laboratory Records Notebook, "my will to
disorder is not so great (it was after all a matter of technical curiosity,
of predicament, a measuring)" (LRN 52). Even in Writing Writing, the ra-
tional incoherence enacted by his verbal structures is based on premises
that differ significantly from Stein's. "The Feeling of Language in Poetry"
echoes Stein's Two stylistically and thematically. Its long sentences,
wandering elegantly among the "snakelike coils of syntax," embody his refus-
al of too-restrictive "arranging" and "defining," but the reasons for the
refusal diverge sharply from Stein's. Stein chose to abdicate the role of
an active, self-expressive center in order to function as a passive receiver
of chaotic external experience; Duncan describes multiple, fragmenting
selves, resisting the fiction of the "effortful pretension of identity in
purpose." Words, too, replete with signification and tenuous in their for-
mal coherence, are "barely contriving [their] surviving singleness and dou-
bleness." The composition of a sentence is a fragile and momentary contain-
ment of all these centrifugal forces of signification:

> This is the advice of thousands, the roar that we see to our
> delight is united in the words which conquer their sentence as
> their sentence conquers its words and it adjusts all its pro-
> testing in their consenting participants into their straight-
> forward pretension at coherence. (WW[45])

But the tension inherent in this "pretension at coherence," the fiction of
an orderly monologic utterance, explodes, through a surfeit of meaning, into
a final incoherence: "A communication is a working together thru meaning to

understand until there is no meaning that is holding us together." This
essay proposes that writing should "represent" this process in the pattern-
ing of language:

> All men in their commonness repeat sufficiently the inco-
> herent powers of each their own oneness and oneness and oneness
> almost sickening and disturbing and maddening in the real many
> particular forces within them in doing, repeat sufficiently the
> violent incoherence of all that is coherent among them to make a
> sentence thrilling in its simple locomotion. Speech built of
> parts that are coming one after another and untying each word
> from all others it is tied to so that the whole sentence is drif-
> ting apart from itself or running away from itself into their
> selves as words in meaning: <u>this is thrilling in representing
> how we are actually existing in its conquering its own reality</u>.
> (WW [46]) (my underlining)

Duncan's words explode into multiplicity because of his sense that
they come to him "loaded" with their history, their prior uses in the lit-
erary tradition. For Duncan, unlike Stein, words can never simply denote
the "actual," because no language is innocent, no writing, unmediated.
Thus, in the act of imitating Stein, Duncan is, inevitably, operating in op-
position to her theoretical premises. The verbal patterns Stein created, in
her effort to strip her words of all literary associations, have become a
part of Duncan's inherited literary language. "This is the poem they are
praising as loaded," one of the finest texts from Duncan's Stein period, is
a wonderful, ironic evocation of the mediation and the surfeit of meaning
which he recognizes as essential characteristics of language as a medium:

> This is the poem they are praising as loaded.
> This is as it is loaded and thrilling. Loaded
> with death's kingdom which is meaning. Loaded
> with meaning which is gathering the former tenants.
> Loaded with the former tenants speaking which
> brings weeping and fulfilling. Loaded with ful-
> filling which brings crises and then wealthy
> associations. This is the poem loaded up without
> shooting which is an eternal threatening. (D 74)

The poet, using "loaded" words which bring with them their "former tenants,"
becomes, as Duncan says elsewhere, a "crowd of one who writes" (D 90). The
poem, far from a simple univocal utterance, is "An anthology of human be-
ings. A loaded folding up in which history is folded" (74).

Increasingly, this sense of repletion of signification--of selves, of

words, and of objects--drew Duncan away from the theoretical presuppositions
of Stein's writing. Even while he was imitating her stylistic and structur-
al procedures, he began reinterpreting the significance of these logically
disordered verbal structures. In Writing Writing, recalling Rimbaud, he
comments, "Not a derangement of the senses, but, yes, there is an occult
other sense of meaning in all disarrangements (Dis in his arranging)" (D 77).
When "disarranging" becomes "Dis" (the god of the underworld) "arranging,"
Duncan is already far from the "concrete chaos" of Stein's deliberately dis-
ordered literary universe. In Letters, his interpretation of the logical
"faults" becomes even more emphatically transcendental: "break orderly con-
verse to address divine disorders" (D 131). Continuing to surrender to sound
associations and to follow them through the resulting breaks in rational dis-
course, Duncan increasingly embraced the belief that the association "found"
in language, far from being arbitrary, revealed unsuspected order. In "To-
wards an Open Universe" (1966), he expresses his faith in the natural order
that structures language. Quoting Carlyle's idea that the music of lan-
guage mirrors the harmony of nature, he adds his own assent: "This music of
men's speech . . . has its verity in the music of the inner structure of
Nature" (TOU 140).

    Letters clearly reveals Duncan's thirst for another order of meaning, in
which objects of this world can be read as signs of a transcendent reality:

> I search among the insignificant objects of vision for
> signs. (D 125)

> When silence blooms in the house, all the paraphernalia
> of our existence shed the twitterings of value and reappear
> as heraldic devices. (D 118)

In Stein's writing, the objects she names resist all interpretation; they
refuse to function symbolically, as repositories of human values. Her rose
"is a rose is a rose is a rose"--pure denotation. Duncan was more at home
in the poetic universe of traditional correspondences, in which the rose is
linked, both by sound associations and by a long literary tradition, to Eros:
"Rilke torn by a rose thorn/blackend toward Eros" (OF 67). In Letters rem-
nants of Stein coexist, less than peacefully, with texts that reaffirm the
traditional poetic universe of "Correspondences" (D 126), heraldic symbols,
and personifications ("a poem, a Lady" [D 106]). "For a muse meant" is a

tour de force demonstration of a deconstructive poetics in action:

              : A great effort, straining, breaking up
                all the melodic line (the lyr-
                ick strain?) Dont
                hand me that old line we say
                You dont know what yer saying.

                    Why knot ab stract
                    a tract of mere sound
                    is more a round
                    of dis abs cons
                      t r a c t i o n
                    --a deconstruction--
                    for the reading of words. (D 95)

Throughout the poem, words separate, decompose, and recompose in deliberate-
ly "unpoetic" disarray. But most of the texts in Letters thematically af-
firm "design" and enact their own harmony: "A dictate, the heart of things/
toward wholeness/restores order" (D 123). Duncan wholeheartedly embraces
this thematics and this poetics in his more recent poetry, beginning with
The Opening of the Field, with its reiterated praise of Law and Order:
"Syntax," "The Law I Love Is Major Mover" (OF 10-11).

     In the early 1950's, with Stein as his guide, Duncan plunged into the
radical modernist project, as Foucault describes it, of "disturbing the
words we speak, of denouncing the grammatical habits of our thinking, of
dissipating the myths that animate our words."[12] The deliberate disorder-
ing which Stein and other modern writers used to subvert and disrupt the
habits of thought embedded in the structures of language paradoxically pre-
pared him to affirm the traditional modes of order he chose to discover in
the medium. His apprenticeship to Stein taught him a new attention to the
substantiality of words, an obedience to their sound associations, and a
commitment to writing as a temporal, sequential process. He continued to
use verbal patterning, as she did, to "represent" directly the movements of
consciousness in language. But after 1955, he left behind Stein's material-
istic, deconstructive project in favor of his own search for the secret har-
monies hidden in language and in (the Book of) nature. No longer content
with "writing writing," he reaffirmed the more traditional function of
writing as a "medium for the life of the spirit" (BR [x]).

NOTES

[1] This section of the essay is based on information given to me by Robert Duncan during two interviews on January 6 and 8, 1976. Elsewhere in my text I have used an asterisk (*) to indicate other information I received directly from him. Duncan also showed me his Stein collection and gave me access to his copies of earlier publications, manuscripts, and some unpublished writing from the 1950's. I am grateful for his permission to quote from these unpublished works and for his generous and complete cooperation with my research.

[2] Epitaph, I, 1 (Spring 1938), [21].

[3] Portraits and Prayers (New York: Random House, 1934), p. 169.

[4] Biographical note in The New American Poetry, ed. Donald M. Allen (New York: Grove Press, 1960), pp. 433-434.

[5] "A Transatlantic Interview 1946" in A Primer for the Gradual Understanding of Gertrude Stein, ed. Robert Bartlett Hass (Los Angeles: Black Sparrow Press, 1971), p. 15.

[6] "Composition As Explanation," reprinted in Writings and Lectures 1909-1945, ed. Patricia Meyerowitz (Baltimore: Penguin, 1967), p. 24. Duncan quotes extensively from "Composition As Explanation" in "Rites of Participation" [Caterpillar, I (Oct. 1967), 6-29], the only chapter of "The H. D. Book" which includes more than a passing reference to Stein.

[7] Picasso (1938; Boston: Beacon Press, 1959), p. 49.

[8] Tender Buttons, in Writings and Lectures 1909-1945, p. 195.

[9] The Laboratory Records Notebook, p. 50 (unpublished). Hereafter indicated by LRN and included in text.

[10] From the (unpublished) "Preface for A Copy Book 1953-1955."

[11] Matisse Picasso and Gertrude Stein With Two Shorter Stories (1933; Barton, Berlin, and Millerton: Something Else Press, 1972), p. 106

[12] Michel Foucault, The Order of Things: An Archaeology of the Human Sciences (1966; New York: Random House, 1970), p. 298

A FEW NOTES ON ROBERT DUNCAN

Helen Adam

Of all the poets that I have known Robert Duncan is the most complete-
ly dedicated to his art.

He lives, breathes, and vibrates poetry. It blows around him like a
storm of fire.

It never occurred to Robert that he could or would be anything but a
poet. When he began to write in early youth, one of his aunts, a Rosicru-
cian, told him, "This is very lazy of you. You have been a poet already in
so many lives." Very probably he had. Absolute mastery of a mighty art is
not learned in one lifetime.

Duncan and his friend, the great visionary painter Jess Collins, who
share a fantastic palace of a house in San Francisco, have always seemed to
me like avatars, visiting this ill-fated planet from other more magnificent
and ideal worlds. Not that there is anything self-consciously superior
about them. They are both enormous fun to be with, filled with zest for
life, joy in little things, and an effortless come and go with the whole in-
nocent animal creation.

I remember Duncan reading to his friends, with one of his huge and hap-
py cats purring on his chest with its paws round his neck.

The rich purring followed the rhyme of the poems, and ever since then,
when I hear Robert read, I listen, with the mind's ear, to a feline accom-
paniment, ranging from the softest of purrs to the lion's roar. Though the
owl is his totem creature, Duncan, like almost all true poets, is deeply
akin to the mighty tribe of cats. The playful kitten is in him, and the
royal lion. Like the lion he can at times be ruthless, but he is much more
often both generous and kind, especially with help to other writers.

I personally owe more than I can ever estimate to his encouragement
when I first met him, in San Francisco, in the fifties, and he responded to
my ballads, even though, with their simple traditional rhyme, they were at
the opposite end of the spectrum from his own immensely sophisticated art.
He even said that I am the true god mother of his "My Mother Would Be A
Falconress," one of the great ballads of the language.

In San Francisco I had the joy of acting in many of Duncan's plays and
masques, which he wrote for the pleasure of himself and his friends. They
contain, in my opinion, some of his most extraordinary poetry.

Probably because of his continual come and go in the astral worlds of
dream and inspiration, Duncan often refuses to realize the hazards of Earth.
He is tremendously stubborn. Once he is set on a track nothing will turn
him.

He has a passion for mushrooms (not the sacred sort, just straight
mushrooms) preferably gathered by himself fresh from the slopes of Mount
Tamalpais. I believe at one time he even belonged to a group of rash enthu-
siasts dedicated to this form of Russian roulette. Over and over again I
warned him that a few years ago the greatest mushroom expert in France died
of toadstool poisoning through gathering and devouring some small daemonic
toadstool that had disguised itself to look so like a mushroom that the
great expert was decoyed to his doom. But Duncan remained unimpressed. He
only said that his passion for mushrooms was such that in pursuit of them
he would enjoy dying of toadstool poisoning, and that anyway it would be a
fine strange vegetable death for a poet. Fortunately the Tamalpais toad-
stools have not yet accepted his challenge.

I can't presume to write in detail of Duncan's poetry, of its power, and
splendor, and scope . . . from little songs, lovely and inevitable as flow-
ers, to the great bursts of heroic rage against war. The songs are always
born with their own tunes, and he sings them like the wandering bards of old.

I never use the word genius lightly. I think that, in poetry, the
twentieth century has been rich in many wonderful talents, but that so far
it has produced only two poets of genius, W. B. Yeats and Robert Duncan,
transcendent spirits, speaking at their highest, with the pure voices of the
morning stars.

Don Byrd

In 1947, Charles Olson left Washington, D.C., for the west coast to do research for a project which he variously conceived as a long poem or a prose narrative with poetic intent, perhaps something in the genre of Williams' In The American Grain. A year later, proposing it to the Guggenheim Foundation, he described it as a study of the differing ways in which the Indian, the white man, and the Negro had created human societies in the American West. In Call Me Ishmael, he had written, "I take SPACE to be the central fact to man born in America, from Folsom cave to now."[1] The new book was to be the historical confirmation of the literary proposition. From the beginning Olson was a literalist.

While he was in Berkeley, reading the papers relevant to the Donner party and the early gold strikes, Olson met Robert Duncan, whose work he had read and admired in Circle. It was the beginning of a friendship which was to remain crucial to both men until Olson's death in 1970. Duncan was in the midst of writing Medieval Scenes. In tone, in the angle of its grasp on the real, it was the opposite of Olson's white-heat scholarship. Although he was trained as a historian--unlike Olson, whose education was largely literary--his imagination was fictive. Some years later he would write, "But realities give birth to unrealities. As Plato discovered, or St. Augustine discovered in the City of God, unrealities, fantasies, mere ideas, can never be destroyed" (NAP 401). And Olson would lambast him publicly, saying, "the poet cannot afford to traffick in any other 'sign' than his one, his self, the man or woman he is."[2] The fictionalist versus

the literalist. They were, however, beginning to articulate a sense of
form which was large enough to contain their oppositions: they were both
devoted to a poetry which reveals a world that can be inhabited, fully,
physically. In pursuit of that world, they both came into a zone where fact
and fiction mingle, the one completing and confirming itself in the other.

In 1960, Duncan quotes from Olson's strictures in "Nel Mezzo del Cam-
min di Nostra Vita," a poem which celebrates Simon Rodia's Watts towers:

> "The poet,"
> Charles Olson writes,
> "cannot afford to traffic in any other *sign* than his one"
> "his self," he says, "the man
> or woman he is" Who? Rodia
>   at 81 is through work.
> Whatever man or woman he is,
>   he is a tower, three towers,
> a trinity upraised by himself.
>   "Otherwise God does rush in."   (RB 22)

On the manuscript of the poem which he sent to Olson in a letter (January
4, 1960), he wrote:

> as all ways
> you come into it: not as rules
> (tho the fools may be misled) but because
> you provide out of them broken
> such a glitter of
> mosaic laws for all of
> my towers.[3]

In the pun on "mosaic," Duncan defines precisely his relationship to Olson.
Olson is Moses, the law-giver, but one among many whom he recognizes in the
patterns of his work. "I am ambitious," Duncan writes, in another passage
which drew fire from Olson, "only to emulate, imitate, reconstrue, approx-
imate, duplicate" some forty writers whom he lists (NAP 406-407). He has
made the gathering of diverse influences into a poetic.

Few of Olson's sources are literary. He recognizes Melville, of
course, the late Shakespeare, D.H. Lawrence, Ezra Pound, and, somewhat
grudgingly, William Carlos Williams. He does dedicate a poem in <u>Maximus</u>
<u>Poems</u> <u>IV</u>, <u>V</u>, <u>VI</u> to Duncan, "Who understands / what's going on."[4] And in
"West," he takes a figure of Duncan from "A Poem Beginning With A Line By
Pindar," Olson writes:

> and Duncan who trot-mocs
> in with the light of seance and the golden light
> of those paintings he knows what the dream
> may be carries a fowling piece like the possible
> World Travelers imagine Duncan in doe-skin
> and with his fowling piece--between
> those romantic paintings and not Peter Rabbit Robert
> Duncan in fringed jacket against the bad sunset
> from all across the intermediary space. . . .[5]

The West is for Olson always romatnic, essentially foreign to his own
northern European literalness, and it is perhaps for that reason he was
never able to make much headway in his treatment of the frontier material
which was a life-long fascination for him.

For Olson, the only genuine mode of poetry is epic, or at least of
epic scale, and it was with the appearance of Duncan's "Passages" that he
was moved to say: "Unbelievable, these new *Passages*. *Passages 33* is what
I think--I mean where Duncan--he's now about 49 or 50 . . . I mean he's
moved into a--almost a status or something, if I may use that word--a con-
dition of status. I don't mean stasis, I mean literally STATUS. He's be-
come a BIG poet, like Yeats."[6] Duncan as Yeats, to his own Pound; the
poet of imagination and the poet of history.

Since Poe, American poetry has addressed itself to the gap which open-
ed when life in the United States failed to sustain a homogeneous culture.
The formal situation of <u>Leaves</u> <u>of</u> <u>Grass</u> can only <u>contain</u> Whitman's contra-
dictions. In the <u>Cantos</u>, those contradictions begin to turn destructive.
Pound in Pisa and St. Elizabeth's is the image of the American poet trap-
ped in the failure of the national experience to cohere. In the poetry of
Duncan and Olson, the endless contradictions which are hidden in such gen-
eralities as chaos, the masses, or the People become the source of crea-
tive energy.

                                      I

"I had met Olson in 1948 . . . , no 1947," Duncan says in an inter-
view. ". . . but I did not know him as a poet. In our first conversation
Charles made some reference to his Maximus, and in that first conversation
we talked about ecology." Although Olson was Duncan's elder by eight years

(Olson was thirty-six; Duncan twenty-eight), he would not have been known at
the time as a poet. The Maximus was already on his mind, but he would not
write "I, Maximus of Gloucester, to You" for more than two years. His early
work--some of which had appeared in Harper's, Atlantic, and Harper's Bazaar
during the previous year--would have been of little interest to a poet who
was already capable of sustaining a sequence of poems as complex as Medieval
Scenes. They did, nevertheless, find much to talk about. Duncan proposed
an "ecological" interpretation of the Russian Revolution: ". . . I was very
interested at that time in the idea that cities have to exploit the country-
side in order to get their food, and so two systems grow up, of political
coercion and cultural coercion" (I [3]). Olson would have responded imme-
diately to this kind of talk. He had written of the ecology of the whale
fisheries in Call Me Ishmael, and, though he would come to speak of it dis-
paragingly, in the root sense, as mere house-keeping, his vision of the
continuity of human and natural energy might have been basic to that science
had it not formed alliances with sentimental conservationism on the one hand
and the social sciences on the other. From the beginning they spoke of the
heterogeneity of modern, urban culture which made impossible the old cul-
ture heroes who embodied and redeemed the dreams of all the people.

They also spoke of Ezra Pound. Olson had been visiting Pound more or
less regularly since he was committed to St. Elizabeth's in January, 1946,
and Duncan met with him briefly in 1947. Although they had both addressed
poems to Pound, their radical ambivalence was apparent. In an essay which
Olson wrote in 1948, he says, "One has a strong feeling, coming away from
him, of a lack of the amorous, down there somewhere (I remember that Dun-
can, when he returned to California from his cross-country pilgrimage to
Pound, was struck by it.) E.P. is a tennis ball."[7] Olson defines his kin-
ship with Duncan in terms of their reaction to Pound. They were, he says,
against Pound, instances of "post-Christian man." In one sense, then,
Pound represented for them a dead-end. He was the final revelation and
embodiment of the paradoxes in the cultural order which his work sought to
revive. Pound recalled a culture which required the unselfconscious

obedience of a homogeneous elite, sharing the range of reference defined by
"two gross of broken statues" and "a few thousand battered books," as he
says in "Hugh Selwyn Mauberley." He had made himself the representative of
a culture which has grown internally so complex, so burdened with both the
failures and successes of the past, that the kind of simplification which he
supplied was inevitable and necessary. As a strategy for an epic in the
twentieth century, however, his scheme failed to take into account, as Olson
says, "the sudden multiple increase of the earth's population, the coming
into existence of the MASSES" (O&P 53). For the first time, a powerful
political and economic force which could not be educated to the artifice of
the culture had appeared. It insisted upon knowledge that was active and
immediate.

   In the decades during which Pound sought to substitute "Kulchur" for
life, the culture which had been more or less continuous since the Renais-
sance obliged by removing itself from life utterly. The rococo patch-work
of the Cantos was already beyond the end of the epoch which began, as Pound
defines it, when "Gemistus Plethon brought over a species of Platonism to
Italy in the 1430's." Pound was an archaeologist of culture. He read the
troubadors, the neo-Platonists, Confucius, and Jefferson, as he might have
pieced together the excavated ruins of a beautiful city from a magnificent
and hitherto unknown civilization. The paranoia which led him to see Jew-
ish conspiracies in the banking system also led him to a vision of a lost,
transcendent order of culture. It fell to Olson and Duncan to retrieve a
way of life which arises directly from the physical body and the space
which it inhabits.

   At the end of World War II, the younger writers found themselves with-
out a meaningful past. After what they had witnessed, they could not make
the modernist's appeal to the Tradition. Olson writes:

> Pound and his kind want to ignore [the masses].
> They try to lock them out. But they swarm at the windows in
> such numbers they block out the light and the air. And in
> their little place Pound and his kind suffocate, their fear
> turns to hate. And their hate breeds death. They want to kill.
> And, organized by Hitler and Mussolini, they do kill--millions.
> (O&P 53)

Olson and Duncan found themselves faced with the necessity of a new depar-
ture in which quantity and action would replace quality and stasis.   Only
William Carlos Williams among their older contemporaries seemed to offer
them some guidance.   He had twice in his work imagined great fires which
redeem life from the excessive presence of the past.   Pound's perfections
as a poet, however, gave the lie even to his fear and hate.   He had allowed
Browning and even, grudgingly, Whitman, into the house of culture.   They had
arrived at the point where the articulation of image, character, story, and
idea verge into an ordering of language.   In their work, the burden which
had been carried in language and through language--the freight of sentences
and paragraphs--began to lose itself in the decision between this word and
that one.   The cultural medium through which forms of vision, or psychology,
or narrative, or thought passed into language fell away, and language in its
crude being asserted itself.   Santayana and Plato make the same objection:
the poets cannot get beyond their words.   It is impossible to "think" Leaves
of Grass and The Ring and the Book, as it is impossible to "think" the Iliad
or the Odyssey.   It is possible only to say them.   The Cantos contests the
limit of the speakable at every point, trying to push beyond what might be
said, to the totalitarian clarity which for Pound was exemplified by Dr.
Soddy's essay in Butchart's Tomorrow's Money or the precision of definition
in medieval scholastic philosophy.   Though the occasion of the Cantos has
passed--even the possibility of creating a culture as Pound imagined it has
disappeared--it remains the most cogent evidence of an apocalypse which is
not yet over.

It was the early Pound to which Duncan and Olson turned, as if to en-
gage Pound's process at a point before it had gone awry.   Characteristical-
ly, they were attracted to different aspects of his work.   Duncan's early
poem, "I Tell of Love," carries the sub-title, "Variations upon Pound's
Essay *Cavalcanti* and his translation of Cavalcanti's canzone *Donna Mi
Priegha*."   In Pound's The Spirit of Romance, Duncan found the statement of
a literary tradition of which he was a part, and much of his prose work,
including "The H.D. Book" and the essay on Dante, is an attempt to clarify
that tradition and define his own place in it.   Unlike Pound, Duncan finds

the tradition usefully carried on by Shakespeare and the poets of the nine-
teenth century. Many of his poems, the ballads, "Variations on Two Dicta of
William Blake," "After a Passage in Baudelaire," "Shelley's *Arethusa* set to
new measures," "A Set of Romantic Hymns," the poems after Verlaine, and the
translation of "The Chimeras" of Gérard de Nerval, are conscious definitions
of a continuing romantic tradition. From the beginning, however, the roman-
tic Pound was of little interest to Olson. After one of his visits to Pound,
he writes, "I . . . feel now the Canto on love [i.e. Canto XXXVI, the trans-
lation of Cavalcanti's canzone] is an intellectual performance, but the
Artemis hymn against Pity is true, straight out of Pound" (O&P 71). For
Olson, northern Europe was the middle ground between the New World and the
ancient, eastern Mediterranean sources of culture. In 1948, he quotes
Chaucer's "The Nun's Priest's Tale" as a corrective to the romantic excesses
of Cavalcanti, and in the Maximus, Pytheus' travels to Ultima. Thule will
by-pass the whole of Romantic culture, John Smith appears as the true dis-
coverer of America, and the Norse emerge as the carriers of all of the
significant tales. Olson was attracted to Pound the historian and the in-
stigator of poetic methodology.

The cultural traditions which lay a-shambles in the Cantos had created
a space in which the external world and the realm of the spirit could meet,
transform one another, and interfuse one another with energy. It was an
artifice, but it did offer a place in which the tenuous intercourse between
body and spirit might be revealed. At what cost that space had been cleared
is the subject of Olson's essay, "Human Universe."

In deriving their poetics Olson and Duncan both develop unrealized
possibilities which Pound generated in his effort to arrest the multi-
faceted cultural decay which he encountered. Olson addressed himself fun-
damentally to the question of authority: on what authority can the poet
legitimately ground his work? In one of his earliest published essays,
Olson assumes the mask of Yeats to castigate himself and his contemporaries
for their failure to respond actively to the problems which the modernists
had left unsolved:

> It is the passivity of you young men before Pound's work as
> a whole, not scripts alone, you who have taken from him, Joyce,
> Eliot and myself the advances we made for you. There is a court
> you leave silent--history present, the issue the larger concerns
> of authority than a state--Heraclitus and Marx called, perhaps
> some consideration of descents and metamorphoses, form and the
> elimination of intellect. (O&P 30)

Olson sought to untie the vicious knot by which Pound had joined poetry to

the political enforcement of a cultural order. If Pound's work is seminal

because it reopens the channel through which the passage from word to object

is made, Olson grasps for the object and the relationship of man to object

implied in Pound's work; Duncan creates a space in which to work that is

nearer language and the subjective centers which condition language. In his

contribution to The Artist's View (1953), Duncan says: "It is the marvel-

lous of the Pisan Cantos that reassuress me. Even after a lifetime of the

struggle for publication and importance, because of his love for poetry, for

song and for Romance, Pound dwells in the innermost enchantment of the mind.

He has been initiated into a world transformed and inhabited by spirits"

(NAP 402). The essay as a whole is an elucidation of the relationship of

language to psyche and the ways in which language arouses the innermost

enchantment of mind.

The wisdom of the cultural order had been decorum, moderation, the

scrupulous practice of the golden mean. Only in such a cool arena could

body and spirit appear on the same stage. Olson and Duncan began to explore

the extremes. Olson seeks to engage geography with an intensity which bends

the physical back into physiology and psychology. Duncan seeks to take up

residence in language so exclusively that actual objects become notes in a

music which emerges in its sensuality as the ultimate physiological and

psychological experience. As their developing work makes evident, the

practice of either the outside or the inside arrives, as it were on the

backside, at the point where the two halves of the world appear as versions

of one another.

II

The contact between Olson and Duncan during the first years after their

meeting was relatively limited. Olson sent a copy of Y&X, his first small

book, to Duncan in 1948. Duncan read it and discarded it. Nor did he in-
itially find much of interest in Olson's essay, "Projective Verse": ". . .
when I read it at that time," he says, "I thought that all it was saying was
that we should read poetry aloud, which we were doing in San Francisco. I
thought, 'Well, they are catching up in the East that you should read poe-
try aloud.'" In 1951, however, the Olson issue of Origin appeared, carry-
ing a substantial selection of poetry and prose which was written just at
the time that Olson was beginning to find his true way as a poet. "I, Max-
imus of Gloucester, to You," "The Gate and the Center," and "Adamo Me" ob-
viously indicated that Olson was a writer to contend with. Recalling the
Origin pieces, in 1969, Duncan says that it "was certainly the most exciting
writing one had seen" (I [1]).

     The first book of the Maximus appeared in 1953, and, with it, Duncan
began to feel, as he would say at the Berkeley Poetry Conference in 1965,
that Olson was one of the poets "I know I must study . . . because at every
turn I am back at those texts in order to get information I need, to find
something that is not a matter of literature but of my own inner reality of
life."[8] When he began the reading of the Maximus which would lead to his
"Notes on Poetics Regarding Olson's Maximus," he writes to Olson (June 6,
1954), describing his intended essay: "On the one hand to make clear how
the poem seemed available to my own anarchist persuasions and on the other
hand (thus against this: look at this foto, and on this) the poem moving
thru its sympathies (ideals) toward its forces (reals)." There is much in
the Maximus to offend anyone of anarchistic persuasions, and Duncan obvious-
ly struggled with this aspect of the poem. About six weeks later, August 8,
1954, he says, ". . . since I'm trying to write about the view of man in
the poem I have to weed about in my anarchist prejudiced mind to get back
to the poem." In a sense, Olson, especially in the earlier parts of the
Maximus, is as much a totalitarian as Pound. The insistent, literal fact
of Gloucester, as it appears in the poem ("this foto"), like Maximus' demand
for absolute obedience to that utterly objective space-time, leaves little
room for the kind of imaginative play which Duncan finds most attractive.

The lines from the first ten letters of _Maximus_ which come most readily to mind are directly to the point: "there are only/ eyes in all heads,/to be looked out of," "these things/ which don't carry their end any further than/ their reality in/themselves," and so forth. Of course, the source of the totalitarian authority, as Olson understands it, is space, or the cosmos, rather than the state, but Olson was no more an anarchist than D.H. Lawrence.

Duncan differentiates between those poetic strategies which find their opportunity in restoring an objective world and another possibility which he identifies as his own. Both Imagism, he says, from which Olson stems directly, and surrealism, with which Olson has a stronger kinship than may be immediately recognized, "define what can't be clarified" (letter, June 6, 1954). Such, of course, is the direct implication of Olson's "Projective Verse": "Objectism is the getting rid of the lyrical interference of the individual as ego, of the 'subject' and his soul, that peculiar presumption by which western man has interposed himself between what he is as a creature of nature (with certain instructions to carry out) and those other creations of nature which we may, with no derogation, call objects" (HU 59-60). In his discussion of his own engagement with poetry, Duncan is much closer in spirit to Mallarmé or Gertrude Stein, whom he was at the time explicitly imitating in a sequence of poems: "I am aroused," he says, in the same letter, "as I find myself referring to no feeling other than the feeling of writing. . . . Poetry leads me to poetry; words to words; talking concerns talking."

The nearest equivalent of Duncan's understanding of the poem as a self-begetting process to be found in Olson is Edward Dahlberg's dictum which is one of the three axiomatic principles in "Projective Verse": "One perception must immediately and directly lead to a further perception." This formulation as well as the one which Olson borrows from Creeley--"Form is never more than an extension of content" (HU 52)--is essentially imagistic and leads to a definition of "what can't be clarified," rather than the articulation of language as an order of music. Duncan's essay on Olson, which was finished in 1955, does not seek to resolve this dichotomy but,

rather, allows it to inform and enrich his discussion of the poetic process.
He quotes Dewey: "Order, rhythm and balance simply means that energies sig-
nificant for experience are acting at their best" (PNAP 188). It is the
action of the poem as an imagistic/linguistic continuum which receives the
weight of his attentions. By steadfastly following Pound's distinction
between phanopoeia and melopoeia, he manages to open a gap between Olson's
"eye's in all heads/to be looked out of" and his "by ear, he sd," in which
his own musical transformations can take place.

Although he makes occasional allusions to music, uses some musical
terms in "Projective Verse," and dedicated a poem to Pierre Boulez, Olson
had very little knowledge of, or interest in, music. His work has the
shape of an immense monologue. Olson's medium is not music but talk. Max-
imus is a talker. He says:

> I measure my song,
> measure the sources of my song,
> measure me, measure
> my forces.[9]

Song is the issue of the engagement, not the base. It rises from forces,
self, and sources. Nevertheless, Olson has a genuine respect for music.
When, in "Against Wisdom as Such," he takes Duncan to task, it is neither
for his musical sense of form, nor for his persistent workings in that lin-
guistic zone which is thoroughly interior. Rather, it seems to him, that
Duncan's mistake is to measure himself by some possibility of wisdom which
he admits his work does not attain: ". . . he chastises himself as either
more or less than he is, because of some outside concept and measure of
'wisdom.' Which is what is wrong with wisdom, that it does this to per-
sons" (HU 67). As Olson understands him, Duncan believes that one must
proclaim oneself a fool or a child in order to find a freedom in which the
imagination can manifest itself as play and do its proper work. He speaks,
somewhat wistfully, of a poetry that will remain, "when poetry no longer
has any cultural value," a poetry "cherished only by the unimportant people
who love or adventure" (NAP 402). It was, as we can now see, a necessary
assertion for Duncan to make. To the fictive imagination, everything must

first be fiction, before it can come to inhabit the reality of the fictive
world. In the introduction to Bending the Bow, Duncan writes, "Working in
words I am an escapist; as if I could step out of my clothes and move naked
as the wind in a world of words. But I want every part of the actual world
involved in my escape." By 1964, Olson's warnings themselves had been
incorporated, hanging from Duncan's real fictional cosmos by an "as if"--
perhaps the most characteristic form in Duncan's syntax:

> Charles Olson, how strangely I have alterd and used and
> would keep the wisdom, the man, the self I choose, after your
> warnings *against wisdom as such*, as if it were "solely the
> issue of the time of the moment of its creation, not any ul-
> timate except what the author in his heat and that instant in
> its solidity yield." (BB 38-39)

To a poet engaged in a poem which proposes a hero who is destined to
draw a city and ultimately the earth itself into a new found coherence by
no force other than the act of creation, as Olson was, however, it would
have seemed that Duncan was underestimating the power and usefulness of po-
etry. He returns in "Against Wisdom as Such" to a vocabulary which he had
used earlier in his discussion of the lack of the amorous in Pound: "In-
side he is like light is, the way light behaves. In this sense he is light,
light is the way of E.P.'s knowing, light is the numen of him, light is his
way." In Williams, however, he sees another principle. Thinking of the
great conflagration in Paterson, he says: "Maybe fire is the opposite prin-
ciple to light, and comes to the use of those who do not go the way of
light. Fire has to consume to give off its light. But light gets its
knowledge--and has its intelligence and its being--by going over things
without the necessity of eating the substance of things in the process of
purchasing its truth" (O&P 100). By 1954, he was prepared to assert ab-
solutely that "Light is reductive. Fire isn't. Or--to get rid of any of
those pleasures which paradox and sectaries involve themselves in. . . .
I said to Duncan, 'heat, all but heat, is symbolic, and thus all but heat
is reductive" (HU 70). In this Heraclitean insistence on the primacy of
fire, Olson brackets the tradition which we usually call "western culture"
and sets it aside as a failed experiment in the clarification of conscious-

ness. The Apollonian intelligence, in its glorification of light, had
articulated a world without interior, without the inner-virtu which objects
as <u>mere</u> objects possess. As a result, the dynamic relationships of things
had ceased to generate a world and had been replaced by man alone, ". . .
the egocentric concept, a man himself as, and only contemporary to himself,
the PROOF of anything, himself responsible only to himself by the exhibi-
tion of his energy. . ." (HU 20-21). The reservoir of energy which power-
ed the culture had been man's own, his will, his ability to simplify and
control. It is man in this attitude, which he calls "humanism," that
Olson finds at the root of the present cultural impasse, and, in order to
find a superior model of human behavior, he returns persistently to the
second millennium B.C.

Pound had turned away from the energy which was given to him by vir-
tue of his own work, and he had turned away from the legitimate authority
with which the order of his work invested him. Olson feared that Duncan
was in danger of making a related mistake, of withdrawing from the respons-
ibility of his acts as a poet by locating an external wisdom, which is so
overwhelming and complete as an expression of the real that it allows an
independent dimension for the imagination.

Duncan's first response to Olson's essay, in a letter dated August 8,
1954, is complex. Although it is not defensive, he moves toward an incor-
poration of Olson's argument and toward a reaffirmation that his work must
hew to the interior centers of the imagination, that they are to be taken
as seriously as Olson takes the objective--or, as he says here, the actual
--world:

> I just picked up Black Mt. Review at the Pocket Book Shop and
> read the Wisdom as Such piece. If it reprimands in part I ain't going
> to rise in defense of my bewilderings--this matter of clarification is
> too important and, if there were no other measure of it, I shld. say
> that it is the keener excitement in writing backs up your point.
>   But moral urgency, the hearty man-to-man gusto--might also dis-
> semble? Anyway: the whole realm of spirit I distrust if it is not
> at play--and a play is a sleight-of-mind, dissembling in that sense--
> I wld. not disown it. . . .
>   First to go on record:
>   Knowledge and control (don't mean domination) in actual life is

subject to an unremitting clarification. For motion to be free and energies just here: the real must be distinguished from the unreal. Things must be discriminated and acknowledged.

--Sects, religions, Platonics etc. don't countenance it: wld. rather fuck a dream walking than actually fuck. And they lead to all kinds of clarifications about what it is like to fuck a dream but fewer about the act.

But in made-up things, in the imagination the will has a range of a different kind. Words like genuine and false, truth and lie, up and down (where ther is nor up nor down but as it's named) great and small are anything and everything we design. . . .

The giant-bodied I may be the world but the actual world is the actual world including me.

Olson incorporates, literally, the authoritative requirements of objective behavior in time and space; Duncan demands that the actual world include his own anarchistic imagination.

The processes in which Olson and Duncan engage share a common point like tangent circles. At the meeting place they find Pound, as later they find Whitehead and Jung. Taken differently the meeting place is the physical body and the formal demands which the poet's being a body make on the poem. In a letter dated August 9, 1954, Duncan adds a footnote to his previous letter:

> Came to mind: "wisdom as such" is perhaps a digestive disorder? or of the digestive order. Internal, that is: the brain, lungs, stomach, intestines, heart, liver, etc. a complex of equilibriums; the rhythmic interaction measure up or don't. Why it is not "what" is in the head by the tone that tells. Self-improvement hence linked to breathing exercises, dietary disciplines, anti-
> sex or action expression or invention since these are external, active not digestive.
> Writing: an affair of hand, eye, ear. O.K. I know you have said it already. "By ear, he sd." and "Polis is/eyes." Aye. And hand is suggested in carpenter--Hartley--etc. . . .
> One language is ingested (known) "in the blood" I think Rilke sez (only he wants writing out of the "blood") an inter-action
> of making with language (which is an exterior fact--an "in the airness" or "on the pageness" of language--hence reading out for a phrase etc.) subject to the brain's sympathies. Rhythmic "abilitys."
> Writing on a too-full stomach, writing with a stomach ache, writing on an empty stomach
> the activity is of the hand, eye, ear, hence or therein

having "no end no more than their own" hence "attention" and
"care" count or discount.

Of course, Olson had begun to take the physiological as the condition of
the poem as early as 1949-50, in "Projective Verse," but Duncan's insist-
ence here on language, rather than the object, as the content of the
informational circuit, opens directly into a space which is perfectly con-
gruent with the space of the Maximus, but never more than implied by it.
Olson and Duncan were coming to share a sense of form which was, at base,
organic. The metaphor of the organism which everywhere informs Romantic
criticism is replaced by the literal organism, and the dynamics of the
poetic form are coincident with the evolutionary process of consciousness.
In "Notes on The Structure of Rime" (1961), Duncan recalls the passage in
which Pound compares the Cantos to Bartok's "Fifth Quartet" on the grounds
that they both exhibit "the defects inherent in a record of struggle."
Duncan comments: "Just this incorporation of struggle as form, this
Heraclitean or Lucretian or Darwinism universe as a creation creating it-
self, that drew us to Pound's Cantos and continues to draw me, alienated
its author, for in this process of self-creation out of self his own con-
flict and distress in the complexity and heterogeneity of his world was
everywhere active there" (M 49).

Olson's formulation of this morphological possibility--or his formula-
tions, as both he and Duncan try again and again to clarify it as a basis
for a sense of the world--uses different terminology, but it is different
in no essential:

> If order is not the world--and the world hasn't been the
> most interesting image of order since 1904, when Einstein showed
> the beauty of the Kosmos, and one then does pass on, looking
> for more--then order is man. And one can define the present (it
> does need to be noticed that the present is post the Modern) as
> the search for order as man himself is the image of same.[10]

The failure of Pound and Eliot to reconstitute in art the culture which had
disappeared from life--like Williams' and Crane's failure to constitute a
nation which never existed--reveals a condition, confirmed by Whitehead's
organicism and Jung's psychic dynamicism, in which the present is the point

of genesis and the primordial beginning of the poem—and life—coincides with a struggle which involves in its potentiality the whole of the past. This center is shared by Duncan and Olson not as a source nor as an end. Rather, they move toward it and away from it in the unique processes of their masterful workings in the zones that have been given to them.

III

In the spring of 1956, Duncan returned from Majorca, where he had been living, to teach at Black Mountain College. This period, actually only a few months during the spring and summer of 1956, was the only time when he and Olson were in close personal contact for more than a short visit. Their relationship was largely through the mail.

When Robert Creeley came to Black Mountain to teach and edit The Black Mountain Review in 1954, Olson had the feeling that they were less in touch than they had been before. "Crazy to have Creeley here," he writes to Cid Corman. "Crazy, that we never talk (in any large sense). It's great: all fast, like telegrams. And what a contrast to the volubleness when we are 500 miles off."[11] One suspects, reading Duncan's account of his stay at Black Mountain, that a similar situation developed while he was there. During his Black Mountain tenure, Duncan wrote a play, "The Origins of Old Son," which he inscribed "to Charles, who—as here—provides the/fulcrum for whatever practices out of a geometry/this imaginary one might move a real world by." In fact, however, Duncan seems to have found the atmosphere at Black Mountain somewhat stifling:

> Students at Black Mountain at that time would have, let's say, a library of ten books. They'd have the *Cantos*, *Paterson*, Charles' work and mine. Also they'd have of Lawrence—Charles and Creeley like *The Plumed Serpent*, which outside of its first chapters I've thought a dud of phantasy. But students would know Lawrence's later poems. There'd be no Henry James, no Joyce. It was thought pretty wicked to read *Finnegans Wake*.[12]

Although Olson taught a course on Whitehead, history, and poetics during the time Duncan was there, he and Duncan had agreed not to attend one another's classes, and they seem not to have talked very much about what they were doing. It was not until 1957, when Olson gave a series of lectures on

Process and Reality in San Francisco that Duncan began to feel the impact
of Whitehead. On October 5, 1957, Duncan writes: "Haven't you, from Of
Wisdom As Such on given me myself. . . . And this last year, uplifting
again the heart--you gave that news of the primordial out of Whitehead's
Process and Reality."

Faced literally with a situation in which the poet could no longer go
on writing without questioning the very grounds on which he stood, Olson and
Duncan created not a school of poetry but a spiritual/physical place in
which the poem could exist. In a letter of January 7, 1967, Duncan writes:

> Well, here I am today forty-eight and the sun has decided
> to shine bright for it all. And a hero of Olson's West; as you
> in the dream were a worker of the East. Along with me. And
> since it was clear it warn't Einstein or grandaddy Freud and you
> were the Doktor, as I remember it you and I were equally having
> to work (and not having more than the need to go by) the shaman's
> task to release those springs. And they can be too the springs
> of my own heart, and I will have always the joy that you are
> with me "to feed the heart."

The continent had come to replace the culture which had slipped through
Pound's fingers.

Duncan visited Olson at New York Hospital only a few days before
Olson's death. In a letter to Jess Collins shortly thereafter, he writes:

> It was not grievous or sorrowful; he was fiercely
> concernd about the stage he is in: "You put it on me, that
> I was not Zeus, but Prometheus"--(as at that Poetry Conference
> I had said he was the man who stole the fire for us) "I want
> you to tell me what to do. What does Prometheus do?" But then
> he went further than the person of Prometheus: "What does the
> liver mean, the live-her--the doctor said it's a female disease,
> cancer of the liver." And the Liver he saw or projected in
> his talk as Mother Liver. "Then you are in the House of Mother
> Liver" I said and that, as I do, I see him always along a way
> (the way or quest of what those of us who set out in 1950 with
> a mission in poetry were promised to) I had come to know this
> scene of a story I was concerned with. Certainly I knew nothing
> about Mother Liver.[13]

They had arrived at the point where fiction and the literal, physical world
join in a seamless whole. The mission in poetry which had begun in the
1950's was certainly not completed, but it had created the grounds from

which a human community, if not a culture, in Pound's sense of the word, might grow. For the first time, at least since the Renaissance, Olson and Duncan have returned to a place at which our visions and our history both bear directly upon our actions.

NOTES

[1] (San Francisco: City Lights Books, 1967), p. 11.

[2] Human Universe and Other Essays, ed. Donald Allen (New York: Grove Press, 1967), p. 69. Hereafter included in text as HU.

[3] The passages from the letters are quoted by permission of Robert Duncan. I would like to thank both him and George Butterick, Curator of the Olson Archives at the University of Connecticut, who made the letters available to me.

[4] (London: Cape Goliard Press, 1968), n.pag.

[5] "Two Poems (fr 'West'--possibly)", Archaeologist of Morning (New York: Grossman Publishers, 1971), n.pag.

[6] "On Black Mountain," Maps, 4 (1971), 32.

[7] Charles Olson and Ezra Pound: An Encounter at St. Elizabeths, ed. Catherine Seelye (New York: Grossman Publishers, 1975), p. 99. Hereafter included in text as O&P.

[8] In Charles Olson, Causal Mythology (San Francisco: Four Seasons Foundation, 1969), p. 1.

[9] The Maximus Poems (New York: Jargon/Corinth Books, 1960), p. 44.

[10] The Special View of History, ed. Ann Charters (Berkeley: Oyez, 1970), p. 47.

[11] Letters for Origin, ed. Albert Glover (New York: Cape Goliard Press, 1970), 1970), p. 137.

[12] Quoted from an interview in Ann Charter's "Introduction" to The Special View of History, p. 9.

[13] "Letter to Jess after His Last Visit to Olson in New York Hospital, 1970," Olson: The Journal of the Charles Olson Archives, 1 (Spring, 1974), 4-5.

A BOOK OF FIRST THINGS: THE OPENING OF THE FIELD

Michael Davidson

        Go write yourself a book and put
        therein first things that might define a world   (OF 79)

                              I

     The inaccessibility of "first things" to the one who yearns for them
remains a particular concern of Romantic thought. The myth of an Edenic
or Atlantean civilization, the cult of the child, the various permutations
of Rousseau's "noble savage," the Hegelian dialectic of the Spirit, Blake's
reduplicating historical cycles and even Nietzsche's philological revalua-
tion of cultural values reflect preoccupations with an original wholeness
that has been displaced. Reconstituting this primordial condition through
poetry invariably reminds the poet of its distance while offering a me-
diating structure in its place. In Robert Duncan's Romantic stance the
intuition of natural and cosmic order begins a return to that original dis-
placed intent. Access to this world comes fitfully by preeminently what
Pound called "charged" language. To "define a world" creates the realm of
values in which "first things" become necessary at all.
     But language conceived as a series of transparent signs leading to
archetypal or immutable concepts restricts its generative powers. The
history of much of literary modernism and of post-modern poetry challenges
the ideas of permanence, stasis, origin and presence, substituting for
these notions a poetics of immanence and process. Standing significantly
within this evolution is Robert Duncan's The Opening of the Field with its
themes of Edenic parentage, an ever-renewing Atlantean civilization, an

                              56

Yggdrasillic unity of nature and its Whitmanesque vision of America's
poetic potential. And through these inaugural events continues a medita-
tion on poetic beginnings:

> Poems come up from a ground so
> to illustrate the ground, approximate
> a lingering of eternal image, a need
> known only in its being found ready. (OF 60)

The reflexiveness of this activity can be found in the book's title
which indicates the entry INTO a field as well as the field's own expan-
sion into areas of one's life. The image of the field recurs throughout
the book, derived from a childhood dream. Duncan calls it the "Atlantis"
dream, referring to its powerful evocation of a primordial flood which he
associates with the death of his mother at his birth. In an unprinted
preface to the book, he writes:

> In this book I take the field as a theme or rather reference
> point; it is the field which appeared in my earliest remembered
> childhood dream where children danced and an omen came of blow-
> ing grass where no wind was and a king of the game was chosen,
> followed by terror, deluge, by what I do not remember.[1]

The central value in this world of emergent potentialities (and traumas)
is "permission," the trust that the world of the poem will yield signif-
icant form. It stands both for the dreamer's entry into the world of his
unconscious and the poet's willing participation in the terms of the poem:

> OFTEN I AM PERMITTED TO RETURN TO A MEADOW
>
> as if it were a scene made-up by the mind,
> that is not mine, but is a made place,
>
> that is mine, it is so near to the heart,
> an eternal pasture folded in all thought
> so that there is a hall therein
>
> that is a made place, created by light
> wherefrom the shadows that are forms fall. (OF 7)

The idea of the poem as a "field" which the poet enters and to which
he gives "certain bounds" resonates with Charles Olson's "composition by
field" as formulated in "Projective Verse." Duncan had encountered this

seminal essay in 1950 and again in 1952 but had, at first, regarded it as
a polemic on reading poetry aloud. After further reading of The Maximus
Poems he knew the essay established a new "permission" for poets of his
generation to create a poetics of multiple ratios and events; it provided
space for a unified field of interrelated poems like that of The Opening
of the Field:

> It is the field projected by the poem as its own form (ex-
> tended here to the field of the book projected by the poem)
> an effort towards projective verse as initiated by Charles
> Olson.[2]

Olson's concern that the poem be a "high energy construct," utilizing the
physiognomy and metabolism of the poet was certainly attractive to Duncan,
as was the development of a poetry based upon the syllable as quantity
instead of discrete measure. Perhaps the most important contribution for
Duncan was the proposition that the poem creates the terms by which it
shall proceed. As Olson says, once the poet "ventures into FIELD COMPOSI-
TION--puts himself in the open--he can go by no track other than the one
the poem under hand declares, for itself."[3]

Duncan's use of the term, "field," has a series of earlier meanings
which pre-date his awareness of Olson. His reading of Norbert Wiener's
Cybernetics, Siegfried Giedion's Mechanization Takes Command and Wolfgang
Köhler's The Place Of Value in World of Facts, as well as his interest in
the music of Stravinsky and Schoenberg provided paradigms for systems of
interrelated parts directed toward the coherence of the whole. The "serial
poem," practiced by poets in San Francisco during the early fifties (Jack
Spicer, Robin Blaser and others) was an alternative version of the "field"
poem. Its coherence depended upon a poetic series, each poem of which
referred to and generated the others.

For Duncan, the field derives largely from a psychological and biolog-
ical model. Its functions include dreaming and cell-making, both of which
draw from and affect the surrounding environment. Likewise, the variable
field and ground of gestalt psychology (which Duncan had studied in depth
during the forties) contribute to the poet's apprehension of organic

continuities.

> But now the poet works with a sense of parts fitting in
> relation to a design that is larger than the poem. The
> commune of Poetry becomes so real that he sounds each
> particle in relation to parts of a great story that he
> knows will never be completed. (BB vi)

The poem as field does not imitate but enacts natural and cosmic orders:
it does not seek to "contain" meaning but to discover immanent meanings.
Terms of visionary events like "gathering," "inbinding," "equilibriation"
in Duncan's statements contrast with Olson's scientific teems, like "vec-
tor," "projection," "intensive."

But Duncan's variation on Olson's congruence can be felt most strong-
ly in his treatment of dreams, derived essentially from a Freudian perspec-
tive. Olson maintains a strong Jungian focus, preferring the enduring
archetype over the shape-shifting, anagrammatic dreamwork. And the pres-
ence of the "Atlantis" dream provides the most basic source of the field
for this book. It reappears throughout the poems ("A dream of the grass
blowing") much as it had appeared in the poet's childhood.

> It is in the dream itself that we seem entirely creatures,
> without imagination, as if moved by a plot or myth told by a
> story-teller who is not ourselves. Wandering and wondering in
> a foreign land or struggling in the meshes of a nightmare, we
> cannot escape the compelling terms of the dream unless we wake,
> anymore than we can escape the terms of our living reality un-
> less we die. There is a sense in which the "poet" of the poem
> forces us as writer or reader to obey a compelling form, the
> necessities of the poem, so that the poet has a likeness to
> the dreamer of the dream and to the creator of our living re-
> ality; dream, reality, and the poem, seem to be one.
> (H.D. I, 5, 18)

In the dream-text, the loss of the mother, a field of waving grass and the
persistence of a childhood circle dance become primary images of loss and
ritual remembering. The dream becomes an inscription of an early trauma,
the interpretation of which becomes another layer of the conglomerate:

> The dream that was called my Atlantis dream was not some-
> thing I thought up or that derived from the talk of my elders.
> The sequence remains emblematic and puzzling. Had my parents

been Freudian instead of Hermeticists, they might have called
it my birth-trauma dream. My first mother had died in child-
birth, and in some violent memory of that initiation into life,
she may be the mother-country that had been lost in legend.
But for me, the figures of the dream remain as if they were
not symbolic but primal figures themselves of what was being
expressed or shown. Memory of Atlantis or memory of birth-
trauma, phantasy of Isis or play with words--these are not
what the heart fears and needs, the showing forth of some power
over the heart. (H.D. I, 5, 18)

These images inform a number of poems: "Often I Am Permitted to Re-
turn to a Meadow," "The Dance," "Nor Is the Past Pure," "At Christmas,"
"Yes, As a Look Springs to Its Face" (both versions), "A Poem Beginning
With A Line By Pindar," "Atlantis," "Under Ground," and a number of the
"Structure of Rime" prose pieces. The book as a whole provides an elab-
orate reading of this "first" dream. And the "making-up" of a childhood
world through story and dream combines with the poet's making-up of ac-
tuality through the poem. In Jess' frontispiece to the book, a photo-
graph of children dancing in a ring extends into a drawing which includes
the title, providing a visual instance of the dream's ability to structure
a reality beyond it.

This dream parallels myths central to the romantic imagination: the
loss of Eden, the dissolution of an Atlantean continent, Psyche's search
for Eros. The need to restore that prelapsarian state stimulates a
meditation upon the origins of culture and language. Ethics, as Eric
Havelock notes, emerge from the "ethea" or laws of the lair. Duncan's
own establishment of a new household in San Francisco during the period
of this book may have directed his attention to the mythology of the
primal hearth as a source of cultural origins:

        the kin at the hearth, the continual cauldron that feeds
        forth the earth, the heart that comes into being through the
        blood, the householder among his familiar animals, the
        beloved turning to his beloved in the dark

            create love as the leaves
            create from the light life (OF 17)

Duncan's reading of Fustel de Coulanges's The Ancient City during the

early fifties provided a description of Greek and Roman law, having its
base in the household--literally beneath the hearth where the ancestors
were buried.[4] And in the Zohar by Moses de Leon, Duncan found the descrip-
tion of another field. In the section called "Haye Sarah," Abraham comes
upon the field of Machpelah and its adjacent cave which, like pasture and
hall in the "Meadow" poem (OF 7) arise suddenly before him. A quotation
from this section appears in "Yes, As a Look Springs to Its Face,"

> a life colors the meadow.
> "This is the place," Abraham said.
> *The field and the cave therein arose,*   (OF 60)

In the cave, Abraham discovers Adam and Eve who explain that this will be
the burial place for his wife, Sarah, and himself. The field of Mach-
pelah and its cave, holding the beginnings of civilization in the form of
its first parents, are "folded" into history:

> The term *Machpelah* belongs properly neither to the cave nor
> to the field, but to something else with which both were con-
> nected. The cave belongs to the field, and the field to some-
> thing else. For the whole of the Land of Israel and of Jeru-
> salem is folded up beneath it, since it exists both above and
> below, in the same way as there is a Jerusalem both above and
> below, both of the same pattern. . . .[5]

The persistence of this field as both a cultural and personal myth of or-
igins is "folded" in time like a "disturbance of words within words" be-
longing to poetry itself.

Duncan's periodic entrance into the story of origins (his "permis-
sion") accompanies his willing entry into the language of his poem. But
he also realizes that language, like the land of Israel in the Zohar,
exists beyond the poem as a field of shared cultural and social exchanges.
The appearance of language as "other" demands that the poet struggle with
it until it yields what it has to say. This Duncan figures in the story
of Jacob wrestling with the Angel:

> Look! the Angel that made a man of Jacob
> made Israel in His embrace

                    was the Law, was Syntax.

                         Him I love is major mover. (OF 11)

    This interplay of personal creativity with a system of cultural and
historical laws and codes (an inherited syntax and lexicon) adds one more
dimension to this ever-opening field. He sees his poetic act as synec-
dochic for larger processes of creation and destruction.

                                    II

    Jacob's wrestling with "Angelic Syntax" provides a metaphor for the
poet's engagement with poetic form. In "The Dance," Duncan's precise hand-
ling of enjambed short and long lines recreates the ritual of dancers mov-
ing to the spell of music:

                            THE DANCE

            from its dancers circulates among the other
                dancers. This
            would-have-been-feverish cool excess of
                movement makes
            each man hit the pitch co-
                ordinate. (OF 8)

    The use of line-endings and spacings to effect the syncopated dance-
step, the hyphenization of words and the forced enjambment of certain lines
create a poetic equivalent of this dance. In a notebook entry from 1959,
he speaks of this process:

            The tempo of verse is controlled by the line and a new verse
        phrasing in which an observable terminus is given to the line so
        that there is a change of phrase, a suspended pitch at the end
        and a raised stress on the opening syllable of a line following
        the break has made possible a variety of melody in place of the
        unbroken continuum of blank verse or the repetitive organiza-
        tion of conventional quatrains.[6]

As explained in the prose which concludes "The Dance," the poem describes
an actual time of dancing:

            (That was my job that summer. I'd dance until three, then up
        to get the hall swept before nine--beer bottles, cigarette butts,
        paper mementos of the night before. Writing it down now, it is

> the aftermath, the silence, I remember, part of the dance too,
> an articulation of the time of dancing . . like the almost
> dead sleeping is a step. (OF 9)

The poetic translation of the original dance into new measures releases it
from any temporal locus. It moves not from a preordained measure but from
"its" dancers, those who have fallen under the sway of dancing; "co-/
ordinates" are established as the dance proceeds.

Duncan's thoughts on prosody during this period are limited to a few
notebook fragments and reviews. In his important essay, "Notes on Poetics
Regarding Olson's Maximus," of 1956, he outlines patterns of rhythmic con-
tinuity in American poetry in which the "striding syllables" of Emerson's
"Hamatraya" bear significantly upon an "aesthetic based on energies" asso-
ciated with Olson:

> Bulkeley, Hunt, Willard, Hosmer, Meriam, Flint,
> possessed the land which rendered to their toil
> hay, corn, roots, hemp, flax, apples, wool and wood.

Although the essay compares these cadences with Olson's, they appear as
well, in "A Poem Beginning With A Line By Pindar,"

> Hoover, Roosevelt, Truman, Eisenhower—
> where among these did the power reside
> that moves the heart? What flower of the nation
> bride-sweet broke to the whole rapture? (OF 63)

Like the action painter's, the poet's art proceeds according to continu-
ities developed during composition:

> Metrics, as it coheres, is actual——the sense of language in
> terms of weights and durations (by which we cohere in moving).
> This is a dance in whose measured steps time emerges, as space
> emerges from the dance of the body. The ear is intimate to
> muscular equilibrium. The line endures. It "feels" right.
>   (PNAP 190)

Such remarks do not attempt to provide a definitive prosody but illustrate
Duncan's own thinking during the writing of The Opening of the Field. The
variety of poetic styles included in this book (ballads, prose poems, short
lyrics, "open" forms) also indicates that he wished the concept of "book"
to be large enough to reflect a day-to-day range of formal improvisations.
There would, for example, have to be a place for the awkward lines:

> By stress and syllable
> by change-rhyme and contour
> we let the long line pace even awkward to its period.   (OF 51)

And a critic's reservations about Duncan's own poetry are themselves com-
bined in "Poetry, A Natural Thing":

> A second: a moose painted by Stubbs,
> where last year's extravagant antlers
>   lie on the ground.
> The forlorn moosey-faced poem wears
>   new antler-buds,
>   the same,
>
> "a little heavy, a little contrived",
>
> his only beauty to be
>   all moose.   (OF 50)

The critic's quoted remarks about Duncan's "contrived" language are here
isolated to define those qualities in Stubbs.[7]

The book contains an extensive variety of formal and musical possibil-
ities. Besides the more open forms of "A Poem Beginning With A Line By
Pindar," "The Propositions," or "The Dance," with their complex rhythmic
and stanzaic patterning.

There are poems of a greater metrical or stanzaic regularity which
focus on Romantic or theosophical themes: "A Song of the Old Order,"
"The Ballad of Mrs. Noah," "The Ballad of the Enamord Mage," and "This Place
Rumord to Have Been Sodom." More noticeable, however, than the appearance
of patterned repetition and rhyme is the density of syntactic and semantic
variation. In "This Place Rumord to Have Been Sodom," semantic ambiguities
syncopate with the stately rhythms of the four and five-stress lines:

> THIS PLACE RUMORD TO HAVE BEEN SODOM
>
> might have been.
> Certainly these ashes might have been pleasures.
> Pilgrims on their way to the Holy Places remark
> this place. Isn't it plain to all
> That these mounds were palaces? This was once
> a city among men, a gathering together of spirit.
> It was measured by the Lord and found wanting.   (OF 22)

Duncan creates the heretical idea of Sodom as a city governed by Eros
and lost to rumor. The puns and wordplay reinforce the rumor by conceal-
ing other terms, thus playfully participating in the story. The even pace
of the rhythms juxtaposed to the puns on "remark," "men," "spirit," "want-
ing" enforces a slight tension throughout, one necessary to the elevation
of Rumor to "a gathering together of spirit."

In the larger poetic series of the book undergirdings of the later
"Passages" series appear, although Duncan's use of variable spacing and
line lengths, his use of poetic series is by no means new to this book.
"The Venice Poem" and Medieval Scenes from the late forties are based on
an extended series and a complex architecture. Duncan was familiar with
Siegfried Giedion's Mechanization Takes Command in which the art historian
discusses the organic structure of various mechanical devices--including,
of all things, the hammock. Giedion's description could as easily fit
Duncan's characterization of composition in the long series of the forties:

> The whole construction is aerial and hovering as the nest
> of an insect. Everything here is based on mobility, on a system
> of interlocking parts "composed of a number of jointed links or
> boughs and legs and suitable cross-rounds. . . ."[8]

Duncan's use of such biological and mechanical models in discussing
poetic form indicates his faith in the poem as an "event" rather than as an
expressive vehicle, and could be extended to apply to poems like "The Pro-
positions" or "Crosses of Harmony and Disharmony" which are built on vari-
able phrasing and tone but which seem to hover about repeated "leit-
motifs." In such poems, section divisions serve the same function as
movement changes in music, establishing a new tone or mood. Spacing pro-
vides a kind of auditory "scoring" (a space is "held" in proportion to the
lengths of each preceding line). Variable line lengths respond to the
subject at hand, whether indecision,

> We wait.
> It does not come. (OF 36)

or a gradually hardening substance,

```
                              first
              more-than-fire, then liquid stone, then stone . . .
                                    (OF 79)
```

or a catalogue,

```
                    Those who are feeble raising feeble Christs,
                    Those who are kindly raising kindly Christs,
                    Those who are pure raising pure Christs   (OF 84)
```

In such cases, clusters of phrases and spaces occur according to needs
developed at each stage of the composition but are linked thematically and
acoustically to other areas of the poem.

III

The matter of a new prosody brings up the question of beginnings once
again. Poetic origins (language-making) and biological origins (genetic-
cell making) proceed according to a skeleton which evolves intrinsically.
Form emerges from the process of composition, not prior to it. Duncan ex-
plores this question of evolving poetic form and its relation to organic-
ism in "The Structure of Rime" series which originates in The Opening of
the Field.

Begun initially during a reading of Rimbaud's Illuminations at Black
Mountain College, the open-ended series of prose poems seems to invoke
those demons and angels of a post-deluvian prophecy. Its task seeks to
discover the nature of poetic form from within language itself. For this,
Duncan creates "persons of the poem," figures who embody aspects of his
composition, syntax and verbal style: the "Master of Rime," modelled on
Nietzsche's Zarathustra, "the woman who resembles the sentence," the "Lion"
of the creative imagination, and so forth. He describes the process of
developing these voices as part of a "constantly changing theory of rime,
measure, correspondences, as kosmos," and reiterates their identifica-
tion with the "language world itself,"

> . . . like Perse--trance-projection (entranced by language) like
> the shaman--[a soul-trip] [only the poet was to go not into the
> spirit world but into the language world itself] let the persons
> of the Language speak thru me; to send myself into the Language.
> (M 45)

In this series, "Rime" does not imply repetition, necessarily, but correspondence in its largest sense (including opposition). When the poet in "The Structure of Rime II" asks, "What of the Structure of Rime?" the response is given: *"An absolute scale of resemblance and disresemblance [which] establishes measures that are music in the actual world"* (OF 13). The scale is "absolute" because it must structure all relationships extendable from it. Duncan does not imply a transcendental or ideal "forma" but rather a variable form answering to its own necessities. That a tone does not "fit" the scale proposed defines the boundary by which "tonality" may be verified, a boundary which circumscribes the difference between "resemblance" and "disresemblance."

"The Structure of Rime" series with its various voices explores the laws ("scales") by which the poet transforms his world into a world of language-events. The fact of prose underscores its role as a skeletal foundation for the poem. This physiological metaphor mirrors Duncan's belief in "Rime" as "morphological intuition," the apprehension of correspondences and affinities. What governs such an intuition is the emotive charge generated by each moment, a fact which Duncan finds congenial in Whitehead's philosophy and which one discovers throughout the "Structure of Rime" series:

> From a nexus in the Impossible a tear flows, absurd grief
> that is a Universe. (OF 70)

> My Spirit is like a reservoir that cannot draw up its
> knees. I crave the visible disturbers--lightning,
> the naked gods, the falling of buildings. (OF 71)

Here, what Whitehead calls "a lure for feeling" becomes the law of the poem. During the composition of The Opening of the Field, Duncan had been reading Whitehead's Process and Reality, brought to him through Olson's lectures on the philosopher held in San Francisco in 1957.[9] "The Philosophy of Organism," as one of its chapters is titled, with its explorations of organic cohesion and growth, its emphasis on process and change over static categories, agreed largely with Duncan's earlier readings in James and Dewey and Köhler.

Olson's use of Whitehead differs somewhat from Duncan's, at least in terms of the direction taken with the philosophical system. The interpenetration of events (prehension) and the applicability of this process in developing an historical perspective were extremely interesting to Olson. The fact that a single moment has a potential to infuse all others provides Olson with a usable definition of history as "the practice of space in time." How the citizens of Gloucester, Massachusetts, use their town has ramifications for the history not only of that town but the country as a whole. This attention to the extensiveness of the local distinguishes Olson's historicity in The Maximus Poems.

Duncan's concern with Whitehead also derives from the description of an "extensiveness" of events and objects, but it is more the philosopher's use of the body, memory and perception as systems of interconnectedness which attracts him. In the chapter of Process and Reality titled "The Propositions," Duncan found confirmation for his view of the poem as a field wherein feeling emerges:

> A proposition is an element in the objective lure *proposed for feeling*, and when admitted into feeling it constitutes what is felt. The *imaginative* feeling . . . of a proposition is one of the ways of feeling it; and intellectual belief is another way of feeling the proposition, a way which presupposes imaginative feeling. 10

Propositions, like poems, occupy an interstitial realm between potentiality and actuality. Duncan's application of such terms coincides with his genetic-cellular view of nature whereby an organism evolves towards its form, not from it.

Attempting to make concrete application of Whitehead's terms, Duncan's poem "The Propositions" explores the condition of love within the specific context of physical pain. A friend's hospital stay provides the focus; the sights of injury and suffering encountered there become the "lures" for more intense feeling which are juxtaposed to the physician's skill:

> the precision the hand knows
> necessary to operate. (OF 30)

His "incisive line" follows the unique configuration of the wound just as

the poet's line must follow the contours of an emotion (and as the sea
"seeks verification" in the "shore lines"--sure lines--created in concert
with the Moon). Physician and poet participate in a world of extremes:
the ability to make discriminations and precise choices surrounded by "vi-
olent imperatives."

The entire poem corrects the traditional love lyric. At one point,
the poet mentions a dream in which "The Masters of Cruelty" offer a hideous
choice:

> Shall we
> tear out *your* eyes . . . or *his*?
>
> "No! No, tear out *my* eyes." But what is terror?
> It flows both ways. (OF 33)

The horror of the choice reflects the power of love in which the anguish
of seeing the lover's pain equals one's own physical pain. No rational
choice can be possible, a fact which Whitehead incorporates into his dis-
tinction between propositions and judgments. Rational decisions, made
under the terms of judgments become tools of the logician. Propositions
imply a multiplicity of choices: "It is a gathering of crows,/omens, that
animates the artifice."

In Olson's The Special View of History, based largely around White-
head's philosophy, love is defined as one of the four qualities. Duncan's
exploration of love includes its power to generate pain as well as life:

> might I deny the force that drove me to the ground
> prime reality?
>
> Have you never come to grief
> in which love holds   reciprocal pain
> of heart? (OF 33)

Love becomes a proposition, composed of "hurt and healing." The demands
of sexuality create an absolute law which Duncan portrays through the vi-
olence contained in romantic story, "that threw up Knights and Demoisel-
les/that did desire the Heart to eat." That love would be directed
entirely toward the "good" fails to recognize its power to hurt and its
ability to "in-/form demand." And, as if to illustrate the danger, Duncan

draws portraits of Van Gogh's madness, William Morris's cultural despair,
Nietzsche's syphilitic last days and Artaud's "poses of crisis."

Another poem in which Whitehead's philosophy appears, "Crosses of
Harmony and Disharmony," refers to the concept of "presentational immed-
iacy," a mode of perception which takes into account the extensiveness of
each spatial region. When we look at an object in a mirror, Whitehead
says, we see both the delusion of the mirror's reflection and the area
behind the mirror at the same time. Such perception does not participate
in discriminations as to what is real or delusory; it accepts the "immed-
iacy" as presented. "It thereby defines a cross-section of the universe,"
Whitehead says, echoing the "cross" which Duncan makes his leit-motif in
the poem.[11]

Whitehead describes this mode of perception by reference to "double
vision, due to maladjustment of the eyes," a condition which affects Dun-
can's own sight. His crossed vision involves the ability to see both near
and far at the same time, a physiological equivalent of the numerous puns
which flood the opening lines:

> "Gladly, the cross-eyed bear"--the cross
> rising from the eye a strain of visible song
>   that Ursa Major dances,
>   star notes, configurations
>   from right to wrong
>   the all night long body stretchd bare
>   sleep's guy in the fame of musical shares,   (OF 44)

Contained in the wordplay of these lines lies a view of complex perception
by which a group of stars in the distant sky may, at the same time, provide
the outline of a bear held in the mind. The stars create a "scale" by
which an image or theme appears, made up of "star notes." No act of per-
ception is simple any more than any act of language "says what it means."
Duncan's poetry incurs such doubleness ("a game of musical shares") in a
belief that the poetic act is semantically generative. He "Gladly" bears
the cross of this double vision (metaphorically and literally) to avoid the
positivist reduction of events to simple causes. The poet, like Dr. Sea in
"The Propositions" "cuts the meat but sees/anatomies." Likewise,

Whitehead's philosophy seeks to include a complex of occasions, "the multi-
fariousness of the world--/the fairies dance, and Christ is naild to the
cross" just as the poet seeks it in his poetry.

For Duncan, Whitehead's view of the propositional nature of reality
provides a link with the poetic act. The poem creates time in the form of
measured language:

> Let
> it have no earthly importance.
> It is a proposition from which
>
> > time flows and takes on umbrage of
> > ultimate things, trans-
> > mutations, crossings over,
> > the tremblings of love. (OF 45)

IV

The potential of language to yield realms of cosmic and divine poten-
cy returns again and again in Duncan's work as a form of hermeneutic. The
Rabbi meditating on the hidden significance of letters in the alphabet, the
psychoanalyst interpreting the patient's dream, the child reciting a nurs-
ery rhyme each participates in this reading act. And by this activity,
the reader participates in the presence of "first things" embodied in a
text.

Duncan's "adopted" parents (as he refers to them) had been involved
in a theosophical movement, presenting their children with stories from
Greek and Egyptian myth along with more traditional Christian versions.
His syncretism began at an early age. "Truth was for my parents primord-
ial and spiritually dangerous"(TLM 9). But this Truth (Gnosis) had been
lost through a catastrophe and was supplanted by what we call knowledge.
In the "Pindar" poem, Psyche appears as "Scientia" when she seeks to dis-
cover the identity of Eros, science being the modern version of gnosticism.
The unravelling of the tale, the reading of forms in clouds, the decipher-
ing of anagrams in Shakespeare's plays, Freud's "rebus" of the dream in
each case participate in a ritual act of decoding, translating, inter-
preting and making-up by the adept in order to reach that original Truth.

        Rabbi Aaron of Bagdad meditating upon the Word
            and the letters Yod and Hé
        came upon the Name of God and achieved a pure rapture
        in which a creature of his ecstasy that was once dumb clay,
                the Golem,
        danced and sang and had being. (OF 81)

The appearance of Christ in The Opening of the Field coincides with
this aspect of the Divine which the Rabbi reads out of letters in the
Hebrew alphabet. Christ, as Logos, embodies a generative principle in
language which links him with Thoth, the Egyptian scribe and inventor of
writing. In "The Structure of Rime VIII" Duncan combines him with Chiron,
the centaur teacher of Achilles, Herakles, and Asklepius.

        How uncertain when I said unwind the winding. Chiron,
        Cross of Two Orders! Grammarian! from your side the
        never healing! Undo the bindings of immutable syntax! (OF 70)

Duncan could also be thinking of the "Chi-Rho" monogram which fuses the
first two letters of the Greek Khristos. In any case, the "letter" is
primary to Christ's nature. In "Another Animadversion," Christ becomes
the likeness of Eros, "ever remembered Lord of Sensualities." In "The
Maiden," he becomes a young girl; "He had solitude." And in "At Christ-
mas," as Wendy MacIntyre has shown, he participates in the act of birth-
giving, his sacrificial agony reflected in "the severing of the hymen and
in the labors of birth."[12] Christ, through his various avatars in history,
is folded INTO history; his nature demands that he be revived.

An important poem in terms of this translation of the creative in
Christ is "Another Animadversion." Duncan quarrels (animadverts) with
"those who tell us Christ was a higher-type man" and who establish a
hierarchy of salvific values to be levelled on others (Duncan's antipathy
to the organized Christian church--or any other orthodoxy--can be found
throughout his writings). His mystery may be found in the things of the
world, "deliberate committed lines of stone or flesh,/flashings of suf-
fering shared." This diffusion of Christ into the world agrees with the
Hermetic-Theosophical view of a fragmented original intent revived by
readers who see a Divine Logos in the writings of certain authors. An old

lady who reads this primordial Christ in Whitman participates in his
being by seeing him "freed from the bondage of old ways." Duncan himself
performs the same act in his "Pindar" poem, reading a lost visionary poten-
tial in "old poets" like Whitman, Williams and Pound. The larger cosmology
of this diffusion appears later in the poem:

> Now let me describe the agony,
> the upward toppling from--was it a simple feeling?
>   into stylistic conglomerations of power,
> the devouring giant race that mistakes us
>   opening certain likeliness
> so that the gods that had faces of being
>   fell apart into one thought   (OF 87)

Such "stylistic conglomerations of power" become consolidations of
poetic styles by "noysome poets" seeking an authority of single doctrine
against the idea of the natural. But even this vision of the natural
finds its source in words:

> *Feld, graes or gaers, hus, daeg, dung*
> in field, grass, house, day and dung we share
> with those that in the forests went,
>   singers and dancers out of the dream. (OF 87)

Each word (in this case, the Anglo-Saxon base) joins in creating the "book
of the Earth," a process of gathering-together versions of the creative.
The manhood of Christ represents the ultimate potential for each person to
participate in this gathering.

Christ's role as generative principle coincides with his participa-
tion in the ritual of death of suffering. What has "died" returns to that
fructive field of potential renewals. Time becomes vegetative, the past
providing a kind of mulch upon which future projects grow.

> The realized
> is dung of the ground that feeds us, rots,
>   falls part
>
> into the false   (OF 41)

An earlier version of this poem ("Nor Is The Past Pure") [13] deals with
masturbation as an act which participates in withheld potency and blocked
fulfillment. But the act does not fall under condemnation. Rather, it is

celebrated within the context of "the pure urge," the same principle upon
which "The realized" becomes "dung of the ground that feeds us." Although
the final version leaves the act somewhat obscure, its potency and "readi-
ness"

> > > > O happy actor
> > > who in the offices of self seeks
> > > > > that which prospers:
>
> > > the full burgeoning, ripeness that is ready,
> > > > the generous falling
> > > into the raptures of heroic death,   the ground,
> > > > the mulch, the right furrow.   (OF 42)

In "Under Ground," a similar pattern occurs. Monuments and epitaphs
which celebrate the dead become "kept dimensions" for that which has gone
under ground. Duncan draws upon a variety of such monuments: Shakespeare's
dedication of the Sonnets to Mr. W.H., Pindar's "Ode to Hippokleas" in
Pythian X, Cheops' pyramid, Charlemagne's tomb, etc. Each of these trib-
utes celebrates the existence, not the death, of someone; as such, they
become "first things that might define a world." Their presence in a poem
called "Under Ground" only suggests that the world is composed of such
memorials, testaments to being, as figured, for example, in the story of
Swift's final days:

> > > Enraged Swift
> > > upon his housekeeper's removing a knife
> > > > as he was going to catch at death
> > > shruggd his shoulders and said:
> > > > *I am what I am*
> > > and in about six minutes, repeated the same
> > > > two or three times.   (OF 80)

Elsewhere, Duncan remembers a former friend, Jeff Rall, whom the poet
had known in anarchist circles during the forties. The poem becomes a
"cenotaph" for Jeff Rall "who/in youth fell/at Dunkirk, because war was
more real/than Blenheim's/in the Village" (Rall was not actually killed,
although Duncan did not know it at the time). The poem itself becomes
such a memorial by remembering both the person and the memorial, standing
"for" while at the same time participating in "a hidden liaison with spring-
time,/an allegiance to the unmentioned."

In "The Structure of Rime XII," the same reverence for that which has returned to earth emerges as a revival. Small creatures and insects of the ever-present field through their hunger provide a continual pattern of eating and "clearing" the field:

> Under the Permission, O yes, under the Permission, at the
> edges of light, the perpetual thriving, our clearings there--
> The handsome builder has torn up the pampas grass that was
> a lord (a tree) of the lower garden--
>
>   our dreams, as the cat too, in those casual nests!   (OF 82)

This theme of renewal out of death and destruction comes to focus in the final poem, "Food for Fire, Food for Thought." Here, Duncan develops the metaphor of the primitive hearth where orders of household and culture begin. Around this central fire, child and householder alike see figures and stories reflected in the flickering light just as Leonardo saw them in stains upon a wall. The fire becomes "the genius of the household, as if the secret of our warmth and companionship were hidden in a wrathful flame" (TOU 142).

Like the spontaneous freeing of such stories from the flames, Duncan's poetic language is "obeyed" rather than being forced to accommodate: "Language obeyd flares tongues in obscure matter." This provides a kind of epilogue to the book which has proposed a world accessible through language:

> This is what I wanted for the last poem,
> a loosening of conventions and return to open form.   (OF 95)

The wood which provides the food for the fire and the word which "flares tongues" reduces the terms for age and youth to simple oppositions. As a form of cosmic nourishment, wood and word further the idea of firstness:

> We are close enough to childhood so easily purged
> of whatever we thought we were to be,
>
>   flamey threads of firstness go out from your touch.
>
>   Flickers of unlikely heat
>   at the edge of our belief bud forth.   (OF 96)

V

The belief in language as "obeyed" finds its most exhaustive treat-
ment in "A Poem Beginning With A Line By Pindar," a poem which participates
in all of the themes discussed thus far. At its center lies a story of
loss and re-discovery (Apuleus' tale of Eros and Psyche) generated by a
line from Pindar's "Pythian Ode I": "The light foot hears you and the
brightness begins." Pindar, by initiating the poem in Duncan's mind,
becomes one of a multitude of poets whose theme sounds beginnings.

Other layers are introduced: the ritual dance celebrating the gods,
a painting of Cupid and Psyche by Goya, Whitman's vision of an American
democratic potency, Psyche's purgatorial tasks, the American westward
movement as romantic legend, the counter-clockwise movement of Jason in
his attempt to return with the Golden Fleece, and finally the "Atlantis"
dream with its vision of children imitating great cycles of birth and
death, creation and destruction in their circular dance.

The poet's personal participation in each detail binds such disparate
parts together. Autobiographical elements fuse with the mythological.
The act of reading Pindar participates in the ritual dance which lies
behind the poem. Pindar's poem, Duncan explains in a prose section, "was
not a statue, but a mosaic, an accumulation of metaphor." Duncan's art
is also an accumulation (collage) lacking a specific telos but directed
toward areas in which ideas of resolution and periodicity have failed.
The qualification of this failure is stated as part of the prose commen-
tary:

> But if he was archaic, not classic, a survival of obsolete mode,
> there may have been old voices in the survival that directed
> the heart. So, a line from a hymn came in a novel I was reading
> to help me. Psyche, poised to leap—and Pindar too, the editors
> write, goes too far, topples over—listend to a tower that said,
> *Listen to me!* (OF 69)

This comment helps to answer one of the crucial questions of the
poem's opening lines: the problem of the "you" that the "light foot"
hears. This "you" becomes the endlessly shifting witness of story through-
out time: the Dionysiac dancers responding to "torso-reverberations of a

Grecian lyre" as well as the contemporary poet reading late at night.   The "you" is the one who listens, a fact which Duncan discovers in Apuleius' tale. To obtain Eros, Psyche must leap from a cliff, despite the danger. So, the poet of open forms obeys the instructions of a previous and compelling language world, whether contained in Whitman or in the modulations and rhythms of his own poetry. To go "too far" implies a commitment.

Duncan's invocation of earlier poets recognizes that their commitment shines through "their faltering/their unaltering wrongness that has style." Whitman's "glorious mistake," his vision of an American democratic potential seen through Lincoln, affirms that "the theme is creative and has vista." As Roy Harvey Pearce has remarked, ". . . Duncan sees that Whitman as poet succeeded not as he portrayed failure, but rather as he gave us the means to measure success, thus to know that our forebears' failures, and our leaders', may well be our own."[14]

The "old stories" emerge out of their power of heart-felt expression, but Duncan wonders at America's inability to maintain the force of that democratic potential which Whitman projected. In the catalogue of presidents, the dispersion of this potential, like Psyche's seeds, among inept men is apparent:

> Where among these did the spirit reside
> that restores the land to productive order? (OF 64)

Presiding over this grim catalogue of failed leadership is the youthful persistence of Cupid and Psyche, "workers of a fiction in the art of poetry" (H.D. I, 3, 67). Their drama of union, loss and search as enacted in Apuleius' tale from The Golden Ass (and later in Goya's painting from the Marquis de Cambo's collection) contains resonances of earlier tellings. Throughout the poem, Psyche's (the soul's) acts parallel those of the poet. For each reenactment, the poet stands like Psyche, "poised to leap." He stands before Love as Whitman stood before America, surrounded by a cacophany of accusing and jealous voices warning him of Love's demonic powers.

Psyche's "first permission" becomes her willing acceptance of Eros, described by her sisters as a serpent or demon. The equivalent act for the

poet in Whitman's footsteps is his ability to project what a nation (or a
poem) might be. Such a projection establishes boundaries around which the
values and laws of a society (for the poet, a poetics) may gather. In the
opening lines, Duncan pays homage to Hermes, god of the boundary: "god-
step at the margins of thought,/quick adulterous tread at the heart." In
"Toward an Open Universe" he clarifies:

> I had mistaken the light foot for Hermes the Thief, who
> might be called The Light Foot, light-fingered, light-tongued.
> The Homeric Hymns tell us that he devised the harp of
> Apollo and was first in the magic, the deceit, of song.
> But as Thoth, he is Truth, patron of poets. (TOU 144)

The tricky quality of Hermes echoes those earlier poems in the book in
which an under-handed or deceitful presence maintains the natural order; in
his poem, sight once again crosses:

> I see always the under side turning,
> fumes that injure the tender landscape.
>   From which up break
> lilac blossoms of courage in daily act
>   striving to meet a natural measure. (OF 64)

The transition of "fumes" to "lilac blossoms," albeit a radical shift
(embodying visions of an industrial waste as well as Whitman's elegaic
flowers), asserts a necessary conjunction of the two much like those seen
in "Nor Is the Past Pure" and "Under Ground." These lines, following upon
Whitman's "double vision" of openness and regulation ("The theme is crea-
tive and has vista."/"He is the president of regulation.") continue the
series of oppositions which form the background for each expressive act.
By the end of the poem, the "under side" refers to the globe which turns
inexorably upon its axis, revealing its dark side to the light.

The poem's four sections orchestrate themes and patterns developed
throughout the book, not so much along a linear pattern but rather in terms
of a geological or topographical layering. If there can be said to exist
an over-all pattern, it would be in imitation of the Psyche and Eros story:
discovery, dispersion, purgatorial tasks and, finally, re-constitution
through memory.

Section one announces the return of primordial beginnings through art.

The Grecian lyre, pre-dating Pindar, surfaces in his poem of praise for
Hieron's chariot in the Pythian games of 470 B.C. But the athletic con-
test is unimportant next to the sounds and textures of Pindar's opening
line and Duncan's own intimation of much earlier ritualistic forms con-
tained. This same early music and ritual, mediated by a romantic and re-
demptive vision, re-emerges in Goya's canvas of the two lovers at the mo-
ment of Psyche's recognition. Duncan focuses on the point that the land-
scape of Goya's painting is that of story itself:

> But they are not in a landscape.
> They exist in an obscurity. (OF 62)

All elements of the story, the "wind spreading the sail," the "jealous
sisters," the "dark," the fatal hot oil which arouses the sleeping Eros,
serve the primal drama, a fact which " The Propositions" makes vivid in
its recounting of scenes antagonistic but necessary to the larger config-
uration of love.

The dispersion of this tale among its tellers (Apuleius, Pindar, Dun-
can and Goya being only four) in section II reflects the loss of Eros,
the god of love and desire, once Psyche has recongized him. As Duncan has
said of her,

> Psyche before her sin is a dilettante. To read, to listen,
> to study, to gaze was all part of being loved without loving,
> a pleasure previous to any trial or pain of seeking the beloved.
> The light must be tried; Psyche must doubt and seek to know;
> reading must become life and writing; and all go wrong. There
> is no way then but Psyche's search, the creative work of a
> union in knowledge and experience. At the end, there is a new
> Eros, a new Master over Love. (H.D. I, 3, 69)

If this tale is, as Duncan insists, primordial, it must inhere in the work-
ings of other kinds of fictions. He sees in the dispersion of Whitman's
dream for America among its presidents the loss of an original optimism.
"A disturbance of words within words," Duncan calls the informing power of
charged language in the poem and he provides a vivid example of this in the
aphasic speech of an aging William Carlos Williams, following his debilita-
ting stroke:

> A stroke. These little strokes. A chill.
> The old man, feeble, does not recoil.
> Recall. A phase so minute,
> only a part of the words in-jerrd.

> *The Thundermakers descend,*

> damerging a nuv. A nerb.
> The present dented of the U
> nighted stayd. States. The heavy clod?
> Cloud. Invades the brain. What
> if lilacs last in *this* dooryard bloomd? (OF 63)

Possessed by the vision of an atomic cloud as well as the failures of
speech, Williams struggles in his old age toward a renewal of love (par-
ticularly in poems like "Of Asphodel That Greeny Flower") and a mythic
version of American political life (in Paterson). Williams' stroke, in the
lines quoted above, becomes the painter's brushstroke as well; "aphasia"
becomes "a phase," as though Duncan wished to transform the physical mal-
ady into art: an act which "serves" the story.

But if this "old poet" is Williams, who becomes his Lincoln? Eisen-
hower? Duncan asks, "What/if lilacs in *this* dooryard bloomd?" In Wil-
liams' halting speech Duncan finds a presence of an original clarity:

> It is toward the old poets
> we go, to their faltering,
> their unaltering wrongness that has style,
> their variable truth, (OF 63)

Whitman's love for Lincoln must undergo qualifications in terms of sub-
sequent history: a testing and challenge, and so the poet joins Psyche in
her search.

Section III, dedicated to Charles Olson, describes the task of re-
construction of that dispersed power. Williams's concern for the partic-
ular and the local, Pound's use of precise language and Olson's demand for
an energetic poetic work combine with Psyche's task of "gathering the gold
wool from the cannibal sheep."

> These are the old tasks.
> You've heard them before.

> They must be impossible. Psyche
> must despair, he brought to her
> > insect instructor;
> > (OF 65)

Pound, too, ("The old man at Pisa") had been brought to a sight of small
things in The Pisan Cantos. The ants and lizards and natural processes
which dominate these purgatorial cantos occur as salvific values for an
imprisoned Pound, "a lone ant from a broken ant-hill" of postwar Europe.

The struggle to re-constitute a displaced power by Psyche and "the old
poets" occurs in terms of Jason's counter-clockwise return to Thessaly
from Colchis with the Golden Fleece, an attempt to bring home the light by
a difficult passage:

> There is the hero who struggles east
> widdershins to free the dawn and must
> > woo Night's daughter,
> sorcery, black passionate rage, covetous queens,
> so that the fleecy sun go back from Troy,
> > Colchis, India . . . all the blazing armies
> spent, he must struggle alone toward the pyres of Day. (OF 66)

Light pervades this section: The Golden Fleece, the Symplegades (wandering
rocks) which "swim below the sun," the "light that is love," the "diffuse
light" of the romantic western painters (Bierstadt, Remington?), and most
importantly, the light from the lamp of "Scientia," or that curiosity of an
innocent Psyche "driven by doubt." The "light foot" of the poem's opening
line has been expanded to include the illumination of a primordial soul.
In "Often I Am Permitted to Return to a Meadow," the field or poem is a
"made place, created by light," suggesting both processes of photosynthesis
and the painter's chiaroscuro. [15]

Psyche's use of light to verify the legend of her demon husband repre-
sents the first appropriation of energy transforming the presence it was to
reveal into the absence which lies at the heart of the problem of origins.
For the poet of open forms, the struggle becomes a need to "penetrate the
seeming of style and subject matter to that most real where there is no
form that is not content, no content that is not form" (TOU 138).

The reconstitution of an original, mythic universe emerges through the

Atlantis dream in section IV. The tone of the entire section is exalted, differing from the more halting progress of the previous section in which

```
                                                 West
         from east    men push.
                                  The islands are blessd
         (cursed)     that swim below the sun.  (OF 66)
```

Now the appeal is directed toward the essential pregnancy of each moment. The "light foot" becomes the "foot informd," transformed through poetic work:

```
            that foot  informd
       by the weight of all things
            that can be elusive
    no more than a nearness to the mind
            of a single image

              Oh yes!    this
    most dear
            the catalyst force that renders clear
    the days of a life from the surrounding medium!  (OF 67)
```

What has been evoked in terms of a light-dark patterning, an effort and struggle, now becomes the acceptance of an essential wholeness, gleaned from the children's dance. Here, Pindar's poetic art and the dreamer's vision combine in one circle with the returning sun:

```
    the information flows
         that is yearning.  A line of Pindar
    moves from the area of my lamp
         toward morning.

    In the dawn that is nowhere
         I have seen the willful children

    clockwise and counter-clockwise turning.  (OF 69)
```

Duncan's faith in the childhood world ("before our histories began") and its expression in song and dance ("Finders Keepers we sang") occurs along lines similar to those involved in defining the field:

```
    To be a child is not an affair of how old one is.  "Child"
    like "angel" is a concept, a realm of possible being.  Many
    children have never been allowed to stray into childhood.
    Sometimes I dream of at last becoming a child.  (NAP 404-405)
```

The "Pindar" poem is the central poem for Duncan's poetics and cosmo-
logy, circling as it does around those "old stories" as if to locate the
"scene" of writing. "It's the universe suspended by the human word," he
says in "Atlantis." The sense that decisions of cosmic significance have
their base in the minute articulations of one's language lies behind "that
foot informd," his projection of Pindar's single line into a cosmology.
The Opening of the Field challenges the idea that events attain meaning
through their analogy to processes beyond us and attempts to re-constitute
meaning as an infinitely displaced presence. This presence ("a nearness to
the mind") exists, like the story of Eros and Psyche, "in an obscurity"
which must endlessly be sought in and through language.

Duncan's dialogue with the past, which I have discussed in terms of a
problematic of origins, provokes a confrontation with the present. And the
confrontation is essentially linguistic, the poet finding in the minute
differences between individual phonemes and words, resonances which lead
the poem forward:

> Central to and defining the poetics I am trying to suggest
> here is the conviction that the order man may contrive or
> impose upon the things about him or upon his own language
> is trivial beside the divine order or natural order he may
> discover in them. (TOU 139)

We may recognize in this position an Emersonian faith in the essential co-
herence of nature--and in the poet's power to uncover it. The poet "reads"
the order of things as a great book, full of portents and omens. A child-
hood dream offers him a text constructed on its own terms, a design which
is "read" as it is "written" into the poem. The Opening of the Field
writes the discovery of this design out of other texts: myths of origin,
Romantic tales, The Zohar, the Bible, a film by Bergman, a painting by
Rubens. In them is contained an immanent presence that, for Duncan, hovers
at the borders of comprehension. Duncan's book becomes an event in itself,
tied to the dances, dramas, rituals, wars and excavations which make up its
contents. It solidly inhabits its own duplicities, extending a broad vista
of Whitmanian potential while recognizing its insufficiencies. A "book of

first things" cannot be created solely out of assurances and continuities
but must accept the vulnerable threshold upon which beginnings are based as
well: "It's the universe suspended by the human word."

NOTES

[1]Notebook A, p. 102.   Notebooks in the Bancroft Library, University of
California, Berkeley.

[2]Notebook A, p. 102.

[3]Charles Olson, "Projective Verse" in Human Universe and Other Essays, ed.
Donald Allen (N.Y.: Grove Press, 1967), p. 52.

[4]Fustel de Coulanges (Numa Denis), The Ancient City; A Study of the Reli-
gion, Laws and Institutions of Greece and Rome (N.Y., 1873).

[5]The Zohar, trans. Harry Sparling and Maurice Simon (London, 1949), Vol.
II, p. 16.

[6]Notebook A, p. 97.

[7]Letter from John Crowe Ransom to Robert Duncan, 14 Aug. 1957.   Quoted by
permission of Washington University Libraries.
   I have read this verse of yours with interest.   I don't think we could
   quite use it; . . . you get some difficult things said poetically. Some-
   how it seems a little heavy, a little contrived, but you are a good
   prospect.

[8]Siegfried Giedion, Mechanization Takes Command (Oxford: Oxford University
Press, 1948), p. 476.

[9]Charles Olson, The Special View of History (Berkeley: Oyez, 1970), p. 12.

[10]Alfred North Whitehead, Process and Reality (1929; rpt. New York: Harper
& Row, 1960), p. 285.

[11]Ibid., p. 186.

[12]Wendy MacIntyre, "Robert Duncan: The Actuality of Myth," Open Letter,
Second Series, No. 4 (Spring 1973), 47.

[13]"Masturbation: For the Innocence of the Act," R. C. Lion, No. 3 (1967),
46-50.

[14]Roy Harvey Pearce, "Whitman and Our Hope for Poetry," in Historicism Once
More (Princeton: Princeton University Press, 1969), p. 327.

[15]The "Meadow Poem" was first published in Ark II, Moby I (1956/1957),
[10], in which the relationship between field and poem is made explicit.

SOME DUNCAN LETTERS--A MEMOIR AND A CRITICAL TRIBUTE

Denise Levertov

In the early spring of 1948 I was living in Florence, a bride of a few
months, having married American literature, it seemed, as well as an Amer-
ican husband. Both of us haunted the U.S.I.S. library on the via Tornabu-
oni--Mitch to begin rereading at leisure the classics of fiction he had been
obliged to gallop through meaninglessly at Harvard, I to discover, as a
young writer of the British "New Romantic" phase of the 1940's, the poetry
of what was to be my adopted country. I had read at that time a minimal
amount of Pound (anthologized in a Faber anthology) and Stevens ("discov-
ered" in Paris a few months before when Lynne Baker lent me a copy of The
Blue Guitar). William Carlos Williams I had found for myself in the Amer-
ican bookstore on the Rue Soufflot, near the Sorbonne, but though I knew
with mysterious certainty that his work would become an essential part of my
life, I had not yet heard enough American speech to be able to hear his
rhythms properly; his poems were a part of the future, recognized but held
in reserve. The rest of American poetry was terra incognita, except for
Whitman (in the William Michael Rossetti edition of 1868) and a few poems
by Emily Dickinson, Robert Frost, and Carl Sandburg--again, anthology pieces
only. I had read Eliot; but like most English readers at that time, I
thought of him as an English poet (and of course, the fact that it was pos-
sible to do so was precisely what made Williams so angry with him, as I
later understood). Also I had read and loved, at George Woodcock's house in
London a year or so before, a few poems from Rexroth's Signature of All
Things.[1] Those were the limits of my acquaintance with U.S. poetry.

The American library was not, to my recollection, rich in poetry; but

among my findings were some issues of <u>Poetry</u>, Chicago; and in one of these,
a review by Muriel Rukeyser of Robert Duncan's <u>Heavenly City</u> <u>Earthly City</u>.
Both these people, then just names to me, were to become, in varying ways,
close friends who influenced my history--as did Dr. Williams. Thinking
back from the present (1975) I realize how destiny was sounding the first
notes, in that cold Florentine spring, of motifs that would recur as domin-
ant themes in the 50's and 60's (and in the case of Muriel Rukeyser, with
whom I visited Hanoi in 1972, into the 70's) and which, indeed, are so inter-
woven in my life that whatever changes befall me they must be forever a part
of its essential music.

In Muriel's review of <u>Heavenly City</u> <u>Earthly City</u>, she quoted:

> There is an innocence in women
> that asks me, asks me;
> it is some hidden thing they are
> before which I am innocent.
> It is some knowledge of innocence.
> Their breasts lie undercover.
> Like deer in the shade of foliage,
> they breathe deeply and wait;
> and the hunter, innocent and terrible,
> enters love's forest.

These lines, and the whole review, so stirred me that I convinced myself no
one in Florence needed that particular issue of <u>Poetry</u> more than I did, and
I not only kept it out for months but, when we left for Paris, took it with
me. It is the only such rip-off I have ever committed.

Retrospectively, I see that I was drawn to Duncan's poems of that
period not only by their intrinsic beauty but because they must have formed
for me a kind of trans-Atlantic stepping-stone. The poems of my own first
book (<u>The Double Image</u>, 1946) and those that Rexroth included in <u>The New
British Poets</u> (New Directions, 1949) belonged to that wave of Romanticism
which Rexroth documented, an episode of English poetry that was no doubt
in part a reaction against the fear, the drabness, and the constant danger
of death in the daily experience of civilians as well as of soldiers in W.W.
II. While the subject matter of the poems of the "New Romantic" movement
may often have been melancholy and indeed morbid, the formal impulse was
towards a richly sensuous, image-filled music. When the war ended, English

poetry quickly changed again and became reactively dry, as if embarrassed
by the lush, juicy emotionalism of the 40's. But though not many individ-
ual poems of the New Romantics stand up very well to time and scrutiny,
they still seem preferable to the dull and constipated attempts at a poetry
of wit and intellect that immediately succeeded them, for their dynamic
connected them with a deeper, older tradition, the tradition of magic and
prophecy and song, rather than of ironic statement. And it was to that old,
incantatory tradition that Duncan, then and always, emphatically (and, as
I did not then know, consciously) belonged. So here, I must have intuited,
was an American poet whose musical line, and whose diction, were acces-
sible to me. It must have made my emigration, which I knew was not far
distant, seem more possible, more real. Lines of my own (from a poem in
The Double Image which Duncan—years later—read and admired) may serve to
show some of the affinity I felt:

TO DEATH

        Enter with riches. Let your image wear
        brocade of fantasy, and bear your part
        with all the actor's art and arrogance.
        Your eager bride, the flickering moth that burns
        upon your mouth, brings to your dark reserve
        a glittering dowry of desire and dreams.

        These leaves of lightness and these weighty boughs
        that move alive to every living wind,
        dews, flowers, fruit, and bitter rind of life,
        the savour of the sea, all sentient gifts
        you will receive, deserve due ritual;
        eloquent, just, and mighty one, adorn
        your look at last with sorrow and with fire.
        Enter with riches, enviable prince.

In a 1964 letter, after talking about a then new poem of mine called
"Earth Psalm," Duncan tells how after rereading it that day he had read, or
reread, "To Death" and, "I began to conjure the Tudor, no Stuart (something
between King James's Bible and Bunyan) dimension (a fourth dimensional of
you) with figures from a masque . . . Haven't we, where we have found a
source, or some expression of what we love in human kind, to give it a
place to live today, in our own gesture (which may then speak of nobility
or ardour)—Well, if Orpheus can come forward, so, by the work of the poem,

Death and His Bride in brocade--

    "How many correspondences there are," he goes on to say, "between your
Double Image, 1946, and my Medieval Scenes written in 1947. In this poem
'To Death'--'brocade of fantasy': in 'The Banners' where the 'bright jer-
kins of a rich brocade' is part of the fabric of the spell; or in 'The Con-
querors' compare 'The Kingdom of Jerusalem'. . . ." And after a few more
lines of comment he begins, right in the letter, the poem "Bending the Bow"

> We've our business to attend Day's
> duties, bend back the bow in dreams as we may,
> til the end rimes in the taut string
> with the sending . . .

>   I'd been

> in the course of a letter--I am still
> in the course of a letter--to a friend,
> who comes close in to my thought so that
> the day is hers. My hand writing here
> there shakes in the currents of . . . of air?
> of an inner anticipation of . . . ? reaching to touch
> ghostly exhilarations in the thought of her.

    But here, noting the life-loom caught in the very act of its weaving,
I anticipate. In 1948 I had nothing of Duncan's but those quotations in
Poetry, fragments congenial and yet mysterious; and when I arrived in New
York for the first time in the fall of that year I was too passive, dis-
organized, and overwhelmed by unrecognized "culture-shock" (the term had not
yet been invented) to do anything so methodical as to try and find his book
or books: so that when I did happen upon Heavenly City, Earthly City on
the sale table outside the Phoenix Bookshop on Cornelia St., just a few
blocks from where I was living, it seemed an astonishing, fateful coin-
cidence--as in a sense it was.

    The book enlarged and confirmed my sense of affinity and brought me,
too, a further dim sense of the California of fog, ocean, seals, and cliffs
I was by then reading about in Robinson Jeffers.

> "Turbulent Pacific! the sea-lions bark
> in ghostly conversations and sun themselves

> upon the sea-conditiond rocks.
> Insistent questioner of our shores!
> Somnambulist, old comforter!"

Duncan wrote in the title poem; and:

> "Sea leopards cough in the halls of our sleep.
> swim in the wastes of salt and wreck of ships,"

and:

> "The sea reflects, reflects in her evening tides
> upon a lavender recall of some past glory,
> some dazzle of a noon magnificence".

Much, much later--in 1966, it must have been, when I visted Carmel and Monterey--there was possibly some recall of those lines in a poem of mine, "Liebestodt": "Where there is violet in the green of the sea. . ."

But the impact of Duncan's rich romanticism was perhaps less powerful by the time I found the book, for I was also beginning to get a grip on William Carlos Williams's sound by then, able to "scan" it better now that I was surrounded by American speech, no longer baffled by details like "R.R." (railroad--in England it is railway) or obstructed in reading by the difference in stresses (e.g., the first American menu I saw announced "Hot Cakes" which I ordered as "hot cakes").

Now I was quickly, eagerly, adapting to the new mode of speaking, because instinct told me that to survive and develop as a poet I had to; and Williams showed me the way, made me listen, made me begin to appreciate the vivid and figurative language sometimes heard from ordinary present-day people, and the fact that even when vocabulary was impoverished there was some energy to be found in the here and now. What I connected to, originally, in Duncan, was a music based in dream and legend and literature; and though my love of that music has proved to be enduring, it was not uppermost in my needs and pleasures just then when I was seeking a foothold in the realities of marriage, of keeping house in a tenement flat, raising a strenuous baby, buying groceries at the Bleeker Street Safeway.

Meanwhile Duncan, unknown to me still, was changing too, on the other

side of the continent. There was of course this big difference in us, a
thread of another texture in among those that we held in common: he had a
sophistication in which I was quite lacking, which gave to his romanticism
an edge, not of the type of wit academics of the period cultivated anxiously
--like a young man's first whiskers--but of an erotic irony such as Thomas
Mann adumbrates in his essays on Goethe and elsewhere. He was not only a
few years older than I; he had already an almost encyclopedic range of
knowledge, he had studied history with Kantorowitz, he had read Freud, and
he lived in a literary and sexual ambience I didn't even know existed.
Whatever he wrote was bound to include an element of complex consciousness;
indeed, I can see now that while my task was to develop a greater degree of
conscious intelligence to balance my instincts and intuitions, his was,
necessarily, to keep his consciousness, his diamond needle intellect, from
becoming overweening, violating the delicate feelings-out of the Imagina-
tion; and it was just because his awareness of every nuance of style, of
every double meaning, was so keen, that he has, through the years, been
almost obsessively protective of the gifts of chance, of whatever the un-
conscious casts upon on his shore, of "mistakes" which he has cherished
like love-children.

My first direct contact with Duncan came in the early 50's
and was almost a disaster. By this time I had become friends with Bob
Creeley and Origin had begun to appear. Mitch and I had gone back to Eu-
rope on the G.I. Bill in 1950, when our son was just over a year old, and
in 1951 the Creeleys came to live a mile or two away from us in the Proven-
cal countryside. Sitting on the ground near our cottage, by the edge of a
closely pruned vineyard under the slope of the Alpilles, Creeley and Mitch
would talk about prose, and Creeley and I about poetry: Williams, Pound,
Olson's "Projective Verse" which had just come out, how to cut down a poem
to its sinewy essence--pruning it like the vines. I learned a lot; and am
not sure what, if anything, I gave in exchange, though I know I was not
merely a silent listener. Duncan had not yet met or been acknowledged by
either Olson (with whom Creeley was corresponding) or Creeley,[2] and though
he had not been dislodged from my mind I don't recall mentioning him. After
I was back in New York, and just at about the time Cid Corman included some

poems of Duncan's in Origin ('52) I received a communication from a San
Francisco address signed only "R.D.". It was a poem-letter that (I thought)
attacked my work, apparently accusing it of brewing poems like "stinking
coffee" in a "staind pot." When the letter spoke of "a great effort,
straining, breaking up all the melodic line," I supposed the writer was com-
plaining. How I could have misread what was, as Duncan readers will recog-
nize, "Letters for Denise Levertov: an A muse ment"--how I could have so
misinterpreted his tribute, it is difficult now to imagine. I've never been
given to paranoia; perhaps it was simply that the mode of the poem, with
its puns, lists, juxtapositions (more Cubist than Surreal) was too sophis-
ticated for me to comprehend without initiation. I had at the time not
even read half the people he mentions in the poem as sources, or at any rate
as forming an eclectic tradition from which I thought he was saying I had
unwarrantably borrowed (but to which, in fact, he was joyfully proclaiming
that I belonged): Marianne Moore, Pound, Williams, H.D., Stein, Zukofsky,
Bunting, St.-J. Perse. Of these, I had by then read only Williams, Marianne
Moore and Perse in any quantity; I knew Pound's ABC of Reading pretty well
but had not tackled the Cantos. Of H.D. I knew only the anthologized Im-
agist poems of her youth, and of Stein only "Melanctha"; of Zukofsky and
Bunting, nothing. Duncan also speaks in the poem of Surrealism and Dada:
and I was at least somewhat acquainted with French Surrealism (and the
English poet, David Gascoyne's book about it) but with Dada not at all. So
much of the corresponding intellectual background, in the simplest sense,
was lacking in me as a recipient of the letter.

I wrote to "R.D." enquiring plaintively why he had seen fit to attack
me for a lack of originality for I took phrases like

> "Better to stumb-
> 11 to it,"

and

> "better awake to it. For one
> eyes-wide-open vision
> or fotograph
> than ritual,"

as stern admonitions, when, of all the names he cited, only Williams was to
me a master, and from him I believed myself to be learning to discover my

own voice. I concluded my letter by saying, in all innocence, "Is it
possible that the initials you signed with, R.D., stand for Robert Duncan?
You don't sound like him!--But in case that's who you are, I'd like
to tell you I loved Heavenly City Earthly City, and therefore hope it's
not Robert Duncan who dislikes my poems so much." I quote from memory,
but that's a pretty close approximation. It is a wonder that Duncan was
not furious at my stupidity; especially at my saying he did not sound like
himself. If he had been, I wonder if our friendship would ever have begun?
Certainly if it had not, my life would have been different. But luckily
he responded not with anger (or worse, not at all) but with a patient
explanation (on the envelope he added the words, "It is as it was in
admiration") of his intent, including his sense--central to an understand-
ing of his own poetry--that "borrowings" and "imitations" were in no way
to be deplored, but were on the contrary tributes, acts of faith, and the
building-stones of a living tradition of "the communion of poets." This
concept runs through all of Duncan's books. It is most obvious in the
Stein imitations, or in his titling books Derivations, or A Book of Resem-
blances, but is implicit in every collection, though not in every poem;
and it is closely tied to his recognition of poetry (and of all true
art) as being a "power, not a set of counters" as he put it in a section
of "The H.D. Book" that deals with H.D.'s detractors, the smart, "bright"
critics. If Poetry, the Art of Poetry, is a Mystery, and poets the
servers of that Mystery, they are bound together in fellowship under its
Laws, obedient to Its power. Those who do not recognize the Mystery
suppose themselves Masters, not servants, and manipulate Poetry's power,
splitting it into little counters, as gold is split into coins, and
gaming with it; each must accumulate his own little heap of manipulative
power-counters--thus so-called "originality" is at a premium. But within
the Fellowship of the Mystery there is no hoarding of that Power of Poetry
--and so-called borrowings are simply sharings of what poetry gives to
Its faithful servants.[3] By the light of this concept we can also under-
stand Duncan's often criticized "literariness," i.e. his frequent allusions
to works of literary and other art and his many poems that not only take
poetry itself as theme but overtly incorporate the "languaging" process

into their essential structure--as he does even in this very first "Letter"
in the sections subtitled "Song of the Languagers," and later in such poems
as "Keeping the Rhyme," "Proofs," "Poetry, A Natural Thing" or "The Structure
of Rime" series, and so many others.

Some readers--even deep and subtle ones--object to poems about poems
(or about the experiencing of any works of art) and about writing and lan-
guage, on the grounds that they are too inverted; I have never agreed (ex-
cept in regard to conventional set-pieces "about" works of art, those which
seem written in fulfillment of commissions or in the bankrupt manner of
British poets laureate celebrating Royal weddings). If much of a poet's
most passionate and affective experiences are of poetry itself (or litera-
ture more generally, or painting, etc.) why should it not be considered
wholly natural and right for him to celebrate those experiences on an equal
basis with those given him by nature, people, animals, history, philosophy,
or current events? Poetry also is a current event. The poet whose range
is confined to any single theme for most of a working life may give off
less energy than one who follows many themes, it is true--and if any single
thing characterizes those whom we think of as world poets, those of the
rank of Homer, Shakespeare, Dante, it is surely breadth of range. But Dun-
can, although, in tribute to the Mystery, he is avowedly and proudly "liter-
ary," cannot be accused of narrow range, of writing nothing but poems about
poetry.

It was in 1955 that I first met Duncan. He spent a few days in New
York on his way, with Jess, to spend a year in Europe--chiefly in Majorca,
near to Robert Creeley with whom he had by this time entered into corres-
pondence but still not met. I am not able to locate the letters that pre-
ceded this joyful meeting, nor do I remember our conversation. But the ten-
tative friendship that had begun so awkwardly was cemented by his visit, and
I recall with what a pang I watched him go down the stairs, he looking back
up the stairwell to wave farewell, I leaning over the landing banister.[4]
I gave him a notebook for his journey; he used it as a drawing book and gave
it back to me full of pictures a year later; and still later I wrote captions
for them.

Whatever had passed between us before that time--and Duncan years later claimed that "we must have been in full correspondence by fall of '54"--it was now that the exchange of letters which continued into the early '70's began in earnest. Somehow, in the course of a busy life and many changes of dwelling, a few of the letters Duncan wrote to me have been mislaid, though I am confident that they are not irretrievably lost, for I always treasured them. I have a stack of letters for every year from 1955 to 1972. The written word was not the only dimension of our friendship: from time to time Duncan would come East; in 1963 he and I were both at the Vancouver Poetry Conference; and three times I was in the San Francisco Bay area (in 1969 for six months). At these times we would have the opportunity to "talk out loud" rather than on paper and I have happy memories of visits to museums and galleries, to the Bronx Zoo and the Washington Zoo, and of walks in the Berkeley Hills. Over the years we acquired many mutual friends; and during my son's childhood Duncan and Jess befriended him too, sending him wonderful old Oz books they would find in thrift shops. But it was the correspondence, with its accompaniment of poems, newly finished or in progress, that sustained the friendship most constantly and importantly.

Looking through these letters from Robert I am confirmed in my sense of their having been for me, especially in the first ten years, an extremely important factor in the development of my consciousness as a poet. Pondering what I gave Duncan in exchange, besides responding in kind to his admiration and love, I recall his speaking of how writing to me and to Creeley gave him "a field to range in," and in a 1958 letter he writes of me as serving as a "kind of artistic conscience" (not that he needed one). I had, certainly, the great advantage of not being connected to any "literary world" in particular, and being quite free from the factionalism so prevalent in San Francisco.

Both Duncan and I are essentially autodidacts, though he did have a high school and some college education while I had no instruction after the age of twelve, and the education I received before that was unconventional. I had a good background in English literature, a strong sense of the European past, and had read widely but unmethodically. Duncan read deeply in many fields I was ignorant of--the occult, psychoanalysis, certain areas of science. He did not teach me about these matters, which were not what I was really interested in--but he did give me at least some awareness of them as fields of energy. Because of my family background I knew a little about Jewish and Christian mysticism, so that when Duncan mentioned the Shekinah or Vladimir Solovyóv I recognized what he was talking about. The Andrew Lang Fairy Books and the fairytales of George MacDonald (and some of his grownup stories too) were common ground, along with much, much else-- many loves in literature and art. It was in those areas of twentieth-century literature, American poetry in particular, of which at the time of that first "Letter" I had been ignorant, and--more importantly--in the formation of what I think of as "aesthetic ethics," that Duncan became my mentor. Throughout the correspondence there run certain threads of fundamental disagreement; but a mentor is not necessarily an absolute authority, and though Duncan's erudition, his being older than I, his often authoritative manner, and an element of awe in my affection for him combined to make me take, much of the time, a pupil role, he was all the more a mentor when my own convictions were clarified for me by some conflict with his. Perhaps there was but one essential conflict--and it had to do with the role of a cluster of sources and impulses for which I will use "convictions" as a convenient collective term (though no such term can be quite satisfactory). Although, having written poetry since childhood (beginning, in fact, several years before Duncan wrote his first poems), I had experienced "lucky accidents" and the coming of poems "out of nowhere," yet I needed, and was glad to get from him, an aesthetic rationale for such occurrences--reassurances to counter the "Protestant ethic" that makes one afraid to admit, even to oneself, the value of anything one accomplishes without labor. Nevertheless, then and now (and I fully expect to so continue) my deepest personal commitment was to what I believed Rilke (whose letters I'd been reading and rereading since 1946) meant in his famous admonition to Herr Kappus, the "Young Poet," when he told him to search his heart for its need. The "need to write" does not provide academic poem-blueprints, so there was no conflict on that level; but such "inner need" is related to "having something" (at heart) "to say," and so to a high valuation of "honesty"--and our argument would arise over Duncan's sense that what I called honesty, he (as a passionate anarchist or "libertarian") sometimes regarded as a form

of self-coercion, resulting in a misuse of the art we served. He saw a
cluster, or alignment, that linked convictions with preconceptions and under-
esty with "ought," while the cluster I saw linked convictions with integrity
and honesty with precision. Related to this was my distrust of Robert's
habit of attributing (deeply influenced as he was by Freud) to every slip of
the tongue or unconscious pun not merely the revelation of some hidden atti-
tude but, it appeared to me--and it seemed and still seems perverse of him
--more validity than that of what the speaker meant to say, thought he or
she said, and indeed (in the case of poems of homonyms noticed only by Dun-
can) did say. To discount the earnest intention because of some hinted, un-
recognized, contradictory coexisting factor has never seemed to me just; and
to automatically suppose that the unrecognized is necessarily more authentic
than what has been brought into consciousness strikes me as absurd. Jung
(whom I was reading throughout the '60's--Duncan disliked his style and
for a long time refused to read him)[5] had made the existence of the "dark
side," and the imperative need to respect it, very clear to me; it was Dun-
can's apparent belief that the dark side was "more equal," as the jest puts
it, that I could not stomach.

     However, the first time I find this matter touched upon in one of
Robert's letters it was not in a way that affronted or antagonized me but
one which, on the contrary, belongs with the many ways in which he opened
my mind to new realizations. I had been puzzled by some ballads of his,
inspired, in part, by Helen Adam (to whose fascinating work he soon intro-
duced me). I found them, I suppose, a curious retrogression from the excit-
ing pioneering into the "open field" in which we and a few others were en-
gaged. What was the Duncan of Letters, the Duncan who in a letter of that
same summer (1955) was excited by my poem "The Way Through" (printed in Or-
igin) and who shared my love of Williams, what was he doing being so "lit-
erary"?--I must have asked. For I myself was engaged in "de-literaryfying"
myself, in developing a base in common speech, contemporary speech-rhythms.
"I don't really understand your ballads," I wrote (I quote now from Duncan's
transcription of part of my letter in his preface for a projected volume to
be called Homage to Coleridge), "why you are writing that way. It seems
wasteful both of yourself and in general . . . when I remember what else

you have written, even long since, as well as of late especially, I can't
quite believe they aren't like something you might have written very long
ago." My hesitations about questioning anything he did are evident in the
circuitous syntax and its qualifiers--"I don't really"--"I don't quite"--
"it seems". . . . And in his reply he wrote, ". . . it is the interest in,
not the faith, that I wld take as my clue. Ideally that we might be as
readers or spectators of poetry like botanists--who need not tell them-
selves they will accept no matter what a plant is or becomes; or biologists
--who must pursue the evidence of what life is, haunted by the spectre of
what it ought to be [though] they might be. As <u>makaris</u> we make as we are,
o.k., and how else? it all however poor must smack of our very poorness or
if fine of our very fineness. Well, let me sweep out the old validities:
and readdress them. They are inventions of an order within and out of non-
orders. And it's as much our life not to become warriors of these orders
as it is our life to realize what belongs to our order in its when and who
we are and what does not. I can well remember the day when Chagall and
Max Ernst seemed bad to me, I was so the protagonist of the formal (like
Arp or Mondrian) against the Illusionary. The paintings have not changed.
Nor is it that I have <u>progressed</u>, or gone in a direction. But my spiritual
appetite has been deranged from old convictions." This openness was some-
thing I was happy in; and indeed, in such passages Duncan often sounded for
me a note of "permission" to my native eclecticism that some shyness in me,
some lack of self-confidence, longed for. Yet even this liberation was in
some degree a source of conflict--not between us, but within me. For years
no praise and approval from anyone else, however pleasant, could have re-
assured me until I had Robert's approval of a poem; and if I had that--as I
almost always did--no blame from others could bother me. "The permission
liberates," wrote Duncan in '63 (about a procedure of his own, relating to
a habit of "reading too much the way some people eat too much" as he put it
elsewhere) "but then how the newly freed possibility can insidiously take
over and tyrannize over our alternatives."

　　　Duncan's wit is not a dominant note in the letters but it does flash
forth, whether in jest or in epigram. In September '59 for example, he com-
plains that Solovyóv had been, alas, "a Professor of Philosophy--that hints

or sparks of a life of Wonder can show up in such a ground is a miracle in
itself. What if Christ's disciples had not been simple fishermen and a
whore, and he the son of a carpenter, but the whole lot been the faculty of
some college?" Of a highly cultured friend he wrote in 1957, "he has enthu-
siasms but not passions . . . He collects experience [but he doesn't] under-
go the world." He described San Francisco audiences for poetry readings
(preparing me for my first public reading anywhere, in December '57, which
he had gone to considerable trouble to arrange): "The audiences here are
avid and toughened--they've survived top poetry read badly; ghastly poetry
read ghastly; the mediocre read with theatrical flourish; poets in advanced
stages of discomfort, ego-mania, mumbling, grand style, relentless insist-
ence, professorial down-the-nosism, charm, calm, schizophrenic disorder,
pious agony, auto-erotic hypnosis, bellowing, hatred, pity, snarl and snub."

Among recurring topics are friendships and feuds among fellow writers;
his publishing difficulties (due in part to his very high standards of what
a book should look like and in what spirit its printing and publication
should be undertaken); and--more importantly--his current reading and its
relationship to his work; as well as his work itself. Sometimes poems would
have their first beginnings right there on the page, as Bending the Bow did;
or if not their beginning, the origins of poems enclosed are often recounted.
(These, however, I do not feel inclined to quote; they are, as they occur in
letters, a part of the intimacy of communion, not to be broadcast--not be-
cause they say anything Robert might not say to someone else or to the world
in general, but because in their context they are said in an expectation of
privacy.)

It is not easy to isolate from the fabric some threads of the essential,
the truly dominant theme I have already named--clumsily but not inaccurately
--the "ethics of aesthetics"; for the pattern of the whole is complex: nega-
tives and positives entwined and knotted. Everywhere I discover, or redis-
cover, traces both of the riches Duncan's friendship gave me and of the
flaws in mutual confidence which in the 1970's impoverished that friendship.

Perhaps a point at which to begin this drawing-out of one thread is
what he says about revision. I had read the notebook excerpts, printed in a
S.F. broadside, in which the beautiful phrase occurs, "My revisions are my

re-visions." In the beginning I supposed it to mean it was best never to work-over a poem, but instead to move on to the next poem--the renewed vis-ion. But taking it to myself as the years passed, I have come to know its meaning as being the necessity of constant re-visioning in the very act of refining: i.e., that changes made from outside the poem, applied as a reader would apply (supply) them, cannot partake of the poem's vitality; the valid, viable reworking of a poem must be as much from within, as seam-lessly internal to the process, as the primary working. Duncan himself in May 1958 explicated: "I revise (a) when there is an inaccuracy, then I must re-see, as e.g. in the Pindar poem--now that I found the reproduction we had someplace of the Goya painting, I find Cupid is not wingd: in the poem I saw wings. I've to summon up my attention and go at it. (b) when I see an adjustment--it's not polishing for me, but a "correction" of tone, etc., as in the same poem 'hear the anvils of human misery clanging' in the Whitman section bothered me, it was at once the measure of the language and the content--Blake! not Whitman (with them anvils) and I wanted a long line pushed to the unwieldy with (Spicer and I had been talking about returning to Marx to find certain correctives--as, the ideas of work) Marxist flicker of commodities. (c) and even upon what I'd call decorative impulse: I changed

> "follow
> ~~obey~~ to the letter
> freakish instructions"

to gain the pleasurable transitions of 1 - to 1 - r and f to f - r.

"The idea in back of no revisions as doctrine was that I must force my-self to abandon all fillers, to come to correct focus in the original act; in part there's the veracity of experience (. . . the poem 'comes' as I write it; I seem --that is-- to follow a dictate), but it's exactly in re-spect to that veracity that I don't find myself sufficient. . . . I had nothing like 'I write as I please' in mind, certainly not carelessness but the extreme of care kept in the moment of a passionate feeling . . . My 'no revisions' was never divorced from a concept of the work. Concentra-tion. . . . I've got to have the roots of words, the way the language works, at my fingertips, learned in the nerves from whatever studies, in addition to the thing drawn from--the sea, a painting, the face of

Marianne Moore--before there's even the beginning of discipline. And
decide, on the instant, that's the excitement, between the word that's sur-
rounded by possible meanings, and the word that limits direction."

Copying this out in December 1975 I find the dialogue continuing, for
I feel I want to respond to that last sentence: ah, yes, and here I see a
source of the difference in tendency between your poetry and mine (though
there is a large area in which our practices overlap): you most often
choose the word that is "surrounded by possible meanings," and willingly
drift upon the currents of those possibilities (as you had spoken in "The
Venice Poem" of wishing to **drift; and I most often choose the word that**
"limits direction"--because to me such "zeroing in" is not limiting but
revelatory.

In August of the same year (1958) Duncan resumes the theme: "I've
found myself sweating over extensive rehaulings of the opening poem of the
field and right now am at the 12th poem of the book which I want to keep
but have almost to reimagine in order to establish it. . . . It's a job
of eliminating what doesn't belong to the course of the book, and in the
first poem of reshaping so that the course of the book is anticipated. I
mistrust the rationalizing mind that comes to the fore, and must suffer
through--like I did when I was just beginning twenty years ago--draft after
draft to exhaust the likely and reach the tone in myself where intuition
begins to move. It comes sure enuf then, the hand's feel that 'this' is
what must be done. . . ." He quotes Ezra Pound saying in a 1948 manifesto,
"You must understand what is happening"; and makes it clear the significant
emphasis is on "what is happening," the presentness, the process. "Most
verse," Duncan comments, "is something being made up to communicate a thing
already present in the mind--or a lot of it is. And don't pay the atten-
tion it shld to what the poet don't know--and won't [know] until the process
speaks." He quotes the passage from T. S. Eliot's Three Voices of Poetry
in which Eliot incorporated a line from Beddoes: "bodiless childful of
life in the gloom/crying with frog voice, 'What shall I be?'" and noted
that there is "first . . . an inert embryo or 'creative germ' and, on the
other hand, the language . . . [The poet] cannot identify this embryo until
it has been transformed into an arrangement of the right words in the right
order." And from Eliot he passes directly to a recent poem by Ebbe

Borregard--"What Ebbe's got to do is to trust and obey the voice of The
Wapitis. Where obedience means certainly your 'not to pretend to know more
than he does.' But the poem is not a pretention to knowing; it is not,
damn it, to be held back to our knowing, as if we could take credit for the
poem as if it were a self-assertion. We have in order to obey the inspired
voice to come to understand, to let the directives of the poem govern our
life and to give our minds over entirely to know[ing] what is happening."

     Most of this rang out for me in confirmation of what I believed and
practiced. But I question one phrase--that in which he opposes, to the
trusting of a poem's own directives, the communication of "a thing already
present in the mind"; for unless one qualifies the phrase to specify a
fully formed, intellectualized, conscious "presence in the mind" I see no
true opposition here. The "veracity of experience" does not come into
being only in the course of the poem, but provides the ground from which the
poem grows, or from which it leaps (and to which it fails to return at its
peril). "The sea, a painting, the face of Marianne Moore," are indeed the
"things drawn from." What the writing of the poem, the process of poetry,
the following-through of the radiant gists (in W. C. Williams's phrase) of
language itself, does for the writer (and so for the reader, by a process
of transference which is indeed communication, communion) is to reveal the
potential of what is "present in the mind" so that writer and reader come
to know what it is they know, explore it and realize, real-ize, it. In the
fall of '65, commenting anew on my "Notes on Organic Form" which he had read
in an earlier, "lecture" form, he quotes with enthusiasm: "whether an ex-
perience is a linear sequence or a constellation raying out from and in to
a central focus or axis . . . discoverable only in the work, not before it"
--but in that phrase I meant "discoverable" quite precisely--i.e., not
"that which comes into being only in the work" but that which, though pres-
ent in a dim unrecognized or ungrasped way, is only experienced in any de-
gree of fullness in art's concreteness: The Word made Flesh, Concept giv-
en body in Language. One cannot "discover" what is not there. Yet the po-
em is not merely a representation of the thing discovered--a depiction of
an inscape seen; it is itself a new inscape, the seen and the seer conjoined.
And it is in the action of synthesizing, of process in language, that the

poet is voyager, sailing far beyond that lesser communication, the conveyance of information, to explore the unknown. Duncan seems always on the brink of saying one does not even <u>start off</u> from the known.

At times it seems as if it were his own brilliant intellect he is struggling to keep from domination of his art--beating not a dead horse but a horse that does not exist in me, or in others about whose poetry he wrote. In 1956, writing from a small village in Majorca, wondering if he and Jess can afford to travel to London at Christmas time (their budget was $100 a month) he spoke of "craving the society of English **speech**. My notebooks are becoming deformed by the 'ideas' which ordinarily I throw away into talk, invaluable talk for a head like mine that no waste basket could keep clean for a poem. I can more than understand dear old Coleridge who grew up to be a boring machine of talk; I can fear for my own poor soul. And, isolated from the city of idle chatter, here my head fills up, painfully, with insistent IMPORTANT things-to-say. I toss at night, spring out of bed to sit for hours, crouched over a candle, writing out--ideas, ideas, ideas. Solutions for the universe, or metaphysics of poetry, or poetics of living. Nor does my reading matter help--I have deserted Cocteau for a while because his ratiocination was perhaps the contagion; and the Zohar which irritates the cerebral automatism. Calling up, too, conflicts of poetry's--impulses toward extravagant fantasy, my attempt to reawaken the 'romantic' allegiances in myself, to Poe, or Coleridge, or Blake, are inhibited by a 'modern' consciousness; I grow appalled at the diffusion of the concrete. . . ." And in 1958, "Sometimes when I am most disconsolate about what I am working at, and most uneasy about the particular 'exaltations' that may not be free outflowings of imagination and desire but excited compulsions instead. . . . I feel guilty before the ever-<u>present</u> substantial mode of your work." But of course, it was more than an overactive intellect that he had to contend with; the struggle was often with the sheer complexity of vision. His cross-eyes saw deep and far--and it is part of the artist's honor not to reduce the intricate, the multitudinous, multifarious, to a neat simplicity. In 1961 he wrote, "It's the most disheartening thing I find myself doing in this H.D. study, trying to win her her just literary place--and what I find (when I reflect on it) is that I lose heart (I mean I get that sinking feeling in my heart and lungs, I guess it is, as if I had played it false). I know I can't just avoid this playing it false--you know, direct sentences like sound bridges from good solid island to good solid island; and contrive thought lines like pipe lines to conduct those few clear streams--because the bog is the bog" (he has previously written of "the bog I get into with prose") "and I really want to discover it on its own terms," (my italics) " which must be the naturalist's terms. . . . that damned bog would have to be drained and filled in to be worth a thing, but it is a paradise for the happy frog-lover, or swamp-grass enthusiast--and in its most rank and treacherous backwaters a teeming world of life for the biologist. . . ."

Instances of particular changes made in poems in progress (and here I return to the interwoven theme of revision) occur in many letters, following poems sent earlier. The mind's bog was fully inhabited by very exact, green, jewel-eyed frogs. Here are two typical examples:

"Nov. 29, 1960

Dear Denny, That Risk!--how hard it seems for me to come down to cases there. This time it is not the wording (tho I did alter 'simple' to 'domestic' in 'turning the mind from domestic pleasure') but what necessitated my redoing the whole 3 pages was just the annoying fact that I had phrased certain lines wrong--against my ear. I never did read it 'not luck but the way it falls choose/for her, lots' etc., which would mean either an odd stress of the phrase on 'for' or a stress I didn't mean on 'her.' I was reading it from the first 'choose for her' with the stress of the phrase on 'choose'; and that terminal pitch heightening 'falls' in the line before. And again: What did I think I was hearing when I divided 'I had not the means/to buy the vase' or whatever--was it?--worse! 'I had not the means to buy/the vase' etc.? Anyway, here I was going on like any hack academic of the automatic line-breaking school . . . not listening to the cadence of the thing. My cadence, my care, is changing perhaps too--and I was notating this from old habits contrary to the actual music." Or in March '63 he gives the following revisions for "Structure of Rime XXI": "'solitude' for 'loneliness' . . . 'A depresst key' for 'a touched string'--a depresst key is what it actually is (when the sympathetic sound rings) and also because both 'depresst' and 'key' refer to the substrata of the poem.

'steps of wood' = notes of the scale on a xylophone. . ."

There are also the occasional suggestions for revision--or for more comprehensive change--of my own work (for until the late '60's we probably exchanged manuscripts of most of what we wrote). Sometimes his criticism was deeply instructive; of this the most telling instance concerns a 1962 poem in which I had over-extended my feelings. Hearing that a painter we both knew (but who was not a close friend of mine, rather a friendly acquaintance whose work had given me great pleasure) had leukemia or some form of cancer, I plunged, as it were, into an ode that was almost a premature elegy. An image from one of his paintings had already appeared in another poem of mine--"Clouds"--which Duncan particularly liked. In his criticism of this new poem he showed me how the emotional measure of the first (which dealt with matters "proved upon my pulses," among which the remembrance of clouds he had painted ". . . as I see them--/rising/urgently, roseate in the/mounting of somber power"--"surging/in evening haste over hermetic grim walls" entered naturally, although the painter as a person played no part in the poem) was just; whereas in the new poem, focussing with emotional intensity upon an individual who was not in fact anywhere close to the center of my life, however much his paintings had moved me, the measure was false. Although I thought (and looking it over now, still think) the poem has some good parts, I was thoroughly convinced, and shall never publish it. It was a lesson which, like all valuable lessons, had applicability not only to the particular occasion; and one which has intimately to do with the ideogram Ezra Pound has made familiar to us--the concept of integrity embodied in the sign-picture of "a man standing by his word."

There were other occasions, though, when I paid no attention to Robert's criticism because he was misreading. For example, reading my prose "Note on the Imagination" in 1959, he speaks of "distrusting its discrimination (that just this is imagination and that--'the feared Hoffmanesque blank-- the possible monster or stranger'--was Fancy), but wholly going along with the heart of the matter: the seed pearls of summer fog in Tess's hair, and the network of mist diamonds in your hair. But the actual distinction

between the expected and the surprising real thing here (and taking as
another term the factor of your 'usual face-in-the-mirror') is the contriv-
ed (the work of Fancy) the remembered (how you rightly [say] 'at no time is
it hard to call up scenes to the mind's eye'--where I take it these are re-
membered) and the presented. But you see, if the horrible, the ugly, the
very feard commonplace of Hoffman and Poe had been the 'presented thing'
it would have been 'of the imagination' as much as the delightful image. . .

          . . . The evaluation of Fancy and Imagination gets mixed up with the
description. All these terms of seeing: vision, insight, phantasm, epiph-
any, it 'looks-like', image, perception, sight, 'second-sight,' illusion,
appearance, it 'appears-to-be,' mere show, showing forth . . . where trust
and mistrust of our eyes varies. However we trust or mistrust the truth,
necessity, intent etc. of what is seen (and what manifests itself out of
the depths through us): we can't make the choice between monster as fancy
and the crown-of-dew as imagination." Here the disagreement is substantial,
for the very point I was trying to make concerned the way in which the
active imagination illuminates common experience, and not by mere memory
but by supplying new detail we recognize as authentic. By common expe-
rience I mean that which conforms to or expresses what we share as "laws of
Nature." Hoffman's fantasies, known to me since childhood, had given me
pleasure because they were "romantic" in the vernacular sense (and my edi-
tion had attractive illustrations) but they did not illumine experience,
did not "increase the sense of living, of being alive," to use Wallace
Stevens's phrase. In the "Adagia" Stevens says that "To be at the end of re-
ality is not to be at the beginning of imagination, but to be at the end of
both." To me--then and now--any kind of "sci fi," any presentation of what
does not partake of natural laws we all experience, such as gravity and
mortality, is only a work of imagination if it is dealing symbolically
with psychic truth, with soul-story, as myth, fairytales, and sometimes al-
legory, do. Duncan continues, "Jess suggests it's not a matter of either/
or (in which Fancy represented a lesser order and Imagination a higher or-
der . . .) but of two operations or faculties. Shakespeare is rich in both
imagination and fancy . . . where Ezra Pound totally excludes or lacks fan-
cy. . . . George MacDonald [spoke] of 'works of Fancy and Imagination.'

But I think he means playful and serious. Sometimes we use the word 'fancy'
to mean the trivial; but that surely does injustice to Shelley's landscapes
or Beddoes' Skeleton's Songs or the description of Cleopatra's barge that
gives speech to Shakespeare's sensual fancy," and here I think the differ-
ence of views is semantic; for I indeed would attach the words "playful"
and sometimes "trivial" and frequently "contrived," "thought-up," to the
term fancy, and for the instances cited in Shelley or Beddoes, would employ
the term fantasy. The description of Cleopatra's barge is neither fancy nor
fantasy but the rhetoric of enthusiasm accurately evolving intense sensuous
experience; an act of imagination. Fantasy does seem to me one of the func-
tions of the imagination, subordinate to the greater faculty's deeper needs
--so that "In a cowslip's bell I lie" and other evocations of faery in the
Midsummer Night's Dream, for example, are delicate specifics supplied by the
power of fantasizing for the more precise presentation of an imagined, not
fancied or fantasied, world that we can apprehend as "serious"--having sym-
bolic reality--even while we are entertained by its delightfulness and fun.
The more significant divergence of opinion concerns "the presented thing,"
as Duncan called it--for there he seems to claim a value for the very fact
of presentation, as if every image summoned up into some form of art had
thereby its justification; a point of view he certainly did not, does not,
adhere to, and yet--perhaps, again, just because he has had always so to
contend with his own contentiousness and tendency to be extremely judgmental
--which he does seem sometimes to propound, almost reflexively. "What I do,"
he wrote in January '61, "--in that letter regarding your essay on Imagina-
tion, or yesterday in response to your letter and the reply to _____'s
piece . . . is to contend. And it obscures perhaps just the fact that I
am contending my own agreements often. . . . Aie! . . . I shall never be
without and must work from those 'irritable reachings after fact and rea-
son' that must have haunted Keats too--" One of the **ways** in which what Dun-
can says here seems, unfortunately, to be true is manifest in this very
statement, which assumes without due warrant (I think) that just because
Keats saw in Coleridge that restless, irritable reaching, he himself was
subject to it. Yet, however contentious, Duncan is often self-critical in

these letters--as above, or as when he speaks (Sept. '64) of "my . . .
'moralizing,' which makes writing critically such a chore, for I must vomit
up my strong puritanical attacking drive. . . . this attacking in others
what one fears to attack in oneself. . . ." And in the midst of arguments
he was often generous enough to combine self-criticism, or at least an ob-
jective self-definition, with beautiful examples of his opponent's point of
view--for instance, in the Oct.'59 letter already referred to, discussing
Fancy and Imagination, he says, "Jess said an image he particularly remem-
bers from Tess is stars reflected in puddles of water where cows have left
hoof tracks--But, you know, I think I am so eager for 'concept' that I lose
those details. Or, more exactly--that my 'concept' lacks details often.
For, where you or Jess bring my attention back to the 'little fog' inten-
ser 'amid the prevailing one' or the star in the cowtracked puddle: the
presence of Tess and Angel leaps up. . . . But for me it's not the per-
ceived verity (your seed pearls of summer fog from Tess; or Madeline Glea-
son years ago to demonstrate the genius of imagination chose a perceived
verity from Dante where the eyes of the sodomites turn and:

> e si ver noi aguzzavan le ciglia,
> come vecchio sartor fa nella cruna.

'towards us sharpened their vision, as an aged tailor does at the eye of
his needle) I am drawn by the conceptual imagination rather than by the
perceptual imagination. . . ."

There were other times when Robert objected to some particular word in
a poem of mine not in a way that instructed me but rather seemed due to
his having missed a meaning. He himself was aware of that. In October
'66 he writes: "And especially with you, I have made free to worry poems
when there would arise some feeling of a possible form wanted as I read.
Sometimes, as in your questionings of the pendent of Passages 2, such quer-
ies are most pertinent to the actual intent of the poem. And I think that
even seemingly pointless dissents from the realized poem arise because
along the line of reasoning a formal apprehension, vague but demanding, has
arisen that differs from the author's form. In a mistaken reading, this
will arise because I want to use the matter of the poem to write my own

'Denise Levertov' poem. Crucially astray." He wanted me to change an
image of grief denied, dismissed, and ignored, in which I spoke of "Always
denial. Grief in the morning, washed away/in coffee, crumbled to a dozen
errands between/busy fingers" to "dunked" or "soaked" in coffee, not under-
standing that I meant it was washed _away_, obliterated; the "errands," the
"busy fingers" and whatever other images of the poem all being manifesta-
tions of a turning away, a refusal to confront grief.

The attribution to others of his own intentions, concerns, or hauntings,
an unfortunate spin-off of his inner contentions, occasioned another type
of misreading--a reading--**into,** a suspicion of non-existent complex motives
that obstructs his full comprehension of what _does_ exist. "What is going
on," he writes in July 1966, "in your:

> still turns without surprise, with mere regret
> to the scheduled breaking open of breasts whose milk
> runs out over the entrails of still-alive babies,
> transformation of witnessing eyes to pulp-fragments,
> implosion of skinned penises into carcass-gulleys[6]

--the words in their lines are the clotted mass of some operation . . . hav-
ing what root in you I wonder? Striving to find place in a story beyond
the immediate." In this comment of his I find, sadly, that the "irritable
reaching" stretches beyond "fact and reason" to search out complications for
which there is no evidence. He misses the obvious. Having listed the
lovely attributes of humankind, I proceeded, anguished at the thought of the
war, to list the destruction of those very attributes--the violence per-
petrated by humans upon each other. Because I believed that "we are members
one of another" I considered myself morally obliged to attempt to contem-
plate, however much it hurt to do so, just what that violence can be. I
forced myself to envision, in the process of writing, instances of it (draw-
ing in part on material supplied by the Medical Committee for Human Rights
or similar accounts, and elaborating from that into harsh language-sounds).
There was no need to look for "what was going on" in me, "from what root"
such images came--one had only to look at the violation of Viet Nam. And
from the misreading of this very poem stemmed, ultimately, the loss of

mutual confidence that caused our correspondence to end--or to lapse at
least--in the early '70's. But Duncan had conscious justification for such
misreadings. In a 1967 interview of which he sent me a transcript he ex-
pounded it in terms of what the writer himself must do as reader of his own
poem-in-process--but it is clearly what he was doing as a reader of my (and
others') poems also: "The poet must search and research, wonder about,
consult the meaning of [the poem's] event. Here, to read means to dig, to
let the forces of the poem work in us. Many poets don't read. For instance,
take an awfully good poet like Robert Frost; while he writes a poem, he
takes it as an expression of something he has felt and thought. He does not
read further. It does not seem to be happening to him, but coming out of
him. Readers too who want to be entertained by [or] to entertain the ideas
of a writer will resent taking such writing as evidence of the Real and
protest against our 'reading into' poems, even as many protest the Freudians
reading meanings into life that are not there. The writer, following im-
ages and meanings which arise along lines of a melody or along lines of
rhythms and impulses, experiences the poem as an immediate reality. . . .
I am consciously and attentively at work in writing--here I am like any
reader. But I ask further, what is this saying? What does it mean that
this is happening here like this?" This statement, as always with Duncan,
contains, it seems to me, a valuable reminder of how closely writers must
see what they do, to be responsible for it; and of how readers, similarly,
should not be content with the superficial, the face-value of a poem. But
unfortunately, though his "digging for meanings" results in many felicities
and resonances in his own work, the method often makes him a poor reader of
others, a reader so intent upon shadow that he rejects, or fails to see,
substance.

Meanwhile, if Duncan did not see what was obvious in that poem of mine,
he certainly did see the war. Increasingly, from the mid-'60's on, its
dark, dirty, oppressive cloud pervades his letters. In '65, responding to
a form letter I sent out to gather money and signatures for a full page ad
in the New York Times--"Writers and Artists Protest the War in Viet Nam"--
he had written, "We feel as we know you and Mitch must feel--a helpless
outrage at the lies upon which the American policy is run, and at the death

and suffering 'our' armaments, troops, and bombers have inflicted upon Viet
Nam. Count on us for all protests and write if the protest needs more money.
We will tell you if we can't make it; but we want to do whatever we can."
And along with his sense of helplessness in face of the outrage--where for
all of us the horror itself was compounded by being committed in our name,
as Americans--he began to worry about my increasing involvement in the anti-
war movement. "Denny, the last poem" (it was Advent 1966) "brings with it
an agonizing sense of how the monstrosity of this nation's War is taking
over your life, and I wish that I could advance some--not consolation, there
is none--wisdom of how we are to at once bear constant (faithful and ever-
present) testimony to our grief for those suffering in the War and our know-
ledge that the government of the U.S. is so immediately the agent of death
and destruction of human and natural goods, and at the same time as con-
stantly in our work (which must face and contain somehow this appalling and
would-be spiritually destroying evidence of what human kind will do--for it
has to do with the imagination of what is going on in Man) now, more than
ever, to keep alive the immediacy of the ideal and of the eternal. Jess and
I have decided that we will wear black armbands (as the Spanish do when
some member of their immediate family has died) always and keep a period of
mourning until certainly the last American soldier or 'consultant' is gone
from Viet Nam--but may it not be the rest of our lives? until 'we' are no
longer immediately active in bringing grief to members of the family of man.
I started to wear a Peace button for the first time during the Poetry fest-
ival in Houston, and I found that it brought me to bear witness at surpris-
ing times--a waitress, a San Salvador millionaire, a Texas school teacher
asked me what it meant. And I rejoiced in being called to my responsibil-
ity. Just at times when I was most forgetting myself and living it up."

Just over a year later, again, February 1967--"I have thought often
how, if the outrage and grief of this war preoccupy my mind and heart as
it does, the full burden of it must come upon you and Mitch with Nik so
immediately involved." (Our son Nikolai was by now of draft age.) "And I
was fearful in January that you were having a bad time compounded with that
other constant claim upon one's life the whole literary structure would
make, and where you have a greater exposure in New York. I

think also of how much [anti-] war groups and other organizations would lay claim. . . . it seems to me too that whatever is not volunteered from the heart, even goodness and demonstrations against the war, when it is conscripted is grievous."

There is, I feel, a confusion here. Certainly, as that poem Advent 1966 and others attest, the ever-present consciousness of the war darkened my life as it darkened the lives of us all. Yet Duncan's affectionate anxiety about me and Mitch was in a sense misplaced. Duncan himself suffered, surely, a greater degree of frustration than we did, because we lightened that burden for ourselves by taking on the other burden of action. Duncan did bear testimony with his peace button and black armband; he attended a number of demonstrations, including the rally of writers, artists, and intellectuals at the Justice Department (which led to the conspiracy trial of Dr. Spock and four others, of whom Mitch Goodman was one) and the huge march on the Pentagon the following day, in fall of 1967; and he participated in group poetry readings given as benefits for the Resistance movement. But he did not join with others on a day-to-day basis in organizing anti-war activities. Meanwhile, even though grief, rage, shame and frustration inevitably continued, and indeed even grew as my political awareness grew and I began to see how this war was only one facet of a complex of oppression, I nevertheless was experiencing unforeseen blessings. Not only was ongoing action a relief, an outlet for frustration, however small a drop in the bucket of resistance to that oppression one knew it to be; but--much more importantly--there was the experience of a new sense of community as one worked, or picketed, or even merely "milled around" with comrades. As a good Anarchist from his youth up, Duncan mistrusted group action; and he was just enough older than I to have a ready suspicion of "Stalinism" every time he confronted some action planned or carried out in a way that did not strike him as entirely "voluntarist." This habit of distrust had shown itself to me as far back as 1959, when he expressed hesitations concerning a magazine he otherwise liked (and which in fact was quite non-political in its concerns) merely because of its "exaggerated estimate of Neruda . . . plus the poem by Celan where I suspected the reference to Madrid as standing for Spain in the Civil War" and added that he had sent "a prodding letter" to the editor, "to see if there was any neo-

Stalinism going on there." This fear in him, by being a large factor in keeping him out of more involvement in the Movement during the '60's and early '70's, had two effects: one was that his political awareness, formed in the '40's and early '50's, remained static; and the other, that he did not experience the comradeship, the recognition of apparent strangers as brothers and sisters, that so warmed the hearts of those who did feel it, giving us in the difficult present some immediate token of hope for a truly changed future—a comradeship which depended precisely upon a political awareness that was <u>not</u> static, but <u>in process of</u> becoming. Had he but realized it, the spirit of those days was (except in certain factions not central to the movement) not Stalinist, coercive, and regimented at all, but essentially as voluntarist as he could have desired. But we did gather together, and we did shout slogans—and it was perhaps due not only to ideological difference, but to temperamental distaste, that Duncan did not and could not do so. He was, therefore, isolated in his very real anguish; his blood pressure soared; and he could not see that there was nothing I was engaged in that was not "volunteered from the heart."

But the wedge driven between us by his supposition that I was acting coercively, toward myself and—possibly—towards others (a supposition which had, as I see it, no foundations in truth) had not yet gone very deep. In December 1968, a time of private troubles for me as well as of shared political ones, he wrote, "to reassure you my thoughts are with you. And a prayer . . . not to something I know, yet 'to,' but <u>from</u> something I know very well—the deep resources I have had in our friendship, the so much we have shared and share in what we hold good and dear for human life, and the service we would dedicate our art to. My own thought has been dark this year and in some part of it I have been apprehensive of how much more vulnerable and involved you are: I mean here about the crisis of the war and then the coming-to-roost of the American furies. What we begin to see are the ravening furies of Western civilization. And it corresponds with our own creative generation's arriving at the phase when the furies of our own art come-home-to-roost. Denny, just as I have been carried in my own work to a deeper, grander sense of the ground, I have begun to be aware of gaps

and emptinesses--in my being? in the ground?--and I have now to turn next
to work again on the H.D. book where I had begun to dread having to do with
the inner conflicts I sensed at work there. The World Order essay, as I
wrote, was written in phases of inertia, dread and breakthrus.

"Does it help at all to consider that in part your affliction is the
artist's? The personal pain is compounded in it.

"Well I couldn't speed this off. My sense that I was doing no more
than identifying a brooding center in my own feeling with your inner pain
halted me in my tracks. Only, this morning, to find that my thought as I
woke turning to you still revolved around or turned to the concept of
inner trials belonging to the testing of the creative artist, which we as
poets and artists come to, as surely as the fairytale hero or heroine comes
to some imprisonment or isolation--to dwell in the reality of how the loved
thing is to be despaired of. I am thinking of the story of the forgotten
bride and groom dwelling close to her or his beloved in despised form.

"Only, in this fumbling, to try to say that your dread, pain, and be-
ing at a loss--personal as it must be, is also the share of each of us who
seeks to deepen feeling. Not an affliction in and of itself but belonging
to the psychic metamorphosis--we cannot direct it, or, it is directed by
inner orders that our crude and unwilling conscious self dreads. Eros and
his Other, Thanatos, work there."

That beautiful letter, in which the feeling-tone of an earlier time in
our friendship resounds at a deeper, darker pitch, and which sums up, or
rather, is representative of, the rich, the immeasurable gift given me by
this association, seems almost valedictory. Yet it was not yet so, in
fact, for a month later Mitch and I arrived on the West Coast to spend six
months at Berkeley. During this period, though my teaching job and partic-
ipation in current events (this was 1969, the spring of the Third World
strike and of People's Park) prevented me from seeing Robert as often as I
had hoped, there were some quiet times of reading current poems to one
another (and to Mitch and Jess) and at least one or two walks in the
mimosa- and eucalyptus-scented lanes above Berkeley, a terrain he knew
intimately and seemed curiously at rest in.

It was not until after that, in the early '70's, that our correspond-
ence faltered and jarred to a halt. I will not deal here with the way
every negative element that had ever arisen between us, but especially the
false interpretation begun in his questioning of "Life at War," began to take
over in our letters, each of us taking fierce, static, antagonist "posi-
tions," he of attack, I of defense. It is a conflict still unresolved--
if this is in some sense a narrative, the end of the story has perhaps not
yet been reached. But I think of my Duncan letters as a constellation
rather than as a linear sequence. And in that constellation the major
stars are without question the messages of instruction by means of which
my intelligence grew keener, my artistic conscience more acute; messages
of love, support, and solidarity in the fellowship of poetry. None of my
many poet friends has given me more; and when I look back to Florence,
1948, I know I came then upon what was for two decades a primary current
of my life.

NOTES   1975

[1] Rexroth had struck up a correspondence with me at that time, for he was
editing New British Poets. He was the first American writer I knew person-
ally--but I had not met him except through letters.

[2] R.D. had, however, sent Medieval Scenes to Olson as early as 1948.

[3] This does not necessarily imply that the poet should erase his signature
from his works nor that poetry, or other art work, is best undertaken commun-
ally. To me the sense of chronology, the cumulative power of a life-time's
work, is of profound importance; and it can only be experienced if author-
ship and sequence are known. As for "group poems," I find them superficial:
each individual needs solitude in order to bring his or her experience in
life and language to fruition in the poem, and it is through communion with
ourselves that we attain communion with others. Duncan's own practice seems
sufficient evidence that he would agree.

[4] It is possible Duncan had some half-conscious memory of this moment when
years later he spoke of his special feeling for a poem called "Shalom." The
"man / going down the dark stairs" in that poem was not he, but it has
come to seem to be as much about him as anyone, in the way poems do, with
time, come to admit more than their first inhabitants.

[5] By the summer of '63 he had somewhat relented, however: "Oh yes, it's true I'm most likely to bridle at the mention of 'Jung'. But, while there is an argumentative cast always in Jung that I find exasperating and dislike finally (the having the answer to things in a schema), there is always much and often so much else that I find revelatory. I look forward with the usual mixture of prejudice and expectation to reading the Autobiography."

[6] From "Life at War," see The Sorrow Dance, 1966. (New York: New Directions, 1966), p. 80.

HEROIC SURVIVAL THROUGH ECSTATIC FORM:
ROBERT DUNCAN'S ROOTS AND BRANCHES

Eric Mottram

Duncan dates the work in Roots and Branches from 1959 to 1963, and from the evidence of the poems, those were four years of exhaustive, exhausting reconsideration of the kind of poet he needed to be. The book is disturbed with a responsibility to be gnomic--to re-enter the core of "wisdom as such," in Olson's terms of warning--and to retain a bardic presence of emotionally committed language at every point of argument or discourse. (Myths and gods are to be resuscitated by the Bard, old forms and other poets to be placed within a text which analyzes the "structure of rime." And Duncan required of himself a social function for a poetry whose ecology included the history of cultures, "the rites of participation" as he delineated them in 1967.

> The drama of our time is the coming of all men into one fate,
> "the dream of everyone, everywhere." The fate of drama is the
> fate of more than mankind. Our secret Adam is written now in
> the script of the primal cell. We have gone beyond the reality
> of the incomparable nation or race, the incomparable Jehovah in
> the shape of a man, the incomparable Book of Vision, the incom-
> parable species, in which identity might hold & defend its
> boundaries against an alien territory. All things have come now
> into their comparisons. But these comparisons are the corres-
> pondences that haunted Paracelsus, who saw also that the key to
> man's nature was hidden in the larger nature. (H.D. I, 6,6)

Duncan's citations for comparison are Marx, Darwin and Frazer and their handling of economics, species and magic, ritual and "the gods" towards world commune, world family in evolution, and world cult--towards "a larger community of man." And further: Pound's "all ages are contemporaneous," Stein's "the continuous present" of man composing the process of the contemporary, and Malraux's "our art world is one." Duncan inherits a universalism developed in the mid-nineteenth century, a sense of American culture as the heiress of all the ages.

Roots and Branches appeared at a time when an American had to decide as never before whether to disaffiliate from his imperialist nation, whether to protest, to break the law, or to support official slaughter in Southeast Asia, Orangeburg, Kent State and elsewhere. Duncan would move towards the clarities of Passages. Meanwhile he had a good deal to explore, nervously searching for a language and forms which did not simply inherit rhetoric and procedure. The goal of visionary utterance would have turned into an absurd retrogression into shamanism, a popular primitivism of power-desires among American poets of the '60's.

In Roots and Branches, the reasons for its difficulties of apprehension and for the problems in describing its passage, is that Duncan is working to find containers for a knowledge which does not repeat the limitations of the polemical in Eliot and Pound, nor the romantic egoism of the declining personal lyric tradition. He refuses the provincial and tries for a poetry which will stand with his world-binders of comparative studies. This entails a consideration of any kind of leadership: the book is obsessed with mastery and authority. American imperialism was destroying remaining vestiges of that old dream of American moral leadership in the world. By the time he came to compose Passages, Duncan had entered the international scene then occupied by Ginsberg, Snyder and Yevtushenko, poets with a message directly stated enough to simplify the issues of love, hatred, community and authority, and to cut through the local apologetics for corruption without using a fixed ideology.

Duncan had not reached that state in Roots and Branches. But already erudition had to rest on the elemental--that had been learned from the Cantos as well as techniques of image and melody. The lyric and the song appealed deeply to a poet who needed to make gnomic verses, spells, rhymes of magic compulsion--who wished, in a word, for poetic power. He has often referred to the crucial effect of his reading Carlyle's "The Hero as Poet" in 1961, a chapter in On Heroes and Hero-Worship and the Heroic in History (1841), a work which stems from similar concerns in Hegel's Reason in

History. Hegel embodies active energy in "world-historical individuals" who
choose, rather than happiness, "toil, struggle, work for their purpose":

> The organic individual produces himself: it makes of itself
> what it is implicitly; thus the spirit, too, is only that which
> it makes of itself, and it makes of itself what it is implicit-
> ly. . . . Spirit is this, that it produces itself, makes itself
> into what it is.

For Hegel "great historical individuals" contain "the substantial will of
the World Spirit." They are heroes because they derive purpose and vocation
from "a secret source whose content is still hidden." The source is "a ker-
nel different from that which belongs to the shell." Out of their impuls-
es, heroes "produce a condition of things and a complex of historical rela-
tions that appear to be their own interest and their own work." They "see
the very truth of their age and their world, the next genus, so to speak
which is already formed in the womb of time." At this point they enter the
action which Rimbaud stated for the poet, at the time of the Paris Commune
(his letter of May 13, 1871):

> The world-historical persons, the heroes of their age, must
> therefore be recognized as its seers--their words and deeds
> are the best of the age. . . . For this reason their fellow
> men follow these soul-leaders.

Duncan found that he had to discover his heroes, to ascertain to whom
he could go as a son, to make sure that his predecessors and fathers would
enable him to be "a poet of many derivations" but still develop his own
voice. He could not own allegiance to that long tradition of yielding to
tyranny described in Eric Bentley's A Century of Hero-Worship (1944; 1957),
especially in a time when many Americans had to resist the State's heroic
leaders, and many poets felt the need to act against authority. In the
1950's poets began to perform in public as vatic indicators of public cor-
ruption, and by 1965 prophetic indictment of their country had become part
of the Movement. But they also realized the need for an inner melody of
coherence which was not simply protest. Carlyle speaks of "musical thought,"
an ability which turns on "power of intellect" in the seer:

> It is a man's sincerity and depth of vision that makes him a
> Poet. See deep enough, and you see musically; the heart of
> Nature being everywhere music, if you can only reach it.

For Duncan, Carlyle's words reinforced Pound's concept of _melopoeia_ and
Olson's doctrine of "by ear, he sd"--both used in "Notes on Poetics. . ."
(_Black Mountain Review_, 1956). In "Ideas of the Meaning of Form," he em-
phasizes Carlyle's melody of language, song as the deep structure of vatic
intellect in the poet.

But he also recognized the new public possibilities for the poet in
society and with public readings of _Passages_ from about 1965 onwards en-
tered the Movement decade with authority in the traditional role proposed by
Carlyle. Through his "Heroic Gift" the poet ends that "sceptical Dilettant-
ism" which cripples his power. Like Dante and Shakespeare, the poet will
"read the world and its laws; the world with its laws will be there to read."
The _vates_ combines poet and prophet, penetrates "the Divine Idea of the
World, that which lies at the bottom of Appearance," and shows "what we are
to do [and] what we are to love."

Duncan must have felt this appeal deeply as he came into his middle
powers of 1961: to be able to make Song the structure of the seer and the
lover, and melody the vesture of "inward harmony of coherence," in a time of
confusion and moral decay. "Passionate language" moves naturally to Song--
and Duncan quotes Carlyle's next passage in both "Ideas of the Meaning of
Form" and "Towards an Open Universe." The keys are:

> All deep things are Song . . . _musical_ Thought . . . power of
> intellect . . . the heart of Nature _being_ everywhere music,
> if you can only reach it.

"The Heroic of Speech" emanates from an epic factor in Dante and Shakespeare.
The Song contains history, and its morality lies in the eye not trivializ-
ing as it sees: "no most gifted eye can exhaust the significance of any
object" (a statement also central to Objectivism and its development by
Williams and Zukofsky).

Roots and Branches is a book which explores "heroic vitalism" (Bentley's
term) and its inclination to messianic prometheanism, and the need to create
within what Carlyle, in _The French Revolution_, gives as the Process--"all
embodiment of Force that work in this miraculous Complex of Forces named
Universe--go on _growing_, through their natural phases and developments, each
according to its kind." Writing within Whitehead's extensions of Coleridgean

romantic theology, Duncan says in the second poem of "Apprehensions 5":
"All things are powers within all things. . . . There is only one event"
(RB 41). It follows that poems can never be considered alone, any more
than any object in the universe can be taken apart. In his preface to
Caesar's Gate, he speaks of his earliest commitment to poetry:

> In my commitment, there was a Reality behind the Reality I knew
> in making it up, a Reality to which everything I knew referred.
> The world was a text, the code of many languages, yet to be
> broken. . . . All that I came to sense and to learn of the uni-
> verse and its elements, of the nature of life, and of myself as
> a poet of that reality, I read as the text of an ultimate Poetry,
> beyond me, upon the verge of such a being able to read I write,
> even as a child, I used to make up worlds and populations of a
> play-real upon the shores of the Reality I belonged to. It was
> the happy rite of a fearful belonging. (CG xviii-xviv)

In a section of "The H.D. Book" Duncan says: "Poems are not objects but
events of Poetry, of our consciousness of _making_ a universe of feeling and
language" (H. D. II, 5, 50). The central image of that making, in The Open-
ing of the Field, in Roots and Branches and in Bending the Bow, is the tree,
as the creative commitment to the organic process of human nature within
nature. In 1955 Duncan stressed Olson's "emergence from vitality of facul-
ties" against Joyce's "retreat from his faculties to his mere vitalities"
("Notes on Poetics Regarding Olson's Maximus").

> Olson insists upon the active. Homo maximus wrests life from
> the underworld as the Gloucester fisherman wrests his from the
> sea:
> _the under part is, though stemmed, uncertain_
> _is, as sex is, as moneys are, facts_
> _to be dealt with as the sea is . . ._

Duncan concludes:

> The major address of the poem is to what the act need be--to
>
> facility
> resulting from life of activity in accordance with
>
> felicity
> resulting from life of activity in accordance with (PNAP 192-194)

Olson is characteristically looking for centre and law in this poem--
"ukase," through the center of buoyancy, the right action of behaviour both

in poetry and in building the <u>polis</u>. Duncan recognizes this necessity, but the difference between <u>facility</u> and <u>felicity</u>—if it is indeed Duncan's own rewording—is the difference between his requirement that a poem be a garden of both cultivated and wild, and Olson's more restricted desire for ukase. Both poets, however, were searching at this time for facts to underpin poetic praxis in the absence of usable ideology—in the terms of Olson's poem, buoyancy based on reliable law, in a time of catastrophe. Duncan's later response would be his public reading of <u>Passages</u> 21, 25, 26 and 27. If the last of the <u>Passages</u> of 1965 does conclude with the old Shelleyan hope for Promethean youth against Zeus, Duncan's figures of opposition also include Pegasus reborn from a new Helicon and ambiguous release of "Dionysos, Zeus's Second Self,/Director of the Drama."

How the tree process could be used within this poetic and political action, Duncan suggested a few years earlier, at the University of British Columbia seminar (reported by A. Frederick in <u>Trace</u> IV, 1963-64):

> the event is transformed from the history . . . into the present, a thing still happening. . . This is why it is difficult to 'burn out the roots.' You can chop down a tree (presumably a bad one) but not the poem. His (Dante's) purpose is to restore the tree.

In 1953 Duncan had been impressed by Poe's ability to manifest strong feeling as part of political and social tensions, and Mallarmé's ability to subject materials to "the intensity of conception" through language manipulation, so that "nothing circumscribed the flowing of being into its particular forms." When Duncan came to write on Olson, this became "the discipline of the eye, clarity . . . acknowledged as measure" as the practice of responsibility. Olson's metrics of "how to dance/sitting down" became Duncan's "dance in whose measured steps time emerges, as space emerges from the dance of the body. The ear is intimate to muscular equilibirum." The linking image between tree process and language measure is the garden. Looking back to his 1949 story "Love," in 1963 (<u>Kulchur</u> No. 11. Autumn 1963), Duncan noted the recurrence of "the theme of gardens and gardeners" in his poetry. But the story also connects sexual and chemical forms of energy transformation with metamorphoses of acting and action within the

Carlylean poetic function. "Ideas of the Meaning of Form" (Kulchur No. 4,
1961), summarizes the resultant poetic:

> Taste can be imposed, but love and knowledge are conditions
> that life imposes upon us if we would come into her melodies.
> It is taste that holds out against feeling, originality that
> tries to hold out against origins.

So the poet chose to be "many-fathered" and "mothered in the various chem-
istries of the planets," against the simplified rationalities of "the posi-
tivists and semanticists who would free matter from its inspirational
chaos." The poet is to compose at a pitch of high enthusiasm, underpinned
with science and a sense of the political event in his time and in history.

II

Roots and Branches is divided into two sections, "Roots and Branches
(1959-60)" and "Windings"(1961-63)." The first moves into the possible
inferences of such an extended growth idea as the title offers. But its
opening poem shows how dispersive Duncan's style could be in 1959. It is
a piece of opaque personal rhetoric, a manner of euphoria which needed,
and achieved, substantial pruning in order to generate branches and support
fruit. But the monarch's movement does begin to offer a form for Duncan's
later poetic action: it is multi-dimensional, a poetic which collects news
by tracing roots and branches, woven and broken filaments, connecting with
"intent and easy" profusion, and under excitement, "transports of an inner
view of things" (RB 3). In the book that follows, however, Duncan aims
for abundance of information and form, the extreme opposite, say, to
Creeley's cautious, low-keyed perfecting action of one kind of procedure.
In "What Do I Know of the Old Lore," the Kabbalah is Rabbis "rejoicing in
their common devotions," a woven design--the weave will enable the poet to
exclaim "O, I know nothing of the left and the right" (RB 4). Drawing on
love, he can substantiate the supposition that all myth, legend and fairy
tales store the wisdom the monarch can sip, "flitting into area of aroma"
(RB 3). He leans to the magic of forms, books of wisdom and priests because
a bardic stance refuses the intellectual accidie of current criticism-
poetry. The book Duncan wants is governed by night and the moon, the chia-

roscuro of selective illuminations and excited light. In "Night Scene"
Eros causes birth and rebirth through not only through homosexual love, but
through studying fruitfully the lore of ardour contained in past poets en-
gaged in the metamorphic process: occultists, surrealists, hermeticists,
and Prospero's white magic. Ariel's sucking of the natural toward the fu-
ture making of a hive is part of a recurrence of bee and honey images.
Restoration must be discovered in a usurping time; Eros must infuse Pysche,
and Beauty relieve the Beast: "And from the Beast a man that was Day came/
shaking my heart like a store in old trees" (RB 7). This reappears in the
second song of the Night Nurse further reinforced from lore:

> The Beast is the lord of the heart's need
> He must be hideous.
> His is the Rose
> He is the First One.
> Ask the Sun. Ask the Moon. (RB 61)

The police cars in "Night Scenes" image "the old divine threat" of fixed
Centre to the continuous creation of design, the poet's weave in this case.
Duncan's gods are generally hermeneutic positions rather than Jehovic auth-
orities.

Certain Ovidian procedures of transformations in love and the soul,
present in seventeenth-century English poetry, move within Duncan's poetics
--mainly methods of presenting human figures diminished to points of valu-
able light and threatened by the darkness of political and religious power,
and of lust, but still capable of that knowledge which can release and ex-
pand. This is the tradition not only of the recusant and metaphysical poets,
but of Bacon and Browne, and such a figure as Prospero, the Ovidian magus of
white magic. Duncan emerges in Roots and Branches already the poet of
counterpower resistant to ideology and the State which will be his stance
in the later 1960's. The American magus is a monarch and an anarchist but
within a sense of social responsibility. Fluidity of form and variety of
procedure have the urgency of having to find forms of energy for both sex-
ual love and for the necessary rebuff of the artist against those repeti-
tions authority demands: "youth spurts, at the lip of the flower/lifts
lifewards"--"we see one lover take his lover in his mouth,/leaping."

Against fatigue: the spire, the fountain, the "single note around which/
the throat shapes!" (RB 7, 8).

In "A Sequence of Poems for H.D.'s Birthday" the archetypes are in-
creased: the advisory Mother, the Prince as lover and alchemical trans-
former, and the risk-taking Poet "moving through here." The tutelary figure
of part two is the seventeenth-century meditational poet--Herbert and
Vaughan, together, as the poet of dawn, the platonic light. It is Vaughan's
ease of intent that is supplicated: "love and judgment" in balance, "all
tones coming forth into one scale/to govern and release the music of our
dance" (RB 11).

Duncan's poetry contains a tough central resistance to nostalgia for
Centre and Universal, only too seductive in a time when the values he needs
to inherit were and are being terrorized. Duncan risks the archaic as he
invents his language and procedures irrespective of fashion, not out of
fatigue or alibi but in a spirit of inheritance and recognition. Part
three of the H.D. poem, then, is a prayer for the achievement of unified
vision under properly conceived authority. The unity evoked is male, its
workings are poems, and the poems take up and further stages and examples
of myth and ritual. Duncan is coming to terms with birth as conjunction of
sexes and poetic materials, so that the term family can be an analogue of
such a coming together. H.D.'s birthday is analogous to his own: the poet
bears poems on his birthday. His own family of birth is replaced--as in
his actual experience as a child--by a family of rearing. Precisely who
"mother" means is bound to be unstable, and this issue recurs in seance
and dream throughout the book, haunting the poems in the form of mysterious
generation in poems. Poems become, like the poet or orphans, made over into
a new family, the analogue of society beyond the family of birth. His
astrological place is his chance of birth in the universe of such conjunc-
tions.

Experience, the poet has discovered, is double: two mothers, two fa-
thers, the life of the cross-eyed, the double-sighted--these are multiples
in "the plan" which provides a definition of "home." But it is a home

agitated by ambiguities of love and terror. The main security is that
female hope of inspiration who, in part six, takes the old Christian form
of the blue-gold virgin radiating light. Inspiration is unpredictable, as
well as unstable, enough to be taken into the prose letter to a carpenter,
which follows, as part of resistance to being moulded into a utilitarian
society where men are parts of a labour system. Any organization force--
Christ, angel, hunting carpenter--threatens the poet's fate, especially
since he is, at this stage, insecure in his vocation, even in dreams. In a
dream, hunted by the carpenter, he becomes a monkey on a chain; the carpen-
ter becomes an angel, a giant authority, who like any ideologue or religious
Centre, searches out potential members:

> You think of it as salvation and you cant see how
> it is slavery for us. You wanted me to give up
> everything, didnt you? and go with you, and I
> couldnt think about my own work in poetry I was
> so scared. (RB 21)

No compromise is possible. Poetry as a fate is part of that image of
a hearth to which Duncan returns to his work--home, his mate, his friends
and his cats. The crisis to be survived is developed in "Nel Mezzo del
Cammin di Nostra Vita"; the Dante title refers to artists in the process of
getting into the second half of their maturity, into another kind of achieve-
ment, another birth. The heroes are: Rodia and his Watts towers, con-
demned by the authoritarian city, "taller than the Church," "Art, dedicated
to itself!"; Gaudi in Barcelona; Olson saying "the poet . . . cannot afford
to traffic in any other sign than his one." So the artist must create his
own resistant autonomy--"Otherwise God does rush in." That this may be a
political act of subversion is implied in the poems' quotation from Burck-
hardt: "Art . . . the most arrogant traitor of all/putting eyes and ears
. . . in place of/profounder worship" (RB 22-23). That the poet needs to
reveal his privacy to the public is the gist of "A Dancing Concerning Form
of Women," a parodic usage of Creeley's short measures and brief stanzas
appropriate to a poet so deeply concerned with breathing his way through
experience like a wary hunter. A poet makes his own rules, says "The Law,"
within his social and literary inheritance, and this is the essence of

Duncan's sense of vocation: "Crime/fulfills the law. *Oedipus* is a/ravish-
ing order in itself./His tearing out his eyes--/a phrase, secretly prepared,
/that satisfies" (RB 27).   Poetic vocation--and Roots and Branches is an
ascertaining of vocation--is a plan wherein law destroys law constantly.
Once again, Shakespeare's theatre is invoked--with grim paradox: "They go
to murder Duncan, who here/is a sleeping King" (RB 27).

      The thirteen pages of "Apprehensions" explore the ancient distinctions
to be made out of nature and culture. Part one affords a glimpse of how the
basically animate could function as intermediate between Earth and Man; part
two takes in architecture and agriculture as cultivation of the natural
(Earth) as prose and verse are: an understanding of grove, house, hearth,
"the dome of many-colored glass," temple, and the "Sage Architect" himself,
who awakens "the proportions and scales of the soul's wonder/of stars and
water." The issue is: what is making within the natural? The poet dreams
of a pre-alphabetic culture in which a man might live unself-consciously
with the rest of the Earth, taken to be a recoverable condition to which a
poet might gain access: "a monument of what I am"--"a house built in the
ancient time" (RB 33-34). In the basis of the natural lies an impulse to
formation which ends in a made architecture within the unmade: house and
poetry are the results of Love, an active agent impregnating what is.   The
movement of confident rhythm and metric holds both anxiety and serenity in
the poet's apprehensions (apprehension--the action of seizing upon, seizure;
the action of taking manual possession; the action of learning, sensible
perception, understanding, anticipation). In part three, the action appre-
hends how the elemental lies in mythology, a central notion in Duncan's
poetry. Here the work looks forward to Passages in its initially confident
inheritance, a stage beyond Pound, H.D., and Eliot, his guardians and
coaches in a drama of the Return of the Gods:

                  The elemental man is a humpt bank where
                     the hair grows, heapt up of time,
                  folded upon fold, lifted up from what he was,
                     a depth of silt, into this height
                        above sea level. (RB 35-36)

Adam Kadmon releases the horde from being a set of giants--primal man as "a

vast dispersed being" with all-consuming appetites; the stabilization of
hunger is structure, holding light and carbon, defined. The poem consider-
ed within this aegis is historical man, a rehearsal and reverence for the
non-individual, the type, in the hands of a transmitter and converter, the
poet. The specifically American poet inherits that part of the world
mythology which makes the grandparents, moving west to Oregon, part of a
collective unconscious--"myth/that Freud says lies in our blood, Dragon-
wise,/to darken our intelligence" the folds of the pre-alphabetic. Surviv-
al is not yielding to such a possible form of Tiamat, the mother-dragon,
but conquest or finding a dream, a vision, so that the play continues.
Men are cast, Duncan puns, so that games and theatre, roles and dice fuse
in one "design toward crisis" (RB 37).

The musical structure of "Apprehensions" itself moves to and fro with-
in the space of this transcultural, translatory, transitory and transrefer-
ential action. But the action is also both archaeology and an excavation
of the caves of the body's self or soul--part of the Earth's need for
release and architecture. In the first of eight Structure of Rime sections
placed here, the subject is casting, now punned as the lost wax process.
This in turn is a version of related images: the jewel of Dung from the
muck of Night, Love uprising in light from the darkness, the man rising
from the boy, theatre out of void, the Morning Star, the valuable object
retrieved from a cave, the poem out of a core of resemblance and rimes.
This creative-destructive necessity leaves scars in the body as it does in
the Earth. In tones reminiscent of Stevens, part five states an eternal
hope, recurrent in Duncan's poetry, "The sun is the everlasting center of
what we know,/a steady radiance." The resurrection comes through a se-
quence of images: the earliest cells still in the body; sperm as sparks;
the "occult egg" challenging law or "doctrine" (RB 40). The poem's
exclamations of wonder echo French convention rather awkwardly, but the
ecstasy is true.

"Apprehensions" states bearings which may locate together dream, wak-
ing experience, the theory of knowledge and a structure of rime; it is
that ambitious. The 1972 preface to Caesar's Gate speaks of everything in
the "field of feelings in which I work" being compacted of passages deep-
ening "the identity of my intention" as "fabricator of identities." The

aim is conscience: "the consciousness and conscience of the poem in rela-
tion to the various fields of meaning in which I recognize the poem to
operate" (CG iii). The personal or historical alone do not make the poem.
Reunion with the lover was threatened by Duncan's "jealous rages," and
the basic fear was of losing home. The problem was to understand "co-
ordinations" of form and content as language enabling the poetic impera-
tive to articulate "the meaning of what was happening":

> Poetry . . . taking up fear and error as its own terms,
> seeking every rumor, every superstition, every promise of
> its own existence as it journeyed into the continent of that
> existence, seeking to regain a map in the actual to come to
> know, part by part, the transformation of a continent into a
> **life.** *"So that there is a continent of feeling beyond our
> feeling,/a big house of the spirit,"* as it came to me in the
> poem *Apprehensions* some ten years later.
>
> What does it mean that in order for it to come real in the
> poem we must *imagine* even what we have actually felt? (CG xii)

The conclusion of "Apprehensions" shows with what degree of affirmation
Duncan would state his poetic at this stage:

> Wherever we watch, concordances appear.
>
> From the living apprehension, the given and giving *melos,*
>
>   melodies thereof--in what scale?
>
> Referring to these:
>
> the orders of the sentence in reading;
> the orders of what is seen in passing. There was the
>   swarming earth;
> the orders of commanding images;
> the orders of passionate fictions and themes of the poet
>   in writing;
> the orders of the dead and the unborn that swarm in the
>   floods of a
>   man embracing his companion;
> the orders of the Lord of Love. . . . (RB 42-43)

The Prince and the Architect are still present, since <u>orders</u> means
both created forms and commands. But it is <u>melos</u> that is the poet's
business as he coordinates the meanings of order:

> There is no life that does not rise
> melodic from scales of the marvelous.
>
> To which our grief refers. (RB 43)

"Sonneries of the Rose Cross" is a celebration and rejection of the false
ritual in the master of Rosicrucianism, Sar Peladan, the poseur, the lu-
dicrously gothic. The reason for celebration is clear in the essay "Ideas
of the Meaning of Form" where Duncan speaks of how "the inspiration of
Reason" countered Renaissance consciousness:

> The neo-Platonism and Hermeticism that had begun
> with Gemisthus Plethon, Ficino, and Pico della
> Mirandola and appeared in the Rosicrucianism of the
> early 17th century carried men's religious thought
> across barriers of right belief, church and civilization,
> into realms of imaginative synthesis. (PNAP 205)

Poetry, not religion, inherits that synthesis, but the religious materials
remain active in Duncan's poetry: its magian impulse to power. "Now the
Record Now Record" has the tree putting out leaves again--"conductors or
translators only"--as an analogue of creative life: "immortal, radiant
energies of one fire" which, through a passage from Lorca, is also the gen-
erative figure of love: *"Verde, verde, que te quiero verde"* (RB 47).
"Variations on Two Dicta of William Blake" shows Duncan's acceptance of
a prophetic tradition of the poet as magus:

> The Authors are in eternity.
> Our eyes reflect
> prospects of the whole radiance
> between you and me
>
> where we have looked up
>   each from his being. (RB 48)

The poem puns on author. Poetry is the legacy of authors. It is both free-
dom and compulsion. An author is authority in both a spirit of compelling
love and of compelling obedience. But: "I am the author of the authors/
and I am here" (RB 49); poetry is responsibility, an access to the eternal.
a duty of restoration as well as creation. Part four presents the neces-
sity of vision as a penetrative mobility between present and eternal. The
figure of the ideal author here shifts from Yeats to Olson, but his vision-
ary ability is also dangerous authority:

> Here, again, I have come close upon what harm?
>   where the honey is,
> charmd by the consideration of his
>   particular form,
>
> as by lines in the poem charmd. (RB 52)

So the poem ends with a simultaneity of withholding an acknowledgement, "the lover's kiss" (RB 53); but the disturbance and uneasiness of the work is carefully maintained without question of debilitating resolution. "Cover Images" shows that the lover's kiss is not a reconciliatory action, since the erotic is a complex of consideration and fury, and the two selves neither stable nor finished. So the next poem, "Come, Let Me Free Myself," takes up a theme in the earlier part of the book: the paradoxes of freedom, a movement between love, obedience and service in both life and art. The American reference is direct enough--Whitman, Kerouac, the mobile "barbarian"; "I am on the road" is the obsession, even at home. It is Whitman's sense of waiting and impatience for outwardness _and_ comradeship, except that Duncan has a more critical sense of self:

> O let me be free now of _my_ way, for all that I bind to me
> . . .
> For I stand in the way, my destination stands in the way!
>   (RB 55)

The punned tension of "in the way" relates to "Risk," a poem in which the theme of freedom and obedience is punned inside a use of Mallarmé. From "a last chance" Duncan moves to "this die's immediacy," "_le hazard_," and "the cast of the dice." Rider Haggard's Ayesha brings through earlier images for the Matrix--She whose passion is imperative, the Goddess of Fortune who must be trusted and cannot be trusted, Luck which controls arbitration and the arbitrary. She is the tutelary daimon of Duncan's cultivated and ill-kept garden. Art must include the unpredicated and unpredictable, and the artist thrown "into the void" (RD 56). Craftsmen in glass, gold and amber, and faience "try us"--those Byzantine temptations of Yeats. But in the garden a rare herb "disturb[s] the mind towards darkness," and the god of the artist as maker is Loki--Mercury, Thoth, Hermes, Wieland--the impulse towards "the incorporate dissatisfaction," the rare or unique which is both autonomous and provocative. It includes in its form of obedience the lure of numbers, the interior action of chance: cards, dice, "painted sticks." The poet has to "cut loose" but also be obedient to the apparent power of "the lost numbers" (RB 59).

Risk is again a theme in "Four Songs the Night Nurse Sang"; the message in legends is risky metamorphosis--the Swan-Lover, for example, the

history-breeding erotics of Leda and Zeus. Beauty's Beast is released by
love under power, and love is risk with the husk of ugliness: fire which
releases the pine cone into generation. Duncan's lyric forms use our
memories of riddle, enigma, the fairy changes in ballads, and the para-
doxes of Blake's songs of innocence and experience. This 1959-60 section
ends therefore with four parts of Structure of Rime, and "Osiris and Set,"
dramatizing the theory and practice of how nature becomes, is made to
become, art--a new coherence within the All, the coherence of "the ever-
lastings." The mandrill is the mask beneath which lies universal energy,
of which a man is part. The Trois Frères type of figure becomes "the man
in the drill dancing,/His form enters the animal form" (RB 65). Bee and
honey enact origins and results. Goethe's Helen, Kundry and the witch are
other forms of the intoxicating risk of mask and bliss. These in turn are
focussed in a relationship between Wagner and Egypt--Kundry, Tefnut and
the Muse. In an interview with Robert Creeley in 1962, Duncan recalls the
effect on him at high school of reading Browning's dramatic monologues;
then Pound's study of heroes and the spirit of romance, and the intense
sense of being alive in Williams. Pound's concentrated nucleus of image
which drew in surroundings, the use of the persona in **"Sordello," H.D.**
speaking in the voice of the gods, and Carlyle's lecture on the poet-hero--
all these went into his **poetry** as a complex vitality. Specifically, in
"Structure of Rime XVIII," Tefnut, he states, is the wild lioness of the
wilderness, the Sun, destructive force who ate the **Egyptians. Kundry** laugh-
ed Christ crucified--which Duncan relates to critics laughing at poets using
such material (the New Critics in particular). The poet must invite the
Muse in which all risks are present--creation is impossible without
destruction: the lioness mask of the Muse.

　　Set is the male equivalent of the disturbing female mask, a reductive
figure who drives us to nature against law. With neat duplicity Duncan
defines his function: "He comes into the court of the law to remind us./
He gives us the lie." But all myths are ways of misunderstanding the body:
"mouth, mask, hand,/the hidden plan of volition . . . in the closed palm,/
in the human face" (RB 68). The poet's drama lies within the dramaturgy of
myth and the body. Duncan's poetry has steadily developed the meanings of

this continuity as the resurrection of the scattered body of Adam Kadmon/
Osiris/Christos through the agency of the figure of renewed wholeness, Isis,
and that pattern of conflict--Horus against Set--which enables conquest:
"the sensory-motor homunculus/subduing the forces of nature" (RB 69).

So this first part of Roots and Branches is an ascertaining of what
possibilities there may be of a serious place to work with melos, the
region which Kadmon coheres again within the history of images of destruc-
tion and creation. The hero is to emerge in the form necessary--in
immediate terms, the form Duncan wanted in America at the beginning of the
1960's as the Carlylean poet, the man of order and risk. As he observes
in the 1956 notes on poetics:

> THE RISK: to suggest that the conquest of babble by the
> ear--to distinguish and organize, to make significant,
> to relate as experience, to name--is the origin of speech
> and emotion. Speech at this level articulates internal
> sensations . . . melopoeia is the passionate system of the
> poem. The conquest of passion by the eye, phanopoeia is
> at once and in the same a physiological gain, a focusing,
> and a gain in meanings. To "see" is to re-form all speech.
> (PNAP 190-191)

But Carlyle's poet is also a "great soul" whose speech contains silence
"like roots, like sap and forces working underground!" Part two of Roots
and Branches is entitled "Windings" and goes deeper into the subterranean
action of the World Poet.

III

"Two Presentations" moves out from the figure of the poet's dead moth-
er. These are poems searching the nature of identity, the enclosure of
self within circumstance. In the first, a cold loneliness thrusts again
at divided life. In a prose note Duncan tells how his first mother died
at his birth. After six months motherless, his second mother "found and
adopted me." So that birth, being found and loved, rebirth, and the Mother
who subsumes all mother-feelings and presences are a persistent material
of his poetry, a basis to which he returns with increasing understanding.
The cold dawn bewilderment of this first poem is a datum from which he
climbs and retrieves, a given with a certain warmth, a motion of descent
and ascent which recurs in his poetry.

The poet also had two names, and this doubleness, combined with

cross-eyed sight, Duncan everywhere converts to positive action. Double
vision is the requisite of the seer, so he sees a certain luck in the
conditions of his entry into the world, part of an essential recognition of
accident and risk in the generative--the ill-kept part of the garden. In
the second poem, he rides a Union-Howard bus in San Francisco--the prose
preface recalls his lost Christian name, Howard--during which the mother's
presence is heard and felt, her voice recalled, "long ago," saying "'You'll
never love anymore'" (RB 76). The **poem concludes etymologically--Great**
Mother: metre: matter: a sense of matrix and measure in the very nature of
being born and engaged now in the generation of poetry. The haunting
unfinished business of "mother" is converted into possibilities of creation
rather than left as divisive obsession, a Fate or harpy.

Then follow three poems of inspiration by derivation. "After a Pas-
sage in Baudelaire" explicitly concerns symmetry played against adventure,
the "precision" of surfaces and reflections against hypothesis. Poetry
rises from movement around symmetry, fate, "this sure thing," and Baude-
laire's usage and theory is directly employed:

> . . . *l'hypothèse d'un être vaste, immense*

> *compliqué, mais eurythmique.* (RB 78)

The movement emerges from characteristic Baudelaire--the languid bite of
images in "Le Chevelure," "Le Beau Navire" and part one of "Le Voyage,"
with their longing for voyage to the unpredictable in love and poetry, the
ship of containment buoyant on the swirling mirror of the sea. In the fol-
lowing poem, the waters are those of the spring of Arethusa in Ortygia.
Shelley's "Arethusa" becomes a rhythmic and chordal inspiration, a source of
changes played on a standard number, a basis from which Duncan may extend
his measures into complexes of short and long lengths, and work at the ef-
fects of near and distant rhyme. Shelley's virtuosic lyricism is a spring-
board for variation, while thematically, the poem reworks the hunt for love
and metamorphoses in form which mutuality demands. The interaction of
waters, landscape and plants tactfully provides a sensuous language of
implicit eroticism, a feature of Shelley's own poem.

The following poem--on the recovery of a lost book of instructions for
productive life--takes off from H.D.'s **Hermetic Definition,** itself

enquiring into Saint-John Perse's writings. To examine the nature of loca-
tion, Duncan relates human time to the direction-finding methods of bees.
How is "the suntrack" lost? how is the generative source located and return-
ed to Instinct, the Queen/Mother/Isis figure, returned as centre of light,
honey and melos--for the poet, "the sun's rime" (RB 84). The presence of
Edith Sitwell nourishes the work--for instance her poem "An Old Woman":

> . . . The child unborn and never to be conceived,
> Home to the mother's **breast,** I sit by the fire
> Where the seed of gold drops dead and the kettle simmers
> With the sweet sound like that of a hive of bees . . .

And the darkness of part three is related to "the dark wild bees" making
honey "against Darkness" in Sitwell's "Eurydice." In "Doves," H.D. is
the Muse in the branches of a tree, a bird, a soul, a grey dove of flow-
ing sound. Bereft of speech by a stroke, she exemplifies the puzzle of
language as our coded necessity of expression, of the expressiveness of all
forms in nature. The branches hold language as both the doves and the wind
in the leaves. In "Returning to the Rhetoric of an Early Mode," Duncan
recalls his own early self, the gardener in his twenties under the tutelage
of Sitwell and Stevens, tending his tree for its future Hesperidean apples
and finding that gardening the master's garden failed to awaken his own
roots and branches--"the form of my tree"--and that the form of the crea-
tive partakes of the uncultivated:

> I found the form of a man in his redundance,
> sun-dancer, many-brancht in repeating,
> many-rooted in one thing, actual only
> in time so fleet the real trembled
> undoing itself. (RB 90)

The angel of scripture misled and "the workings of ecstatic form" remained
hidden in that garden. "Two Entertainments" rework a Scots ballad measure
and rhyme pattern for the theme of divination of energy and power in a
world of lore and spell, and a ballad-derivation using the world of charms
to control energy. Derivation has always stimulated Duncan and his batch
of seven poems shows his need to perform within a metamorphic mask to re-
explore the controls and the intellectual causes of form, both destructions
and reassemblages.

"What Happened : Prelude" is the centre of Roots and Branches, a long
collection of stanzas which evoke the Muse with her two angels, Puss-in-

Boots and Anubis. Osiris reappears as the figure scattering and reassembling the eternal body which holds energy in form. The musical play within which the verses are formed is a stage for the renewal of the Mysteries in San Francisco; the Egyptian field is fused with Bunyan-like figures, all parts of the soul's journey, described by the poet under his patron, Thoth. The prose containing this kind of information appears to be deliberately clumsy, not to say pretentious--the characteristic pretention of mid-century American poets simply picking up parts of archaic cultures, as if archetypes could be dumped in a poem at will, loaded with meanings intended to work automatically. The religious does rush in. At least Duncan recognizes "that not only in the writing but in the betrayal of the play higher orders contend" (RB 98). In the poem itself Mr. Fair Speech and his cousin By-Ends are representatives of those forces of the Southern New Critics who operated as "false adviser," men "against inspiration" and the element of fire, a false tradition:

> The dead
> and the dreamer strive to meet
> in truth, but
> their words are changed. They're
> playd false. (RB 99)

The cousins wish to "humanize Osiris," to harness the Cat (the other "animal fate" of the poem, sacred to the goddess Bastet), to "alter the plot" of "Thrones" or idea-archetypes. The gods must be enabled to return by providing forms of access and entry, so that "The Divine moves in this Comedy" (RB 104). Duncan's complex materials are rather crammed into the relatively simple prosody of this poem, but the gists are clear: the mechanization of poetry by false machinery of critical tradition; the mutilation of vision by enclosures of narrowly defined utility.

The second of "A Set of Romantic Hymns" takes up the Arethusa theme again--"Fountain of forms! Life springs of unique beings!" (RB 109)--but the hymns are addressed to Orpheus in praise of the "melodic torso," _melos_ as the burning lyre, "the male dance under the hornd head." The male muse in the fourth hymn is evoked as the figure of Eros whose art heals.

> _I have suffered a loss._
> _I came into manhood estranged from men,_

It was a dark way in the light of what was.
It was a changing face.

> *to sing my Eros,*
> *My Stranger in Love.* (RB 112)

And in the last and finest of the hymns:

I will always return to this thing,
    to the lonely stance,
    to the Orphic seizure,
    to the loss of my place among the dancers--

and then to the great thousand-ringing moving crowd.
                                        (RB 113)

The orphic poet uses charms and their form is "the sound" of rime: a
central affirmative in the book.   For the potential Poet-Hero, Eros and
Orpheus are united in the Lover who is needed and yet must be lost at the
moment of the creative act:

I sang in the orders of his rime.
I was most isolate in his charm . . . (RB 115)

The earlier multiplicity of meanings for order is fused with the punning
of charm: the song is made under these controls but they enable the poet
"to take my place among the dancers" (RB 115).   Loneliness, love and the
dancers: it is within this trial that Duncan's poetry operates.   It is
there in "Forced Lines"--a presence of fellow poets (Creeley and the writ-
ers of The Mabinogion in the previous poems), and a dialectic between
romantic, sensual coercion and Apollonian control.   Part one exemplifies
the sensuality; part two invokes Olson and Spicer as true advisers against
excess feeling and for "the discrete poem" (specifically Olson's denuncia-
tion of "the sprawl" and Spicer's advice on economy of composition).
Duncan moves into the problems of his own exuberance and his need for
completion as another form of the interaction of nature and cultivation.
The main forces of his poetics spin here: "So, Rome or Byzantium lost at
its boundaries, consuming/whatever oppositions" (RB 119).

     The three sonnets and "Answering," which precede "Adam's Way," invoke
Eros and at the same time clarify homosexual love in order to justify their
place in the sphere of sexuality and work.   Amor is "a worker among men,"
and the poet's "working song" is part of the world of men "working in the
street," "a work of the natural will" (RB 126).   "Adam's Way" is "a play upon

theosophical themes" which takes up the "continual elegy" materials--the
cycle of fall into separation and creative recovery into new wholes--which
is central to <u>Roots</u> <u>and</u> <u>Branches</u>. The historical placing of materials
indicated Duncan's ambition strikingly. Not only does he rework the Eden
myth but he uses those hermetic materials associated with Yeats, the meta-
morphic action of <u>The Tempest</u> (taken up from "Night Scenes" and using
something of Shakespeare's late iambic rhythms), and the spirit-dramas of
the Romantics (<u>Manfred</u>, <u>Prometheus</u> <u>Unbound</u>). That the play is too oblique
in its dramatization of sources is implied in Duncan's "Narration for a
concert reading," presented in 1966, a commentary on the interior action
and the use of "stage" as form. It is clear that he could only partly
alleviate the problems of the closet-drama of Romantic poets:

> We must return to the first power of words to call up scenes,
> at a stage before there was a stage, of worlds that we do not
> know ever were, and move out of phantoms of the mind half
> persons, half ideas, giving them what life they may have in
> being enacted. (A/P 24)

The play moves through three overlapping worlds--a palimpsest along H.D.
lines, with the difference that even the human characters are immediate
metamorphoses of the other regions--Earth Spirits, faeries of the Dark
Wood, and ancient rulers of Atlantis, now become angels and demiurges:
"The two worlds coming together, Atlantis and the Dark Wood, converge
upon the dreams of Adam unborn" (A/P 24).

The proposition is that behind the immediate seance in a "London
backroom in the 1880's" lies a Powys-Lewis past of esoteric science fic-
tion into which it impinges. But this theosophic world is in high danger
of being faded and ricidulous before Duncan attempts to drive life into
it, and the interaction of fine poetry and confused characterization (the
division of argument into separate dramatic voices) is typical of the
literary tradition. For example, Adam is us and our emanation, to use
Blake's terminology: in Duncan's terms, both a who and a what of being.
The roots and branches of the "astral or dream forest" constitute a space-
time extension, stylized like "*the interior of a shaman's tent*" (RB 128).
Here the gods return, after the Flood which destroyed the wholeness of the
Atlantean kingdom. The old gods believe it will return, but Duncan makes

it clear it will not; the speech by Bobbin beginning "They see us as gods" (RB 131) suggests a criticism of Yeats's persistent belief in the return of the world of Faery.

But these ancient faeries understand one thing--again reminiscent of Blake and Yeats--that knowledge presages death because it divides. Gods experience, men know and thereby they fall and atomize. Gods who know, in men's stories, "lose hold." The Moon falls into time. Gods do not even know gods. They live in a timeless present called Eternity--"a forest of the primeval shadow" (RB 134). Men imagine their forms. Once the Moon is no longer a seed it ceases to exist.

Erda's soliloquy summarizes a good deal of a primary meaning in the play and in Roots and Branches as a whole: the seduction of nature. Her language is suitably reminiscent of "Ode to a Nightingale" and "Kubla Khan." Adam must be born from the Pod of nature in the Chapel or Cabinet of Dame Nature. Otherwise the generative is still-born. But once out he is man, a division from nature. Dame Nature generates the new, but Erda sees it as pain--"the green woe! the fresh/suffering, the ever new souls/ this relentless creatrix looses upon the world!" (RB 136). Once again Isis is the double force of creativity out of Earth. The seance itself is an awkward and parodistic access to the spirit world which breaks down the convictions of such materials. It becomes clear that Adam would be born in any case; the rest is a front. But when he is born, Samael and Michael, the bad and good angels, are also born, in division out of Adam's bardo state. The Green Man is reborn but he has to be born "out of nature," as Yeats put it. In more local terms than the mythical, for Duncan it is a creative retention of the natural life within the process of rime:

> Think of our own life-lines or life-time as being
> such a vegetable thing, abundantly flowering and
> putting forth seed pods of what we are, so that
> moments ripen and fall to earth, bursting with new
> planting, of ourselves in us--and these subject to
> mutations, radioactive alterations and misunder-
> standings of our original form, puns, cross messages
> of the first code we come from, and so we go to birth,
> to the leaping aliveness of a new beginning from the
> inertia of the blind wanderings of the plant we are
> in our going to seed. . . . Adam grows inside the Pod

> that swells upon Dame Nature's vine like a sleeping
> eye, a spirit hidden beneath closed lids of sleep
> that sends from the embryonic brain stems of sight
> into the depths of vision where eyes form in the skin
> between the irreal and the actual real. (A/P 25-26)

Read within Roots and Branches, this is Duncan's myth of the ill-kept gar-
den of nature and cultivation. Adam is change. Man is Heaven and Hell.
Love, born with him, is also division: "All single being was torn apart."
The Forest demons of single being cannot resist this evolution. But in
ripping open the Pod for premature birth, they reinforce division--in
personal terms, Duncan is stating the duplicities of his own birth; in
philosophical terms, the single cannot create. He again quotes Olson on
this separation: "God does rush in . . . and art is washt away, turnd
into that second force, religion." Eden divides Adam from God; the
garden is the plot of God, Nature and Man. Once the plot was God and
Nature in a fluid "network of soul" whose located form is Atlantis. But
"in its movement/the dream calld Man was hidden." Atlantis was "a wedding,
/a power, a ring between the earth and sun," the emanation of "God in His
Glory." Now it is "the broken ring," its demonic forces gone underground
(RB 147-48).

Atlantis formed the Eternal. The Garden is made "out of time," but
planned to be eternal, a place of peace. The untimely birth of Man by the
underground forces ends that prospect. Once again in Duncan's work the
gods return, "the ancient War" is perpetuated. Conflict is part of the
universe or God: "the great Imaginer" knows self only by driving the Void
to form, the Holy Spirit to "form and stories into the story to be undone"
--"He is all we know of war, for we are no more than he *contends* we are."
Freedom is to pass beyond "His conditions." Adam as Man is Change, and
Fear is kissed into Time by Lilith (woman) and into Love by Eve (Erda in
her new form). Through Eve, Adam will become fire and light: "Love is the
nature of the Change." She is also "Imagination's child. Wife-man,/
woman." The human pair join the elements--air, earth, fire, fluid. Erda
becomes "Womb-man of Adam's life"--it is clear that such terms as this and
"wife-man" leave space for all kinds of sexual love. Michael enunciates
the garden law, "the law of Eden" as love. Samael, the law of unbalance,

asserts that the magic of love <u>needs</u> Adam. Truth is both laws (RB 148-56).

The garden is finally all the trees and not simply Adam alone. Eve
declares the practical "structure of rime" to which Duncan holds: the
transmutation of thought and feeling into <u>melos</u> and rime, "one living
tree." So Adam can praise the universe (the language draws on Blake's
tyger and Wordsworth's rainbow). Samael teaches Eve risk, singularity,
the ability to see Adam as self--"Love only *him* in him." Through Samael
the Tree enables her to "see thru the magic," "the Tree of the Other Side."
This knowledge she confers on Adam with a kiss--a betrayal into complexity
which is necessary for creativity. In the darkness which encloses Eden,
Dame Nature promises "a little light" in "that Night men call despair"
(RB 159-63). "Adam's Way" recasts into the form of a myth of creation
certain preoccupations which penetrate the whole of <u>Roots</u> <u>and</u> <u>Branches</u>, as
if the poet's own condition and that of his times are a recurrence from
eternity. He can exert at least the control of such composition--but the
recasting is peculiarly near to "wisdom as such." The myths his poems use
paradoxically reassure that the pain of love and poetry is perpetual.
"Cyparissus," for example, versifies Ovid's metamorphic legend of a
beautiful youth who falls in love with a stag-king and inadvertently kills
him--"his song remembers the grief of that wound." Their love is a deeply
homoerotic analogy, and Duncan places himself in close relation to the
changes: "I too . . ./know the bewildering knowledge in the beast's gaze/
that searcht with trust his lover's eyes/and found his own wound repeated
there" (RB 166). A long tradition of love as mutual wounding, a love-
death, mutates into the Ovidian transformation of man into tree, Cyparissus
into cypress, and the tree sings under the aegis of Apollo (<u>Apollo</u> <u>Musagete</u>),
a tree with branches of <u>melos</u> and roots of love and grief (RB 165-67).

These final poems on the origins of composition in love, nature, war
and duplicity include America in their context partly through a sense of
estrangement from fashionable verse theory, to be found, for instance, in
"A Part-Sequence for Change":

                    I shall draw back
                    and among my sacred objects
                    gather the animal power back,

> the force that in solitude
> works in me its leases. . .
>   . . .   (RB 167-68)

The poem ends with a need to create "the blossoming mass" (RB 169) under
the strain of too many spring buds of change, a desire echoed in "Struc-
ture of Rime XIX-XXI": "How to shape survival!"--how to face the neces-
sity of losing your heart, to "let the beat of your heart go" so that new
form emerges: it is the dialectic of "Adam's Way" in another and more
effective expression: "O brother of the confined! O my twin lord of the
net rime has tied in/tongues of fire" (RB 170). The Master of Rime
comprises all the masters and teachers of Roots and Branches, but he re-
appears in order to leave. The new forms must begin their birth. The
tree is now made into "a herm of wood"--a phallic statue of Hermes, god
of artists and alchemists, of the maze, of design, of the coil of cross-
ings, and melody. So the book properly concludes with "The Continent" in
which America is now the form of Dame Nature, Gaia, Earth, the Matrix of
Duplicities. This is a poem to be compared with Olson's poems of geology
and geography as bases for myths of origin, Hesiod transplanted in New
England. The poem reaches beyond the division and despair of "Adam's
Way" into survival as continuous conquests of nature:

> the thought returns
> that we conquer life itself to live,
> survive what we are. (RB 173)

Part four of "The Continent" is a finely composed lyric of condensare in
which Duncan achieves a serenity in placing himself within the continent:
man in nature metamorphosing nature through the continuous act of composi-
tion. "The Continent" is designed to contain sufficient myth, legend and
landscape to make a place for poetry without strain or clutter. The re-
strained short measures speak out of a coming to terms with the stresses of
natural exuberance and the threats of process which make the body of Roots
and Branches such a difficult story. But the poem certainly gains from its
context; in fact, it initially surprises with its movement of quiet affirm-
ation following the growing pains of the preceding works. The exploration
of poetics and personal capability comes to rest with an intelligence which
we can now see presages Bending the Bow:

> I'm not so old but I can put
> the thought away, my foot
> before my foot,
> climbing the hill as if for rime . . . (RB 173)

The Poet Hero is imaged as the Prince of Love sleeping before he comes into
his own at Easter, as the Green Man awaiting his procession of survival,
as the "effeminized" soul awaiting the awakening kiss which will certainly
always come, as dawn comes, as Sunday comes. The poet is confident in the
first of promise, "the one continent, the one sea."

> Things have roots and branches; affairs have scopes
> and beginnings. To know what precedes and what follows,
> is nearly as good as having a head and feet.
>   (Pound: Confucius--Ta Hsio: The Great Digest)

HOMOSEXUALITY IN ROBERT DUNCAN'S POETRY

Thom Gunn

An unusual article appeared in the August 1944 issue of Dwight Mac-
donald's monthly journal Politics. It was by Robert Duncan, described as
"a young poet who lives in New York City," and was entitled "The Homosex-
ual in Society." Something of the complex eloquence of Duncan's later
prose already shows up in his argument that the homosexual, and partic-
ularly the homosexual artist, accepts his separation from society too
readily. Instead of refusing to be rejected, he lives in secrecy, narrows
the scope of his sympathies, and cuts himself off from the wider concerns
of, say, a Proust or a Melville. It was an unusual article in many ways,
not least in suggesting that the homosexual should publicly identify him-
self as such. The author then proceeds to do just that, though aware of
"the hostility of society which I risk in making even the acknowledgment
explicit in this statement."

The hostility of society showed itself pretty soon. Duncan had prev-
iously submitted his long poem "An African Elegy" to the Kenyon Review,
whose editor, John Crowe Ransom, had accepted it enthusiastically in a
letter discussing it at some length. But now, as a direct result of the
article in Politics, Ransom refused to publish it. Looking through the
early issues of the Kenyon Review, I find quite a few contributions by
writers who were well known to be homosexual. But most of them were never
to admit it in public, and Ransom's extraordinary complaint about Duncan
was that he was indulging in something he called homosexual advertisement.[1]

It is well to remind ourselves how little precedent there was for
Duncan's testimony at that time and in that society. Homosexuality was
held in peculiar horror even by liberals who would not have dreamt of

143

attacking other minorities. In the mid-fifties, when I asked my teacher
and friend Yvor Winters why he did not like Whitman's poem about the twenty-
eight young men bathing (Song of Myself, 11), he replied that the homosexual
feeling of the poem was such that he could not get beyond it. (On the other
hand, he was able to consider Billy Budd the great book that it is.) Homo-
sexuality was even, in our lifetime, thought to be contagious: many edu-
cated people believed, at least until the first Kinsey report appeared,
that a single sexual experience with a member of one's own sex was enough
to alter the direction of one's inclinations for good.

Most homosexual writers until at least the 1960's dealt with autobi-
ographical and personal material only indirectly. One method was for a
poet to address his work to an unspecified "you," giving an occasional
ambiguous hint about what was really going on to those in the know only.
(This is what Auden did, and what I was to do later.) Another method of
indirection was to "translate"--either to change the gender of a char-
acter into its opposite, in a play or novel, or by a less conscious proce-
dure to do what Duncan admitted doing in earlier poems: in the past, he
said in Politics, he had "tried to sell [homosexual feelings] disguised,
for instance, as conflicts rising from mystical sources."

But from now on Duncan's homosexuality was a matter of public record.
His early bravery found few imitators for many years. Meanwhile he had won
himself an interesting artistic freedom: he could speak about his sexual-
ity openly but with barely any twentieth-century tradition of such openness
behind him. He had to create it for himself.

*

In the 1966 introduction to his selection from his early poems, The
Years As Catches, Duncan raises the possibility that his sexual and poetic
beginnings may be connected. "Perhaps," he says, "the sexual irregularity
underlay and led to the poetic." The neutral word "irregularity" suggests
that the emerging consciousness, finding its desires out of harmony with
those of the society around it, extends itself into a realm--that of art--
where things are not judged by mere regularity, where the harmonies to be
reckoned with are far more comprehensive, and where one in fact aspires

to the extra-ordinary—the Divine Comedy, King Lear, Ulysses.

But meanwhile he was exploring the irregularity, and its presentation was not a very happy one in these earliest poems, either before or for some time after the article in Politics. He himself notes the prevalence of images of disease in that early poetry, and suggests Auden's most brilliant book, The Orators, as an influence. But they are also the product of the normal romantic gloom of a young man in his early twenties, deepened no doubt by the fact of a world war. At one point even, in properly Keatsian tradition, he refers to himself as "death-wedded."

And there is indeed a disguising, as he says, or maybe a muddling, of the sources of his conflicts. The figure of the lover in the earliest poems has an alarming tendency to suddenly turn into Jesus—a Jesus of the Hopkins brand, you might say. And when it is not grandly religious the love-making in this poetry is something of a sterile compulsion. As late as 1946, he begins a poem,

> Among my friends love is a great sorrow,

and later moves into the lines

> We stare back into our own faces.
> We have become our own realities.
> We seek to exhaust our lovelessness.

> (FD 29)

These are plain statements of deep feeling: their abruptness, their par-allelism, give them the sound of propositions, but they are propositions of ennui and despair. Nevertheless, love is already starting to be his central theme, and he sees himself afterwards as already, in such poems, preparing for "the development of Eros and, eventually, for that domesticated or do-mesticating Love that governs the creation of a Household and a lasting companionship."

This is the year when I see him as finding himself as a poet. In the earliest poems he had been somewhat at the mercy of his material, but from now on the material is his, and he uses it as a secure home-base from which he moves out into unexpected implications and extensions. In the following year he wrote the complementary sets of poems, Domestic Scenes and Medieval

Scenes. There is talk of love, but it is an unspecific and usually un-
satisfied love. It is still a self-regarding desire for love rather than
an immersion in the real thing. In Domestic Scenes, everyday objects and
situations--an electric iron, a radio, a ride on a streetcar--are used as
emblems of the heart. The feeling is sentimental and ironic. He is scared
of getting off the bus at "Reality Street," and later he says with a kind
of worldly self-pity,

> I have playd the horses -- Crucible,
> Nom de Plume, Ecstasy, and Werther.
>   (FD 50)

As a current song has it in 1976, love is just another high.

If there was a deliberate self-limitation in subject matter and mood
in these poems, there is by contrast an opening up of both in the other
group, Medieval Scenes. The poetry is still inhabited by the unhappy and
deprived. But their sorrowings are bright and exquisite, there is rich in-
vention and surprise of detail. The main theme is of separation, the in-
ability of one to "touch" another, at times the inability--even in this
gorgeous and brocaded landscape--to get beyond the self at all, except
maybe in sinister dreams. Inevitably these poems remind one of visual arts:
but the "scenes" are static, as in tapestries or tableaux vivants. A
whole court is frozen in a fixed attitude, elegant and brilliant, but with
all energy to move, to touch, and to change mysteriously blocked.

> The splendid Emperor of Jerusalem dreams
> of the Emperor of Jerusalem in his splendor.
> The poets at their board
> subvert the empire with their sorrow.
> Powerless and melancholy, the young men smile
> evasively and stroll
> along the shores of the slumbering lake. We hear
> the diapasons of a drownd magnificence.
>   (FD 55)

In the writing, however, he reaches beyond the langorous limits of the
scene. It contains a secret energy, which points to possibilities beyond
the subject matter.

Yet anyone who first encountered Duncan through his later work--that

is, the majority of his readers--can see that this particular mode, of the
wonderfully embroidered tapestry, is not one that he sticks with. Having
mastered it, he abandons it as too limited, too "finished." In "I Tell of
Love," of the following year, he turns to another kind of poem which
(though I find the writing less startling than that of the Medieval Scenes)
leads forward in style and subject to the maturity of The Opening of the
Field. Like Cavalcanti's "Donna mi priegha" on which it is a "variation,"
it is about the fleshing of a god, the living presence of that god in the
joining of two people. He transforms and recreates their lives, for he is
the very god that the young courtiers of Jerusalem were unable to conceive
of. Duncan has returned from the sentimental ironies of Domestic Scenes
and the pictorial objectivity of Medieval Scenes to the less defined, less
distanced, more risky, more personal mode in which most of his best poetry
has been composed. There is a sense, however, in which this particular
poem can be seen as rather a statement of intention, a program, than as a
realization. Duncan strains to reach beyond the limits, to immerse him-
self in love, but if he does so here it is by an act of will.

   I referred above to "two people," because homosexual love is merely
the occasion for a poem which would be just about the same if it were
about the relation between a man and a woman. (And this is the poet's point,
surely: that love of one's own sex, just as much as love of the opposite
sex, is the start of that training that reaches to the god's presence.)

   It is in "The Venice Poem," also of 1948, that he is prepared to dis-
tinguish the characteristics of homosexual from heterosexual love. In the
section beginning "Accident will finally strip the king" he explores in
particular the question of narcissism in the love of one's own sex. A man
loving another man beholds somebody like himself:

> Nature barely provides for it.
> Men fuck men by audacity.
> Yet here the heart bounds
>   as if only here,
> here it might rest.
>
>   (FD 90)

But this is only a short section of a long and complex poem in which there —
is little rest. If the poem is about the Venetian empire and the empire of

poetry, it also explores fully the ambivalence of empire-building. The man
approaches his lover,

> eager to love and yet
>   eager to thrive;
>   so too his lover
>   meets him,
> arrogant and alive, his eyes
>   seeing already
>   more than Love's mirror shows.
>   (FD 90)

The lovers see more than Love's _mirror_ shows, that is they are not lost in
the depths of a mere narcissism; but they can also see more than _Love's_
mirror shows--they are "eager to thrive." I think of the saying "A hard
cock knows no conscience."

                                        *

Most of the severely experimental work between "The Venice Poem" and
Caesar's Gate (first version, 1955) is so impersonal that it contains lit-
tle relevant to my theme, so I will pass over these years. _Caesar's Gate_
takes up where my quotation from "The Venice Poem" left off: it is domi-
nated by the hard cock with no conscience. I spoke earlier of a secret
energy in the style of _Medieval Scenes_. Here the energy is everywhere, and,
emboldened by the experimentation of the intervening years, it informs an
extraordinary book. It is about sexual hell, where lust is continuous, and
where neither body, mind, nor spirit can be satisfied. In his 1972 preface
to this book, Duncan speaks of how love, which can lead to the Household,
the place of growth and harmony, also contains a fury. This work, then,
largely focuses on sexual fury, both self-mastering and self-defeating
Afterwards he can see the hell as a place he had to pass through on the
way to the Household, but at the time he can see nothing ahead. There is
more than a little self-dramatization in the book, but it is appropriate,
as it is in Baudelaire, in that it is an integral part of the subject re-
vealed: indeed, self-dramatization is the distinguishing characteristic
of this particular circle of hell.

There are reminders of other writers than Baudelaire: Duncan renders
the punishments of the sexually obsessed in Dantesque terms. "Torches, we

light our way," one poem begins. Another finds the speaker as a kind of
zombie, between living and dead: he says,

> O holy Dead,   it is the living
> not the Divine
> that I envy. Like you
> I cry to be rejoind to the living.   (CG 17)

And there is the repeated image of the worm curled within an eye, a brain,
or the world itself, much reminding me of Blake's worm in the crimson rose.

Action also takes place on the surface of the earth, which coexists
with hell, each seen as it were through the transparency of the other. A
pick-up tells him:

> If you fix your eyes upon my body
>   you will see
> I have no soul at all.   (CG 1)

And in "An Incubus,"

> I . . . seize upon my own cock, hot with blood.
>
> Love, Love, the demon sighd
>
>   fitting his unflesh to my hunger.   (CG 19)

I am reminded of Dante, Blake, even of Rimbaud, but rather of their
concentration than of their mannerisms. If there is horror at the core of
the book, I still feel delight in knowing that a man can render even hor-
ror with such memorable force.

But there is the difficulty of the poem "H.M.S. Bearskin," with which
Duncan tries to come to grips in his 1972 preface. Bearskin is an old
queen, a stereotype, a kind of gay Stepin Fetchit. He lives in a world of
self-caricature, of homosexual affectation and campiness which stylizes all
that enters it into triviality. The poet positively sneers at him:

> Ridiculous, the butterfly,
> avatar of the serious worm,
> he lights upon the merde of Art,
> that swish old relic, self-enamourd

> fly-by-night, he hovers
> among the cafe tables.   (CG 37)

This is characteristic of the writing in this short series-within-a-series:
even though the butterfly-fly-worm imagery holds together neatly, the tone
is uneasy and itself slightly hysterical. I can feel a little more comfort-
able with the Bearskin poems only by trying to invoke a historical sense.
Twenty years ago, when homosexuals found it necessary to be much more
secretive, many were forced into enclaves within society, little ghettos.
All ghettos tend to stereotype behavior, giving fixed styles to its eccen-
tricity, as Duncan already knew in his article in Politics. Coming from a
"salon" in 1944 he remembers "the rehearsal of unfeeling" that he found
there, even in himself:

> Among those who should understand those emotions which society
> condemned, one found that the group language did not allow for
> any feeling at all other than this self-ridicule, this gaiety,
> . . . a wave surging forward, breaking into laughter and then
> receding, leaving a wake of disillusionment, a disbelief that
> extended to oneself, to life itself.

Those of us who chose not to be part of such enclaves did however feel a
certain sense of threat from the effusive stereotypes: they seemed to be
parodying femininity. Were we in fact really like that ourselves, we won-
dered, if we just let ourselves go? Nowadays the thought that they could
be a threat seems laughable; for the more a ghetto disperses itself into
the surrounding society, the more various are the patterns of behavior
available to its members. But at the time the threat seemed real enough.
And we hate what threatens us.

So I can certainly see how Bearskin has a place in Duncan's homosex-
ual inferno of 1955, even though the writing of this section is uneasy and
wavering, and both the feel of horror found elsewhere and really focused
satire are absent.

Duncan speaks of Bearskin in his 1972 preface at some length, but here
too he doesn't convince me. (He even refers to "harpies," like an outraged
newspaper editorial. I wonder if I am a harpy.) The determinedly trivial
person may indeed be **destructive,** but in the Bearskin poems as they stand

without preface, Bearskin hardly strikes me, at least from this distance,
as being "an avatar" of the worm within the world.

The strength of Caesar's Gate is elsewhere, outside of this semi-
social comment, when Duncan is speaking of the internal agonies.   There
is more to its strength than horror: in the midst of torment comes the
voice of defiance,

> All facts deny the way,
> deny I love.   Only I
>
> > remain to say
> > I love.
> >
> > I say I love.   (CG 32)

Men fuck men by audacity, he had said, and perhaps he has to pass through
this hell not only as a price for the audacity but also as a test of it,
in such a way that one can move beyond it.   And certainly the characteris-
tic mode of the book is one Duncan has put behind him: its dramatic and
concentrated intensities contrast greatly with the quieter and even self-
deprecating tone of the concluding poem added in 1972, a poem related to
the rest of the book mainly through its metaphor of "Asia," which lies on
the other side of Caesar's Gate.

To move from the imitations of Gertrude Stein and the inferno of Cae-
sar's Gate to the later books is like moving from a series of rooms into
open country.   The vision introduced by The Opening of the Field is the
reverse of that in Caesar's Gate: it is open, inclusive, expansive.   The
Gate, he has explained, is the pass that prevents the conqueror from moving
into Asia.   Now he, the conqueror and empire-builder as poet, has moved
through that gate into a larger territory that is indeed haunted, as he
had heard it would be, but by spirits that mingle continuously with the
living in mutually pleasing concourse.   (The much later "Tribal Memories
Passages 1," contains the following

> For this is the company of the living
> and the poet's voice speaks from no
> > crevice in the ground between
> > mid-earth and underworld.   (BB 9)

The book can be seen, and was surely intended, as a single poem, each separate unit being part of the mesh (the mesh of Rime) and relating to every other unit. Thus an image may have many references: in "The Structure of Rime I," Jacob wrestling with the angel is said to have "wrestled with Sleep like a man reading a strong sentence." Such references moreover may be taken up elsewhere in the book or in later work. One could point to the quoted line as a kind of model of what happens in this volume: there are multiplicities of meaning that one doesn't get to the end of easily. The ambiguities sometimes cluster very thick, but time after time Duncan's sense of direction draws him clear of what might have been only confusion, and the visions--of which after all the ambiguities are an essential part-- emerge clearly from the very fogs that generated them.

Among the fields, plains, and meadows of this book, "The Place Rumord To Have Been Sodom" is marked out with especial clarity. This is the poem that I think finally compensates for the apparent contempt in the Bearskin poems, by providing a context in which they can be retrospectively understood.

> It was measured by the Lord and found wanting,
> destroyd by the angels that inhabit longing.
> Surely this is Great Sodom where such cries
> as if men were birds flying up from the swamp
> ring in our ears, where such fears that were once
> desires walk, almost spectacular,
> stalking the desolate circles, red eyed. (OF 22)

It seems that Sodom had been inhabited by Bearskins, and others like them, and that God destroyed it as the younger Duncan would have liked to (in his own word) "disown" them. But there is a Bearskin in everyone, and Duncan, or God, can never disown any part of himself. The place "lies under fear" until one can understand that fear is part of the greater rhythm that is Love. (As in Dante, where Love rules seemingly contradictory elements as part of its dominion.) The revelation is that

> *The world like Great Sodom lies under Love*
> *and knows not the hand of the Lord that moves.* (OF 22)

This is what "the devout," "these new friends," have learned, who "have

laid out gardens in the desert" that once was Sodom; this is what the orig-
inal inhabitants were unable to learn. It is one of Duncan's best poems,
echoing the note of the psalmist or of Blake's prophetic books, and moving
with a sustained and sonorous rhetoric from the melancholy of the first
part to the joyful sound of the last four lines:

> In the Lord Whom the friends have named at last Love
> the images and loves of the friends never die.
> This place rumord to have been Sodom is blessd
> in the Lord's eyes.   (OF 22-23)

Elsewhere in The Opening of the Field there is comparatively little
about the love of man for man. The vision of the book, like that of this
poem, is larger than one of mere sexuality, though including it. And it
is here Duncan establishes once for all that his muse is female. Female
because it is the female who gives birth: only from interaction between
complementary opposites, the male poet and his female muse, can the real
poem be born. (Where this leaves women poets I am not sure.)

The muse then is fertile. And fertility is one of the main subjects
of the book, the fertility of the field in its title: "This is the Book
of the Earth, the field of grass flourishing," he says of a meadow but
could equally well be saying of these poems. He sees "evil" as a neces-
sary part of the fertile process. In "Out of the Black," Lucifer is in
love with God. In "Nor is the Past Pure," Kore is "Queen of the Midden-
heap"--which is made of "corrupted" materials. "Corrupted" is a pun,
evil is as necessary to the scheme of love as rotted stuff is necessary to
the ecology of the meadow: "Death is prerequisite to the growth of grass."
So the sterile loves are necessary to the emergence of the productive
loves; so Sodom had to be destroyed to become blessed; and so the conquer-
ing poet had to stop in the hell of Caesar's Gate before he could enter the
great fields of Asia.

I have proceeded chronologically so far, but it would be difficult to
go on in the same way. Duncan's subjects become larger and more inclusive
as he goes along, and it becomes steadily less easy to separate the sexual
themes from the others. Certainly, homosexuality is as central to Duncan's
poetry, to its origins and its realization, as it is to Marlowe's or

Whitman's, whose work can hardly be discussed comprehensively without tak-
ing account of it. Yet, as I have implied, he is no more than they _merely_
a Gay Poet, sexuality being only an important part of his whole subject
matter.

His whole subject matter. Duncan's is poetry that discusses itself
and its possibilities rather as the Chorus in Henry V discusses the pos-
sibilities of the stage he is standing on. In the mature Duncan--that is,
in the work from The Opening of the Field onward--it discusses itself in a
way through which its themes may be seen in continual interaction: sex,
war, art, love, dream, language, etc., and that is indeed his mastering
subject, their interaction.

*

So I would like to abandon chronology, which is less useful in discus-
sing the work of the matured poet, and concentrate on describing three fig-
ures or themes that recur in the next two books and in the scattered but
plentiful work following them. I will call these figures--for they are
human figures--the searcher, the mother, and the lover.

The searcher is above all the adolescent and young man. He is seeking
something out but its shape is still unclear to him. He was the author of
the earliest poems, those of the first half of the 1940's. And he is the
subject of the Moly poems of 1971, in which Duncan is haunted by the ghost
of himself at the age of fifteen. Spring is felt as a rage of expectancy
to which the adolescent's rage contributes. The boy lives in "the incom-
pletion of desires," both longing for the fulfillment of simple lust and
longing for that fulfillment to have meaning. He goes on the long random
walks of adolescence looking for a someone, the ideal who is also on such
a long searching walk, whose random wandering may suddenly intersect one's
own, and whose needs would respond to one's own needs. So Proust wanders
as a youth, hoping by chance to run across a girl from the village. The
village girl is a provisional identity given to that abstract and unre-
alized someone, the raw outline of that Albertine whose space in his later
life is already being opened up and made ready. But the need has to mature:
the lover is not yet to be found.

> I was never there. He was never there.
> In some clearing before I reacht it
> or after I was gone   some *he*
> had laid him down to sleep where Pan
> under his winter sun had roused the wildness with his song,
> and, long lingering,
> the air was heavy with his absence there--
> Lord of the Heat of Noon still palpable
> where late shadows chill the dreaming sand.

He finds on his father's death

> an emptiness in which an absence I call You
> was present.
>   (Moly Poems [4])

It is like an Old Testament prophecy of the Messiah who will some day oc-
cupy the readied space.

    The adolescent is the perfect embodiment of the searcher, but the
theme of sexual restlessness never completely leaves Duncan's poetry, as
it never completely leaves the human being, however harmonious the house-
hold he has in the end assisted in creating. In his nightmare form the
searcher becomes the Frankenstein-like Prince of "A Sequence of Poems for
H.D.'s Birthday" "in his laboratory, assisted by the **boy**" who "experi-
mented in sensations" (RB 10). But he is also the walker in the cities,
walking more purposefully now. "Night Scenes" from the same book starts
with an evocation of the risk, flashy beauty, and headiness of walking the
city by night:

> The moon's up-riding makes a line
>   flowing out into lion's mane
> of traffic, of speeding lights. (RB 5)

The poem's images suggest the search for excitement, but already it is
performed amongst larger patterns of meaning:

> Our nerves respond to the police-cars cruising
> a part of the old divine threat. (RB 6)

But the poem goes beyond: in the second part the innocent boy's orgasm is
seen, simply, as lovely in itself, and in the third part the city is

transformed to a woman, a mother containing men.

I have already pointed to some of the manifestations of this mother-
goddess muse in The Opening of the Field. And presumably in the twentieth
century I don't have to explain the relevance of them to the title of this
essay. But before coming to some of her later embodiments I should say
something about the relation of dream to Duncan's poetic procedures. I have
already mentioned the complex associationism of Duncan's work, particularly
his later work. The procedure has been common in this century, and was per-
haps first used thorough goingly by Pound in the early Cantos. Figure
melts into figure, name into name, image into image. The ship carrying the
kidnapped Bacchus is transformed into a kind of jungle-shrine to the god,
vines tangling the oars, panthers padding round the decks. Helen of Troy
becomes Eleanor of Aquitaine, both separate and individual women, but both
manifestations of the same ideal figure.

The prototype of the experience of shifting identities is to be found
in the dream, in which a friend may merge into one's cousin, who may in turn
merge into some well-known political figure. Much of Duncan's poetry, par-
ticularly what he has published from 1960 onward, has been based on dream-
work. And by acknowledging the dream-basis to so much of his writing, he
gives a peculiar rightness and strength to the associationistic procedure.
One person melts into another in the poem as he did in the dream, but never
arbitrarily, because there is a rationale to the order of the most random-
seeming dream, even though it may elude the dreamer.

A chief concern, then of this later work, has been in the multiplying
manifestations of the Mother: there appears, for example, Duncan's literal
mother (whom he never saw) and his adopted mother, but these in turn relate
to the ideal Mother, who is the muse and the principle of generation, and
who is also the city, and who in one poem becomes in turn H.D. and Emily
Dickinson. In "Achilles' Song," she is the sea, the fetus' mother whose
blood tides around him, both remote and near at hand, undefined because
everywhere.

But in "My Mother Would Be A Falconress," from Bending the Bow, the
mother appears as a distinct and close figure, no less mythical for her
clarity. The images of her as Falconress and him as the obedient little

falcon who is later to break away from her enable Duncan to dramatize the whole series of conflicts involving possessiveness and love on the one hand and freedom and the need for identity on the other. Every detail is strangely right, showing how his life is patterned by her contradictory demands: she holds him by the leash of her will, but she sends him out into the world on fierce errands, to kill the little birds, but he is to return with their bodies without eating them himself, but she rewards him with meat. Her ferocious love keeps him in her control by its very inconsistency.

> She lets me ride to the end of her curb
> where I fall back in anguish.
> I dread that she will cast me away,
> for I fall, I mis-take, I fail in her mission. (BB 52)

And the pattern that she has created is still retained. Years after her death, he still longs both to be her falcon and to go free. It is a startling poem both for what it is and for what it suggests. It suggests, for example, the ferocious goddess who demands sacrifices as her due; and on the other hand it embodies a perfect example of what Gregory Bateson calls the double-bind (typically used by the mother) which he sees as the principal cause of a common type of schizophrenia. Yet these are only implied in the poem, where the mother is merely, completely herself, so living that she is impossible to deny.

This poem, too, originated in dream. A version of its first two lines came to him in sleep, as he records in the prefatory note. And at one point, he the falcon even dreams within the dream:

> I have gone back into my hooded silence,
> talking to myself and dropping off to sleep. (BB 52)

But there is a sharpness of focus to the poem that makes it unusual in Duncan, much of whose success elsewhere in his later work depends on the changing or even blurring of focus. I find it unprecedented in his poetry.

And then there is the male dream image: "the shadowy figure" who appears in "A New Poem":

> I would not be easy calling him
>   the Master of Truth
> but Master he is of turning right and wrong

and

> He will not give me his name
> but I must give him . . .
>
> name after name I give him.   (RB 120, 121)

Ultimately he is a male counterpart to the Mother. But not an exact count-
erpart—rather than the Father he is the Lover. And the figure of the lover
is as important in Duncan's poetry as is that of the mother-muse, though his
 is not a parallel function. (If I had to separate the functions of lover
and mother I could say that he belongs more to the subject matter of Dun-
can's poetry and she belongs more to its source. But it is far from a
clean separation in a poetry that discusses its own sources so extensively.)
He too merges identities, and changes form, function, and name as in a
dream. But "A New Poem" immediately precedes the first three "Sonnets."

The first of these is largely a translation of Dante's passage about
Brunetto Latini, but it leads into Duncan's own comment:

> Sharpening their vision, Dante says, like a man
>   seeking to thread a needle,
> They try the eyes of other men
> Towards that eye of the needle
>   Love has appointed there
> For a joining that is not easy. (RB 122)

This is a good example, incidentally, of the way in which Duncan takes over
another man's work, extending an implication until it becomes his own. The
threading of the needle is Dante's, but it is Duncan who extends the image
into "a joining that is not easy" (recalling "Nature barely provides for it"
of 1948). We are led immediately into "Sonnet 2":

> For it is as if the thread of my life
> had been wedded to the eye of its needle.   (RB 123)

And then he shows us his lover putting together a patchwork quilt, joining
the different colors and textures, the selected materials from past expe-
rience, into a covering for the shared bed. This is no dream: his lover
is there, sitting near the speaker. And he is "a worker," by this activity
working in the shops of both art and love. He too works under the muse,
then, and has, too, helped to create a household within her city.

Later this figure becomes dreamlike again: in the dance of "5th Sonnet,"

> a constant
> First Caller of the Dance
> Who moves me, First Partner, He
>   in Whom
> you are most you.   (BB 5)

And later yet he returns in one of Duncan's most extraordinary and
satisfying poems, "Interrupted Forms." I quote only the last few lines,
but this does the poem something of an injustice, because the themes and
experience presented in it braid together so tightly.

>   I am speaking of a ghost
>   the heart is glad to have return, of a room
>   I have often been lonely in, of a desertion
>   that remains even where I am most cherisht
>   and surrounded by Love's company, of a form
>   wholly fulfilling the course of my life interrupted,
>   of a cold in the full warmth of the sunlight
>   that seeks to come in close to your heart
>   for warmth.   (Moly Poems [1])

It is used as a kind of prelude to the Moly poems, some of which also dealt
with ghosts. The ghost of the lover in the past haunts the place where the
lover still lives, "interrupting" the life that is itself an interruption of
"inertia in feeling." Love necessarily varies in intensity. And the House-
hold is not the home of complacency.

The energy of the poem hovers between hesitations, much as a ghost
hovers between being and non-being. But it is far from the self-dramatiz-
ing energy of Caesar's Gate, and the ghosts are far from the hysterical
zombie who cries to be rejoined to the living. The poem is about the at-
tempt to understand a complex and intense relationship. And it is primar-
ily the work of a poet, of a homosexual poet only secondarily.

This is why I shall end here. I said earlier in this essay that Dun-
can started with little modern American precedent for speaking openly about
his sexuality. There is now a way of speaking about homosexuality, and it
looks back to him as chief originator. It is due more to Duncan than to
any other single poet that modern American poetry, in all its inclusiveness,

can deal with overtly homosexual material so much as a matter of course--
not as something perverse or eccentric or morbid, but as evidence of the
many available ways in which people live their lives, of the many avail-
able ways in which people love or fail to love.

NOTES

[1]The correspondence between Duncan and Ransom is deposited in the Washing-
ton University Libraries, St. Louis, Missouri.

THE PLURAL TEXT : "PASSAGES"

Ian W. Reid   - see structure w/closure

It has become clearer in recent years that a potent mythopoeic drive
is central to Robert Duncan's work, and that it finds amplest expression
in the "Passages" poems, an open series of which the first thirty appear-
ed in Bending the Bow (1968) and the next five in Tribunals (1970).
(Since "Passages 36," included in the Seventeenth Century Suite, 1974,
individual compositions have been left unnumbered and so emancipated from
ordinal placing.)[1] It would run counter to their spirit to give here a
linear account of each poem as if it were a self-contained unit. Duncan
himself, in a prefatory note written to accompany a public reading of "Pas-
sages," tells us that "all its parts co-operate, co-exist. . . . It is
our own Memory-field as we listen. . . . [O]nly elements will remain in
your idea of what you are hearing, in your own recreation of the realm of
the poem, the first things, the first phrases or lines" (M 53). In what-
ever sequence we read them, wherever we begin to gather them, the "Pas-
sages" conjure forth an active field of myth for which Memory is the in-   *
forming muse, in which Love, War and Music are presiding figures, and
through which creativity itself, multifarious, is the fertile ground.

I

The "Passages" have no foreseen terminus; to quote from their epi-
graph, they are "without bounds and there is no way through or out."
But necessarily they have an initial point of entry for poet and reader
alike. As a poem of inception and conception, the first in the series sets

161

moving some of the primordial genetic images that grow radially through-
out the ensuing work. "Tribal Memories Passages 1" draws us into an
address to a muse ("And to Her-Without-Bounds I send," it begins) who takes
shape as matron of the Muses:

> Mnemosyne, they named her, the
> > Mother with the whispering
> > featherd wings. Memory,
> the great speckled bird who broods over the
> > nest of souls, and her egg,
> > the dream in which all things are living,
> I return to, leaving my self.
>
> I am beside myself with this
> > thought of the One in the World-Egg,
> enclosed,   in a shell of murmurings,
>
> > > rimed round,
> > > sound-chamberd child. (BB 10)

There are some fundamental connections here which indicate the distinctive
nature of Duncan's involvement in myth and of his procedures in the "Pas-
sages" poems. That "shell of murmurings" in Mnemosyne's nest brings into
play the etymological speculations which preface Duncan's essay The Truth
and Life of Myth, where he links μύζω, to murmur with closed lips, to
suck in, with μῦθος, myth. (Implicit in this is the suggestion that myth
comes to resonate in one's mind through a murmur, hum, or susurrus of rim-
ing images and correspondent rhythms. By the agency of Mnemosyne, with
her "whispering/featherd wings" and murmurous egg, the poet is taken back,
taken aback, until--as he puts it in an earlier poem --

> > all the old stories
> whisper once more.)   (OF 68)

Mnemosyne can virtually be identified with the woman who appears in the
first of those prose-poem propositions, "The Structure of Rime," to which
"Passages" provide the verse counterpart:

> There is a woman who resembles the sentence. She has a place
> in memory that moves language. Her voice comes across the
> waters from a shore I don't know to a shore I know, and is
> translated into words belonging to the poem. (OF 12)

"A place in memory that moves language": the myth-making activity, for
Duncan, is predominantly retrospective, a return towards first things,
beginnings, derivations, the "primal wave" (BB iii-iv). It works "to
release from memory a passionate order" (OF 85). This is not to overlook
the presence of strongly eschatological elements in what he writes. Rath-
er, it is to observe that in the figural pattern of these poems there is
no absolute finality; last things are consumed in their turn by first
things; the sense of an ending leads reiteratively into the sense of re-
newal. His is essentially a protological vision, a myth of origins and
continuous fertility.

In this first of the "Passages," accordingly, thoughts of Mnemosyne
induce thoughts of the "World-Egg," an image drawn mainly from ancient
Greek lore. According to Orphic cosmogony the first great god, Eros or
Phanes, "springs from the primal Egg which had been fashioned in the ai-
ther by Time," and then generates all else.[2] This love-god, revealer, is
the "child" who emerges ab ovo in Duncan's poem:

> It's that first!   The forth-going to be
> bursts into green as the spring
> winds blow watery from the south
> and the sun returns north.   He hides
>
> fire among words in his mouth
>
> and comes racing out of the zone of dark and storm
>
> towards us.   (BB 10)

This fiery energetic Love from the aither ("blazing heaven") constitutes
one of the three fundamental creative forces celebrated in the "Passages,"
or rather, one of the three analogical forms in which the Creative Force
itself is most often imagined there. In Duncan's art the strongest verb
is "make," poiein, signifying the vital impulse which not only generates
poetry itself but which likewise makes love, makes music, makes war.

II

Often Duncan has linked love and poetry as aspects of a single divine
activity. The opening group of poems in Letters contains this declaration:

> Incapable of love, I have made-up love: I am a servant
> of the Love. Incapable of writing, I have made-up
> writing: servant of the genius that lies in the language
> before which I have no genius.

Ten years later, a section of "The H.D. Book" begins:

> The work, the ground, and Eros lie at the heart of our
> study here. The work itself is the transformation of
> the ground. In this ground the soul and the world are
> one in a third hidden thing in imagination of which the
> work arises. It is the work of creation then. It is
> Poetry, the Making. . . .
>
> If the work has to do with Eros--and for the poet the
> poem is a return to the work in the charged sense we
> would pursue here--the would-be poet stands like Psyche
> *in the dark*, taken up in a marriage with a genius,
> possessed by a spirit outside the ken of those about him.
>   (HD I, 3, 67-68)

Eros reappears in several of the "Passages" poems, most fully in the com-
plex interweaving of "Chords: Passages 14," where he is represented as
"having the seeds of all things in his body." With a characteristic kind
of condensation, Duncan folds this seminal figure into others: Xronos, the
god who, being "father of the ages," can bring us ease (Χρόνος εὐμαρής θεός, in
a phrase lifted from Sophocles' Electra) as--like Eros/Phanes--he contains
and reveals all things; Herakles and Dionysos, powerful sons of Zeus (him-
self the powerful son of Kronos or Cronus, the Titan ruler whose name the
later Greek writers conflated with that of Xronos); and--in apposition
with Dionysos and with "Protogonos" ("first-born," that is, Eros)--Erikep-
aios, an epithet applied to both Eros and Dionysos and also the name of a
bi-sexual divinity mentioned in the Orphic Fragments. The poem then al-
ludes to a variant version of the Orphic creation story, found in Aristo-
phanes' The Birds, where Love comes forth from a Moon-Egg begotten by the
Wind upon Night. This imagery is nodal in "Chords," which opens by extend-
ing from "Passages" 5 and 6 an association of the Moon with love; here in
14 the lunar force or form is seen as mysteriously containing our human
selves within its changing phases. Eros, then, is cognate with us: not

only "First-Born" and "Not-Yet-Born" but also "Born-Where-We-Are." Herme-
neutically alert, Duncan continues to interrogate his own poem as it pro-
ceeds. The need to clarify that link between the love-god's birth and our
own brings about a modulation, by way of referring to the Egg as wind-
wafted (ὑπηνεμιον), from the Eros of Orphic mysteries to the post-classical
Apuleian fairy-tale in which, as Duncan envisages it, the wind-born Eros is
discovered by the wind-borne Psyche-poet:

> What does it mean that the Tritopatores, *"doorkeepers and*
> *guardians of the winds"*, carry the human Psyche to Night's
> invisible palace,   to the Egg
>
>   where Eros sleeps,
>   the Protoegregorikos, the First Awakend? To *waken* Him
>
>   they carried her into   his Sleep,   the winds
>
>   disturbing the curtains at the window, moving
>
>   the blind, the first   tap tap,   the first count or
>
>   heart beat . the guardians of the winds (words)
>
>   lifting her as the line lifts meaning and would
>
>   light the light, the crack of dawn in the Egg
>
>   Night's nature shelters   before Time.

Thus, conveying the human into the palace of divine imagination, lifting
the poet's breath into inspired utterance, the Tritopatores merge into a
creative spiritus,

>   breath of great Nature,   our own,   Logos.   (BB 46-47)

In a sensitive commentary on this "Passage," Wendy MacIntyre draws atten-
tion to the significance of the imagery here:

> Although Eros is himself "the First Awakend," the progenitor
> of all living things, it is the human Psyche who roused
> him to the meaning of love and expansive spirit. . . .
>
> God cannot come into fullness of his own being without
> the intercession of man. . . . Like the human Psyche, the
> human poet strives to awaken himself to a realization of
> God and to awaken God to a realization of Himself.[3]

There is, however, no single definitive revelation of the love-god to
human eyes. He (or "It": BB vi-viii) is plural and mutant. Chapter 3 of

Duncan's "The H.D. Book" traces some of the many guises in which Eros has
been apprehended and misapprehended throughout the history of men's beliefs
and doubts, to the point where he invades the Romance literature of Celtic
legend and Provençal song:

> Not only the primal cosmic power but also the Platonic ideal,
> the First Beloved, but also the most human god that Psyche
> sought, but also the Eros as evil that Church fathers, Catholic
> and heretic, had imagined, but also now the power of a cult
> that remains as a mode in poetry. Eros had become a tradition
> of the poem. (HD I, 3, 79)

Throughout the "Passages," too, there flickers a multiplicity of erotic
motifs, dispersed, glimpsed momentarily, seen as through a glass darkly or
in sudden flashes of illumination, now distorted in pain, now displaying
lineaments of gratified desire. The shapes of this "love that strives to
speak in the poem" (TLM 28) are variform: "lust" ("Passages" 11), "sweet
marriage" (10), "lovesick desire" (12), the descent and uplifting embrace
of Christ (17), the enchanting Orpheus (13) who introduced a homo-erotic
cult into Greece, the "remorseless Aphrodite," the Platonic abstractions
of Lover and Beloved (27), the potentially reciprocal yet sometimes adver-
sative impulses of Eros and AntEros (28, 29). . . . Through accretion and
interplay of these several forms, Duncan would have us come to see Love as
"a Lord over us in spirit who is dispersed everywhere to our senses. We
are drawn to him, but we must also gather Him to be" (HD I, 3, 69).

Apprehended in its contrarieties, Love is Strife; in its orderly con-
cords, Love is Music. Warfare and Harmony are not opposite poles. They
delineate, with Love, the sides of a single cosmic triangle, like the del-
toid Pythagorean symbol alluded to in "Passages" 6 or like a triune deity
from whom all man's makings proceed.

Emerging in many of the "Passages," musical tropes develop most exten-
sively in the twelfth, "Wine," the twenty-forth, "Orders," and the thirty-
first, "The Concert." A less disjunctive poem than most in the series,
"Wine" draws on Baudelaire and Rimbaud to suggest an intoxication of feel-
ings aroused in the improvisatory interplay of guitar and violin. "The

Concert," too, follows the lines of a musician's playing, this time in
terms taken from the mystical theosophy of Jacob Boehme. A large part of
the poem does in fact consist of phrases quoted and adapted from Boehme's
description of the two chief properties of the heavenly state, the Salitter
or divine potency itself, from which issue all "moving, springing powers,"
and the Mercurius or harmonious sound, the "tone or tune" inhering in ev-
ery power.[4] This latter property, by virtue of which "all creation moves
with/a music," is dramatized in an ecstasy of self-transcendence:

The Musician

        has wound up his pegs
    and tuned his strings. He bends his head
    to hear the sound he makes

        that leads his heart upward,

    ascending to where the beat breaks

        into an all-but-unbearable whirling crown
    of feet dancing, and now he sings or it is

        the light singing, the voice
    shaking, in the throes of the coming melody,

        resonances of meaning exceeding what we
    understand, words freed from their origins

        obedient to tongues (sparks) (burning)
    (speech) outreaching the heart's measure. (T 2)

Yet while "to know this [Music] is to know the order of all things/
set together in a key of diversities/is a sweet harmony" (17), plainly not
all people do know this, not all are attuned. Affirming faith in "con-
cords of order in disorder" (24) can hardly avoid glibness unless coupled
with a full-blooded evocation of the negatives which such a faith must
subsume. Duncan's imagination does not eschew those negatives. In
"Orders" (24) he shows the urge towards "contrapuntal communion" to be
threatened by forces of coercion. Allusions to the slaughter of Albigen-
sian heretics and to purges ancient (under Herod) and modern (in Santo

Domingo) lead up to the assertion that even "rage/grief, dismay. . . ./are
themselves transports of beauty," and that the orders of the cosmos, es-
sentially communal, "will not/dissolve . . . at man's evil." Nevertheless
evil is palpably there, no figment or phantom. The credo emerging from
"Orders" does not expunge the fierce antagonisms, the harsh curbing of
individual volition, the brutal invading of communality by violence and
repression. "Orders" is primarily affirmative, but without purporting to
be thematically complete in itself. It is only one of several "Passages"
which explore the meanings of evil and of war. "Passages" 22 to 27 were
indeed first printed separately under the title Of the War, while the same
preoccupations extend into almost all those written subsequently and into
some that happened to precede. "The Multiversity" (21), for instance, is
dominated by huge shapes of evil: "hydra," "dragon"--and "worm," which
brings to mind not only the sinister image of dark corruption in Blake's
"Sick Rose" but also the monstrous fiends of Anglo-Saxon and Norse myth,
the wyrm and the miðgarðsormr. ("Mid-earth," incidentally, in the first of
the "Passages," is miðgarðr; the second mentions a "worm," obviously no
diminutive creature of the soil; the thirteenth imagines a fire-ravaged
countryside like that caused by the dragon in Beowulf; and there are other
references which similarly prepare us for this mythological view of war-
fare.) It is in "The Multiversity" that the etymological significance of
"evil" is elicited, "referrd to the root of up, over." Though it may come
near to moralistic diatribe, this poem is not inveighing against individ-
uals; the sources of disorder are

                    not men   but heads of the hydra

                              . . . .

                              over us   (BB 70)

--over us: that attempt to superimpose, to regulate from above, is the
root of all evil.

What needs to be emphasized, then, in a proper reading of those "Pas-
sages" that follow on from "The Multiversity" is that while they do give
vent to a vehement sense of outrage at American belligerence in Asia they

are not ultimately "about" that topical situation. To see them in a con-
temporary context alone is to misread radically. It is unsurprising that
James F. Mersmann finds difficulty in coming to terms with Duncan's poetry
of the '60's in his book Out of the Vietnam Vortex: A Study of Poets
and Poetry against the War, since he makes the intial mistake of supposing
that Duncan's work is or ought to be "protest poetry." True, Mersmann
does recognize (despite his book's subtitle) that Duncan is neither "merely
against this war in particular" nor "indiscriminately against all war in
general"; but he cannot fully accept Duncan's position, and his uneasiness
at the mythologizing impulse of "Passages" leads to some misinterpreta-
tion.[5] The fact is that these are not anti-war poems but war poems, stud-
ies in struggle. While the Vietnam conflict is of course substantially
present there, a ganglion of pain, it becomes simply the most salient mani-
festation in our day of an abiding social and spiritual reality which
brings to poetry a mythic dimension. War, Duncan writes, is like love
and poetry in that it expresses "the deepest forces and cleavings (adher-
ences and divisions) of Man's hidden nature" (BR vii); and this convic-
tion was operative in his work many years before Vietnam gave it a new
focus. The fine long 1951 poem "An Essay at War," taking the Korean
struggle as its immediate point of reference, is a set of variations on
the same central motifs that move through the later "Passages." Even be-
fore then the preoccupation with war is discernible. Looking back on his
earliest writings from the vantage-point of the mid-'60's, Duncan
remarks in the preface to The Years As Catches:

> The War itself and the power of the State I dimly perceived
> [i.e., already by the 'forties] were not only a power over me
> but also a power related to my own creative power but turnd
> to purposes of domination, exploitation and destruction.
> (YAC viii)

It is in this light that we should read "Up Rising" (25) and "The Sol-
diers" (26): not as wishing simply to repudiate other men's combative
attitudes but as wishing to recreate, or discover the creative essence
of, the antagonism that Duncan finds endemic in man and the universe. A

poem of the '50's, probably his best-known work, had spoken of a decline
in the life of the American polis, depicting modern presidents as rancorous,
but adding:

> I too
> that am a nation sustain the damage
> where smokes of continual ravage
> obscure the flame.   (OF 64)

The same willingness to acknowledge in his own pulses and in the poem's
impulses something of what he finds monstrous in the abuse of political
power gives to these "Passages" a referential range beyond mere invective.
Only a superficial look at "Up Rising" could lead one to regard it as no
more than a tirade against the Johnson administration, though it does in-
corporate that. What is it that "rises up" in the poem? Not only the
overweening arrogance of a president whose "name stinks with burning meat
and heapt honors" but also the fear of "good people in the suburbs" as
they pile food on their barbecue plates; not only the waves of bombers but
also the "deep hatred" of the new world for the old, or for any alien cul-
ture; not only the zeal of the "professional military" for victory but
also the surge of infantile fantasies of destruction; not only America's
present passion for dominance but the half-buried guilts of its past, sum-
med up by the historian Commager (in a phrase Duncan cites) as "America's
unacknowledged, unrepented crimes." "The Soldiers" (26) took more than a
year to compose, and during that lapse of time (reflected in the arrange-
ment of poems in Bending the Bow, where thirty pages of other matter inter-
vene between 25 and 26) some of the imagery enunciated in "The Multiver-
sity" and "Up Rising" shifted again into a slightly different key. A con-
trast develops between the "first Evil," "that which has power over you,"
and its positive counterpart, the spirit which can

> fight underground
>   the body's inward sum,
>   the blood's natural
> uprising   against tyranny   (BB 114)

The first Evil, the primeval power over us, the embodiment of the blind

coercive force "spreading his 'goods' over Asia," is Ahriman, the god of
darkness who in Zoroastrian mythology contends with Ormuzd, god of light,
for possession of the Mundane Egg. The "blood's natural/uprising" is in
part Duncan's own heightened blood pressure, a condition for which he was
receiving medical treatment at that time, just as the image of America tos-
sing and turning in "fevers and panics" recalls the earlier poem "Shadows"
(11), in which the poet lies febrile like the ailing king of Grail leg-
ends, emblem of a waste land. That identification recurs in "Stage Direc-
tions" (30):

> And from the dying body of America I see,
> or from my dying body . . . (BB 132)

III

There is a difficulty inherent in the rhetorical language of these
war poems. Duncan himself is aware of it, remarking that in them he seems
unable "to move outside the almost hypnagogic high tone."[6] To achieve co-
gency, abstract and thematically explicit strands of discourse (such as
"music's divine strife"--29) must be interwoven with sharply specific
images. For an instance of Duncan's attempt to do this we can return to
"Orders" (24), where mercenary violence is counterposed against

> Gassire's lute, the song
>
> of Wagadu, household of the folk,
>
> commune of communes
>
> hidden seed in the hearts of men
>
> and in each woman's womb   hidden.

Duncan's immediate source here is a fragmentary motif in Pound's The Pisan
Cantos, the LXXIVth and LXXVIIth; but, Pound's technique of allusion being
even more parsimonious than Duncan's we must go for full elucidation to his
original source: an African tale collected by the German anthropologist
Leo Frobenius.[6] In bare outline, the story runs as follows. Gassire is
heir to the throne of Wagadu, the four-gated city, but his father the king
continues to live on into a very lengthy old age. Eventually, after years
of waiting, Gassire decides to become a minstrel, to exchange sword and

shield for a lute, because kings and heroes all die some day and are soon
forgotten unless celebrated in song. Gassire has a lute made for him, but
it will not sing. The instrument-maker tells him: "It is you who must
give it a heart. The piece of wood must go into battle with you. It must
resound at the stroke of the sword. The wood must suck in the blood that
trickles down, blood of your blood, breath of your breath. . . ." On
seven successive days Gassire rides into battle, first with his eldest son,
then with the next eldest, and so on; each day he bears back to Wagadu the
body of one of his sons, whose blood drips on to the lute. Then the
people of Wagadu, weary of Gassire's fierce obsession, ask him to leave
with his remaining son and household. That night in a lonely desert place
Gassire wakes from his sleep by the campfire to hear his lute singing. His
anger leaving him, he weeps; meanwhile Wagadu perishes, to be resurrected
in the hearts of men and the wombs of women. "Every time when, by the
fault of man, Wagadu perished, it rose with a new kind of beauty. . . .
Vanity brought with it the songs of the minstrels." Thus strife engendered
music; thus the very actions which led to the destruction of Wagadu led
also to the dream and song through which it renews itself; and thus Duncan
can declare, in a later part of his poem "Orders," that "rage, grief, dis-
may" are

> themselves transports of beauty! The blood
>
> streams from the bodies of his sons
> to feed the voice of Gassire's lute. (BB 79)

Once familiar with Gassire and Wagadu, a reader can more confidently assent
to some of the generalized propositions into which Duncan sets these allu-
sions. Yet access to proper comprehension is not made easy. "Gassire's
lute" (like various items in other "Passages," such as "Erikepaios" and
"the bull Hadhayans," and unlike Homeric or Dantean or Shakespearean refer-
ences) cannot reasonably be thought to belong in the generally recognized
repository of Western literary culture. But even the "Notes" appended to
Bending the Bow, which indicate some sources, are silent about this one;
the implied expectation, then, is that despite the elliptical nature of the
reference readers will initially guess at something of its meaning and

later track it down precisely. To be sure, some general understanding of
what "Gassire's lute" signifies is facilitated by the fact that elsewhere
in the "Passages" there are less recondite images of a stringed instrument
(or weapon) which serve to convey Duncan's intuition of concordia discors.
Heraclitus, frequently cited in Duncan's writings, states the principle
that all things are held in tune by pulling against teach other, and refers
illustratively to the tension and retention of strings in a bow or lyre.
The second of the "Passages" develop this double image in an interweaving
of allusions to both music and battle. An arrow and a melody are released
by similar means, hands pulling in directions, a taut muscular τόνος.[7]
"Bending the bow," this tensile action is called in the poem that gives its
title to one of Duncan's books and immediately precedes there the first of
the "Passages." An analogous attunement and impulsion orders the poem and
the "poetry of all poetries" or universal "It" (BB vii).

IV

"It" continues to traverse the lines. "Dread love . . . ." one of the
latest "Passages" begins, "I've been your battlefield"--and we have seen
that the battlefield is also a domain of Music, where Eros is "faced with
the entire field of sound" (17), and a domain of the poem itself, where the
shape of each composition incarnates the transformations and transactions of
that creative trinity, Love, Music and War. Making, to poiein, is as much
the form of these "Passages" as it is their content. They enact a myth of
making; they exemplify in their very structure Duncan's sense of creativity
as having these aspects: it is processual, regenerative, reflexive, partic-
ipatory, and playful.

Their processual quality is immediately obvious, as it is in much of
his other work. Long before he began to write the "Passages" his readers
had ample evidence that Duncan regards individual poems not as discrete and
perfected products but as incomplete and interacting parts of a mobile whole.
The poetics of process was already explicit as early as 1951, in "An Essay
at War":

>   The design of a poem
>   constantly

```
            under reconstruction,
               changing, pusht forward;
            alternations of sound, sensations;
               the mind dance
            wherein thot shows its pattern:
               a proposition
               in movement.  (D 9)
```

Five years after that, Duncan found in Whitehead's Process and Reality a
philosophical ratification of his own sense of form. And most of the other
scientific or religious philosophers whose dicta come "into the chresto-
mathy" of his work (24) appeal to him through a similar emphasis on the dy-
namics of change: Schrödinger, who observes that a piece of matter may be
said to be alive "when it goes on 'doing something,' moving, exchanging
material with its environment" (TOU 135); Darwin, who, envisaging the or-
igin of species in terms of an evolutionary struggle between contending
life-forms, "enlarged the depth and field of our apprehension of the na-
ture of creation"[9]; Boehme, whom Duncan quotes as saying that "the stars
have their kingdom in the veins of the body which are cunning passages
(and the sun has designed the arteries) where they drive forth the form,
shape and condition of man" (19); Heraclitus, whose panta rei becomes a
principle of poetic form: "Reveries are rivers and flow . . ." (BB, 7):
you can't step twice into the same reverie. An insistence on rapid move-
ment, driving forth, throwing itself forward, is the primary thing that
Duncan takes from Olson's essay on "Projective Verse." "Passages" 31
quotes, and its development exemplifies, one of the tenets of Olsonian
composition by field: that in the very act of writing one perception
"MUST MUST MUST . . . MOVE, INSTANTER, ON ANOTHER!" A poem is felt to
be a field of energetic activity, as in an electro-magnetic field which is
"capable of a vast variety of motion" and in which "the motion of one part
depends, according to definite relations, on the motion of other parts.[10]
Each passage proceeds, then, towards further processes, pushes on so as to

```
            let image perish in image,
                  leave writer and reader
               up in the air
                  to draw
```

momentous

inconclusions . . . (BB 15)

But images perish only to rise up in new imagery, rhythms falter only
to generate fresh rhythms, "the stuff/vanishes upon the air,/line after
line thrown" (2), only to return in subsequent lines, structures collapse
only to allow others to grow. In short, the form of "Passages" is regenera-
tive, like the universal principle of creativity they celebrate. Birth and
rebirth are recurrent motifs in these poems; in the eighth they are central,
combining physical details of parturition with religious symbolism taken
from the Moravian Brotherhood of Count Zinzendorf; in the fourteenth they
are linked specifically with the myths of Eros and of Dionysos, who was
sewn up in Zeus's thigh for ripening and rebirth after making a premature
debut; in the twenty-eighth and thirtieth Chrysaor and Pegasos emerge from
the decapitated Medusa, as if from "the dying body of America" or from the
perishing imagery of the poem itself. "Death is the mother of Beauty,"
Wallace Stevens had proposed; and Duncan goes beyond Stevens's practice by
incorporating regenerative patterns into the very form of the poem.

That form is also reflexive. Duncan consistently rejects the notion
that the language of poetry is instrumental, merely denoting realities
external to itself. For him it is primarily self-referential; and if, as
he himself suggests, the "Passages" constitute a kind of "Speculum,"[11] it
is one in which the poetry reflects itself, creates itself, in its own
image. There is a clear statement of this in Duncan's Ground Work of
1971:

> As a poet I find myself attackt for my being ultimately
> concerned with the experience of poetry and language. . . .
> [I]t is still rank heresy to take language, the pleasure
> and functions of words in their operations as such, as
> being the ground of primary information. Words are supposed
> properly to refer to and to relate, and all the realm of
> their actual presence and the powers of language to use
> every other realm of experience to refer to and to relate
> its own realities . . . is forbidden as the realm of
> Narcissus, whom the neoPlatonists saw as Creator of the
> world in his self-fascination, is forbidden.

> With that animus men would reject the suggestion that the
> poem presents itself as event and as person, and, where it
> refers to a deeper and/or further reality, refers to a
> metapoetry, not to a metaphysics or a metapsychology. [12]

But "the realm of Narcissus" is tense with ambiguities; concepts of art as
mirror have been treated with various degrees of suspicion and excitement
by many writers from Plato to Cocteau and Borges, and by Duncan himself as
early as "The Venice Poem" of 1948.[13] It is possible to misperceive what
the looking-glass shows, to be "wrong about the reflection" (4). One
problem for a poet is that the surface of language is smeary with abuse:
"Passages" 35 depicts

> men with fossil minds, with oily tongues
> "to lick the mirror of Narcissus" (T 17)

--that phrase being translated from Dante's Inferno, XXX.128, where its ap-
plication is to a malicious liar. In this final poem of Tribunals, "Before
the Judgment" (35), there are several references to the doomed of Dante's
Malebolge and particularly to this image of false or sullied reflection.[14]
But opposed to such negative images are some in other "Passages": the
fifth, for example, where the sun "reflects" on the moon "as if with love,"
and the sixteenth, where pendulous emotions are "mirrored depth-dark" in
the water which is an element of words. Though one usually thinks of
reflection as passive, it has in Duncan's work a creative aspect more po-
tent than any act of force; thus, in the final lines of "At the Loom" (2)
the violent Achilles, fighting not for his nation but for personal and
vengeful pride,

> may have his wrath
> and throw down
> the heroic Hektor   (BB 13)

--but Hektor has nevertheless "raisd/[a] reflection of the heroic" in
Achilles' shield; and thus too Perseus, by seeing the baleful Medusa mir-
rored in his shield rather than directly, can slay the gorgon and so re-
lease Chrysaor and Pegasos from her (30). In writing so pun-charged as
Duncan's, this image-cluster can include his use of the Sufi term "Mi'raj"
(17), meaning a moment of mystical transport, "the visionary trance, the

writing on the wall" (HD II, 1, 146; cf. I, 6, 135). Irresistibly the
word suggests mirage, derived from the French se mirer, to look at oneself
in a mirror. Mi'raj, mirage, on the wall. . . . The poet himself, then,
is present in his work neither as lyricist-cum-prophet (like Shelley) nor
as would-be hero of his own latter-day cultural epic (like Pound) but as
"the poet-magician Dr Dee in his black mirror" (27). Speculative, Dr Dee
(D[uncan]) is intent on "seeing &/or reading scenes/hieroglyphs/texts in
a glass."[15]

     Just as the poet is also a reader at our side, studiously scanning
his own lines in the act of writing, so we the readers are co-poets with
him, joining Duncan in the work and making it new in our collaborative
response. The "Passages" are participatory in their form. The first poem
of the series lays plain emphasis on this, locating its muse "among tribes,"
by campfire or domestic hearth, or in an ideal City of kindred spirits.
Elsewhere in the "Passages" analogues of linguistic communion include
marriage, dance, eucharistic celebration, and household--all "rites of
participation," as he describes them in a chapter of "The H.D. Book."[16]
In the form of these poems generally, the "communal consciousness" to which
Duncan would "surrender [his own] individual isolated experiences" has two
aspects: it speaks a language of membership and remembrance in which words
"move throughout the history of man to find [their] kin" in such mixed
company as "Euripides, Plato, Moses of Leon, Faure or Freud," and in that
language it addresses us, its readers, as a priest might address commu-
icants whose responsals are need to complete a sacramental rite. Most
pronounced in the hierophantic incantation of "Moving the Moving Image"
(17), this "rapture of communication" permeates the whole series.

     Pervasive also in the form of these "Passages," as in all creative
activity, is a playful quality:

          By associations, by metaphor, by likeness of the part, by fit-
          ting as part of a larger figure, by interlinking of members, by
          share, by equation, by correspondence, by reason, by contrast,
          by opposition, by pun or rime, by melodic coherence--what might
          otherwise have seemed disparate things of the world as Chaos
          were brought into a moving, changing, eternal, interweaving

> fabric of the world as Creation. It was the multiplicity of
> meanings at play that I loved. (HD I, 5, 16)

With all those shifting possibilities in mind Duncan can speak of his work
as "multiphasic": rather than superseding one another developmentally,
phases of awareness are available simultaneously, jostling together in a
game of mobile consciousness. Even the way his poems take shape on the
page is part of Duncan's openness to "meanings at play"; the many devia-
tions from aligned margins, for instance, in which he follows Larry
Eigner's practice, leads to a dispersal of phrases whose syntactical
interrelations are often not immediately clear to the eye or ear, so that
various conceivable combinations can be multiplied to the utmost. Fancy
releases words from their moorings. In chapter 13 of Biographia Literaria
Coleridge remarks that "fancy" is "a mode of memory." Duncan sees it as
such, too; but for him memory is a more vital energizing force than for
Coleridge, and fancy, instead of being inferior to imagination, is part of
it.[17] In his reply to Olson's "Against Wisdom as Such," Duncan writes
unabashedly of his fondness for "sleight-of-mind"; "the whole realm of
spirit," he says, "I distrust if it is not at play."[18] And since these po-
ems are participatory, their element of play is something we too engage in.
A distinction made by the structuralist critic Roland Barthes between two
types of narrative is applicable to poetry also, and can serve to summarize
the kind of playful experience in which a reader of Duncan's "Passages" is
involved. Barthes proposes that texts can be regarded as either lisible
(readerly) or scriptible (writerly).[19] The readerly is that which we re-
late to in a passive manner; it is there, established for us by the au-
thor's constraining purpose and by its classic contours as a finished
product. We can take it or leave it. On the other hand, the writerly
text is that which licenses, even requires, the reader's creative effort
for it to be apprehended; it hardly exists as a tangible thing; it is a
potential element of play in our reading; it is thus

> ourselves writing, before the infinite play of the world (the
> world as function) is traversed, intersected, stopped, plastic-
> ized by some singular system (Ideology, Genus, Criticism) which

> reduces the plurality of entrances, the opening of networks,
> the infinity of languages.[20]

Being that which may be recognized as plural, "writerly" can designate
with perfect aptness the mode of Duncan's "Passages." Just as the dis-
membered figures of Eros and Osiris and Lucifer need to be pieced
together, so the reader must re-member the images that are passing along
and between the lines, must _gather_ what is going on, must assemble parts
and phases into a never-definitive unity, must keep making up temporary
Gestalt patterns from the unbounded possibilities of the text. In the
Speculum revealed to us by "the poet-magician Dr Dee" there is something
of "the infinite play of the world"; it is a creative mirage, which offers
a glimpse of "the plurality of entrances, the opening of networks, the
infinity of languages."

NOTES

[1] In writing this essay I have been able, by courtesy of Robert Duncan, to
refer to typescript copies of some "Passages" composed since number 36;
these recent poems are mentioned by title in my text. I am grateful to
Robert Duncan for letting me see unpublished poems and for readily discus-
sing his work with me.

[2] W.K.C. Guthrie, _The Greeks and Their Gods_ (London: Methuen, 1950), p. 319.

[3] "Robert Duncan: The Actuality of Myth," _Open Letter_, second series, No. 4
(Spring 1973), 43-44.

[4] _Aurora, . . . or Morning-Rednesse in the Rising of the Sun_ (1634), trans.
John Sparrow (1656), ed. D. S. Helmer and C. J. Barker (2nd edition;
London: Clarke, 1950), pp. 93, 99; cf. pp. 100-101.

[5] For instance, Mersmann approvingly repeats in _Out of the Vietnam Vortex_
(Lawrence: University Press of Kansas, 1974), p. 196, Louis Simpson's
carelessly inaccurate reading of lines in "The Multiversity" which describe
"Chancellor Strong, the dragon claw/biting his bowels, his bile raging
. . .": Simpson writes disparagingly of "Duncan's attempt to present
Strong as a dragon," but in fact no such attempt is made; rather, Strong's
bile attack, afflicting him as he tried to suppress student demands for
free speech, is seen metaphorically as an attack on him by the dragon of
overriding fear and overruling authoritarianism.

[6] Letter to Ian Reid, 28 January 1976. This problematic aspect of Duncan's
work is discussed by David Bromige, "Beyond Prediction," _Credences_, 2
(July 1975), 101-113.

[7]It has recently been reprinted in Leo Frobenius, 1873-1973: An Anthology, ed. Eike Haberland, trans. Patricia Crampton (Wiesbaden: Franz Steiner Verlag, 1973), pp. 140-147.

[8]Cf. Charles S. Sherrington, Man on his Nature (Cambridge: Cambridge University Press, 1940), p. 253.

[9]Duncan, "Notes on Grossinger's Solar Journal: Oecological Sections" (Los Angeles: Black Sparrow, 1970), p. [1].

[10]Sir William Davidson Niven (ed.), The Scientific Papers of James Clerk Maxwell, quoted by Edward R. Fagan, "Field and English," in Rhetoric: Theories for Application, ed. Robert Gorrell (Champaign, Ill.: National Council of Teachers of English, 1967), p. 45.

[11]Letter to Ian Reid, 28 January 1976.

[12]Ground Work (San Francisco: privately printed, 1971), n.pag.

[13]See the section of "The Venice Poem" entitled "Imaginary Instructions" in The First Decade (London: Fulcrum, 1968), pp. 88-94. On the mirror topos generally, see Ernst Robert Curtius, European Literature and the Latin Middle Ages, trans. Willard R. Trask (Princeton: Princeton University Press, 1953), p. 336, n. 56.

[14]The sources of other quotations from the Inferno in this poem are as follows: XXI. 22-23; XXX. 131-132; XVIII. 22-23; XVIII. 49.

[15]Letter to Ian Reid, 28 January 1976.

[16]Reprinted in A Caterpillar Anthology, ed. Clayton Eshleman (N.Y.: Doubleday, 1971), pp. 23-69.

[17]See A. K. Weatherhead, The Edge of the Image (Seattle: University of Washington Press, 1967).

[18]Letter to Charles Olson, c. 8 August 1954, now in the Olson Archives of the University of Connecticut, Storrs; quoted here with the permission of George Butterick, curator of the Archives.

[19]I take the English equivalents from Richard Miller's translation of Barthes' S/Z (New York: Hill and Wang, 1974); the book was originally published in Paris by Editions du Seuil in 1970. For evidence of some compatibility between Barthes's interests and Duncan's, see the latter's note in Credences No. 1 (1975), 2-6.

[20]S/Z, trans Miller, p. 5.

UROBOROS: <u>DANTE</u> AND <u>A</u> <u>SEVENTEENTH</u> <u>CENTURY</u> <u>SUITE</u>

Nathaniel Mackey

I

Duncan's answer to the possible charge against these works that their
occasion is too insistently bookish can be fairly well gathered from his
essay "A Critical Difference of View."[1] Responding to two reviews which
appeared in <u>Poetry</u>--one of Charles Tomlinson's <u>A</u> <u>Peopled</u> <u>Landscape</u> by Hay-
den Carruth, the other of Louis Zukofsky's <u>Found</u> <u>Objects</u> by Adrienne Rich--
he takes Rich to task for criticizing Zukofsky's recurrent use of a con-
stellation of texts. The essay begins with Duncan quoting the following
passage from Rich's review:

> . . . committed to an enormous, self-conscious struggle with
> language and tradition . . . Zukofsky brings to the battle some
> inherited stratagems of Pound (heavy use of allusion and quota-
> tion) and Williams (a short, breath-phrased line, too often
> here a one-word line). One wonders if nature--instinctual wis-
> dom--might not have led him to drop the greaves and breastplate
> of those great old warriors and to step, finally, light and self-
> exposing, into the fray.

Aware of his own susceptibility to this critique, Duncan makes no attempt
to disguise the vested interest his own work has in his rallying to Zukof-
sky's defense. He comes to question, in what amounts to an outright at-
tack, the pontifical air with which Rich would decide for <u>all</u> poets what
their aims and intentions should be:

> I would not want to go on record against Miss Rich's wish for
> "the coming honestly and uniquely by the 'torsion' of grace and
> ungainliness, casualness and splendor" in a poem--it sounds ter-
> rific; but I do have a certain understanding that my own task in
> poetry is something other and less than what Miss Rich is so sure

is "clearly the task of all today" etc. . . . . What is most prob-
ably at issue is that . . . Miss Rich does not have any great
concern for the poetry of Pound or of Williams and what is cer-
tainly at issue is that she would reprove those of us who have
had and do have such a concern. Is she an entirely original poet
beholden to the work of no poets before her? I am unacquainted
with her work so I cannot say. But given that Miss Rich does
indeed write in the high "torsion" that proceeds from no communal
forms but from "instinctual wisdom" even as in Eden before the
Fall, I do not grant that her natural grace has given her any
understanding of what should be the task of Louis Zukofsky or
should have been the task of Williams or is to be the task of me.

No communal forms. Duncan's use of the word communal provides a case
in point of how this "answer" I'm attempting to sketch has to do with cer-
tain themes which inform these two recent works of his. Completing an
Uroboric circuit of justification which borders on cant (in the light of its
etymological meaning of song), the poetry and its poetics are one. What
this means is that throughout Dante and throughout A Seventeenth Century
Suite poetry (to echo Charles Olson) is preoccupation with itself. This
preoccupation, especially throughout Dante, involves a concern with having
poetry and communality coincide. In poem V of Book Two for example:

> In nothing superior
>
>   to his manhood   Dante
>
> Shakespeare likewise
>
>   the great poet
>
> nowhere makes us feel inferior
>
>   but there grows in the soul
>
> in reading   space and time
>
> Life writing   in each mind
>
>   teems,
>
>   his mind
>
> ours   a sublime community.

These are not the first of Duncan's works in which this notion of poetry as communality occurs. In his introduction to Bending the Bow, to cite an example, we read of a "commune of Poetry." This commune, he pretty much makes clear, is none other than Creation--the World or Cosmos--itself:

> All my common animal being comes to the ox in his panic and, driven by this speech, we imagine only man, *homo faber*, has, comes into a speech words mean to come so deep that the amoeba is my brother poet. . . . I'd like to leave somewhere in this book the statement that the real "we" is the company of the living, of all the forms Life Itself, the primal wave of it, writing itself out in evolution, proposes. Needs, as our poetry does, all the variety of what poets have projected poetry to be.
>
> (BB i-iv)

This variegated Poem then--"a poetry of all poetries, *grand collage*," he goes on to call It--is beyond the reach or apprehension of any single poet. But though an act of imagination which Dante calls "apprehension by means of the potential intellect" the individual consciousness proceeds by way of intuitions or intimations of a Whole in whose service its partiality or particularity exists. Its inability to encompass or incorporate that Whole takes the form of a certain "darkness" conducive to--a muse of motivation for--the postulation (if not hallucination) of "light":

> In the poem this very lighted room is dark, and the dark alight with love's intentions. *It* is striving to come into existence in these things, or, all striving to come into existence is It-- in this realm of men's languages a poetry of all poetries, *grand collage*, I name It, having only the immediate event of words to speak of It. In the room we, aware or unaware, are the event of ourselves in It. (BB vii)

This impalpable All reduces any empirical achievement, makes it incomplete, each "completed" poem merely further evidence of the ongoingness, the inexhaustibility, of Creation: ". . . now the poet works with a sense of parts fitting in relation to a design that is larger than the poem. The commune of Poetry becomes so real that he sounds each particle in relation to parts of a great story that he knows will never be completed" (BB vi).

To show how repetitious of earlier insistences <u>Dante</u> in particular
turns out to be it should be sufficient to compare this last-quoted passage
with the following lines from poem IX of Book One:

> how many essential parts of the story we belong to
>   we will never know;
>
>   only in the Imagination of the Whole
> the immediate percept is
>   to be justified-- Imagining
>   this
>   pivot of a totality
>   having
>   no total thing in us, we so
>   live beyond ourselves
>
>   --and in this   unitive.

What I'm getting at is Uroboros again, as brought to mind by Olson at
Berkeley in 1965: "I have arrived at a point where I really have no more
than to feed on myself."[2] And even more explicitly by Williams--quoting
a line from one of his own early poems, "The Wanderer: A Rococo Study"--
in <u>Paterson</u> <u>V</u>:

>   the serpent
>   its tail in its mouth
> "the river has returned to its beginnings"
>   and backward
>   (and forward)
>   it tortures itself within me
>   until time has been washed finally under

An unwelcome sense of exhaustion creeps into these two recent Duncan works
(a sense intensified by the poetics' promise of an escape from closure).
The ordeal of limitation--in this case (from <u>A</u> <u>Seventeenth</u> <u>Century</u> <u>Suite</u>)
limits on communion, the ability to share--becomes a recurrent concern:

> I do not as the years go by grow tolerant
>   of what I cannot share and what
> refuses me. There's that in me as fiercely beyond
>   the remorse that eats me in its drive
> as Evolution is in
>   working out the courses of what will last. (M 30)

Mingled with such admissions as this, intimations of an unconditioned Source
project a cosmic Poem, the very commune of Poetry which is again and again
invoked as the solvent this ordeal of limits impels towards:

> O Starry Net of Lives
> outflung! And our little lives at last
>   among them realized! Elohim-Cloud of bright
> expectancies, quickening hunger for worlds
>   out of boundless Source seeking Its bounds,
> the ground of all Immensities, tremendous thruout,
>   agony of striving energies thruout, devouring
>   self thruout. Our little household and its
>   inner court of our repose found hidden there.   (M 39)

A conspiracy or a co-sponsorship exists between the claims of the fact of
bounds and the aim, if not the fact, of unboundedness.

   The Source gains access to us, Duncan argues, through the mediacy of
speech. Dante begins with his quoting from and elaborating upon De Vul-
gari Eloquentia:

> "We will endeavor
> the word aiding us from Heaven,
>   to be of service
> to the vernacular speech"
>
> from "Heaven" these
> "draughts of the sweetest honey-milk",
>
>   *si dolcement*
>
> from the language we first heard
>
>   endearments whisperings
>
>   infant song and reverie
>
> a world we wanted to go out into,
>
>   to come to our selves into,
>
>   organizations in the sound of them
>   verging upon meaning,
>   upon "Heaven"

One of the cornerstones of Duncan's poetics is the notion of language,

both written and spoken, as a communal, or a communalizing, act. "To write
at all," he remarks in "Rites of Participation," is to dwell in the illu-
sion of language, the rapture of communication that comes as we surrender
our troubled individual isolated experiences to the communal consciousness."[3]
However, the commune presided over by the rules of grammar, syntax and se-
mantics constitutes a contraction of that less anthropomorphic commonality
a more primal (thus "vulgar") eloquence addresses us to. In the course of an
unpublished interview conducted by L. S. Dembo in 1967 Duncan observed that
that concern with _meaning_ from which these rules derive has the effect of
binding us to an adult, oppressively human or societal order. But rapt at-
tention to the _sound_, the music or utterance-impact in words, he goes on to
remark, moves us into the animal, essentially cosmic realm of the child:

> Meaning is us. That's man, you know. The thing we think we're
> dealing with in language. But when you get into poetry and you
> become more excited about the sound, that's already got beyond
> what you think is your very human area. You share it with ani-
> mals, babies and so forth. And that one then, I would say, is
> the larger area of the poem. . . . After all, the universe
> shares with the poem . . . projections of space and things that
> are sounds.

Positing this latter use of language as "primary,/natural and common,/
being 'milk'" (for which read "galactic"), he writes, again the opening
poem of _Dante_:

> from the beginning,   color
> and light, my nurse; sounding waves
> and air, my nurse; animal presences,
> my nurse; Night, my nurse .
>
>   out of hunger, instinctual
>   craving, thirst for "knowing,"
>
>   toward oracular tits.

The second poem in _Dante_ takes up the idea of grammar as an instance
of social coercion, a secondary impulse or imposition Duncan sees aimed at
a domestication of humanity's inborn cosmicity:

> Secondary is the grammar of

> constructions and uses, syntactic
> manipulations, floor-plans,
>
> spellings and letterings of the word,
> progressions in writing, stanzas,
> conservations and disturbances in meaning

And at the poem's conclusion:

> . . . Insufferable
> are those masters of grammar
> who have denied their illiterate nurses.
>
> Out of dry dugs of their own?
>
> Clonkt lightning!

The line of argument running through the early poems in the book, Urobor-
ically enough, retraces that of the comment to Dembo I quoted above, empha-
sis moving away from "meaning" by way of sound through the animal/child
realm to the world at large. Poem III of Book One begins:

> I know a little language of my cat, tho Dante says
> that animals have no need of speech and Nature
> abhors the superfluous. My cat is fluent. He
> converses when he wants with me. To speak
>
> is natural. And whales and wolves I've heard
> in choral soundings of the sea and air
> know harmony and have an eloquence that stirs
> my mind and heart, they touch the soul.

And poem IV of Book One:

> Everything speaks to me! In faith,
> my sight is sound. I draw from out
>   the resounding mountain side
> the gist of majesty. It is at once
>   a presentation out of space
> awakening a spiritual enormity, and still,
>   the sounding of a tone
> apart from any commitment to some scale.
>
>   The sea
> comes in on rolling surfs
>   of an insistent meaning, pounds
> the sands relentlessly,   demanding

                    a hearing. I overhear
               tides of myself all night in it.

The reversion to what are by now patently Duncanesque assertions is another
case in point of what I meant by a sense of exhaustion. Duncan, that is,
appears to have come, as Olson said he had, to where there's none other
than himself to feed upon. What's interesting is that this should have oc-
curred in the context of works given over to variations upon the works of
others.

     A Seventeenth Century Suite Duncan describes as "imitations, deriva-
tions, and variations upon certain conceits and findings made among
strong lines," lines found in Robert Southwell's "The Burning Babe," George
Herbert's "Jordan (I)" and "Jordan (II)," Ben Jonson's Hymenai, John Norris
of Bemerton's "Hymn to Darkness" and Sir Walter Ralegh's "What Is Our Life?"
His method throughout the Suite is to quote in full (with the exception of
Hymenai) the seventeenth-century poem in question and follow it with his
own variations upon specific themes, expressions and images to be found in
the poem. Ralegh's poem, for example, begins: "What is our Life? a play
of passion,/Our mirth the musicke of division. . . ." Duncan's variation
not only echoes its opening question but also updates its answering figure
of life as theatrical performance with a figure of life as cinematic projec-
tion: "What does this life most seem? But shadows upon/a moving picture
screen. . . ." Dante he describes as études drawn from Dante's prose,
specifically De Vulgari Eloquentia, De Monarchia, the Convivio and the epis-
tles. A certain process of communion wherein the distinction between Dante
and himself dissolves informs his sense of what these "studies" are about:
"Gists, yes, I have meant these études to come from and return to gists of
my intention in Dante's intention. . . . His is not a mind researcht in
the lore of another time, for me, but immediate, to the presence of the idea
of Poetry. . . . I draw my 'own' thought in reading Dante as from a well-
spring." Duncan has been saying things to this effect for three decades now,
so it's clearly not about newness any more than about the archaic or the
antiquarian. The concern is with where the timely and the timeless coincide.
At any such point (conceivably any point at all) phylogeny recapitulates
ontogeny and the individual life proves to be but a localization of supra-

local traits. This is very much the gist of many lines in A Seventeenth
Century Suite:

> faltering in our resolve, resolute in faulty cause,
>   heirs of ancient accusations, hidden in our bones
> long plotted designs of our poor demise.
>
> Our persons are but closets that such skeletons conceal
>   the species dreads, as in our graves
> we lay down the law and return
>   the grievous courses of our lives
> to swell the sentence after our parts are done.   (M 18)

This pun on the word sentence bears directly upon the concern with
grammar, syntax and semantics one finds in Dante. In poem II of Book One,
for example, the same punning use of the word occurs:

> a felt architectonics then of the numinous
>   that drives us beyond us, thruout,
>   tries us in the sentence . . .

The phrase tries us in the sentence makes a verdict of guilty a foregone
conclusion, the "trial" itself something of a punishment to be endured.
Guilty of what, though? one wants to ask. The answer would appear to be,
Guilty of limits:

> It was very like that coming to know
>   my mother was at war with what I was to be,
> and in the Courts of Love I raged that year
>   in every plea declared arrogant
>   and in contempt of Love.
>
> I do not as the years go by grow tolerant
>   of what I cannot share . . .   (M 30)

This accounts for the death-wish which pervades these works, where death
comes as not only a disclosure of our mortality--

> In death alone we are sincere;
> we'll not return to take our bows or read reviews.
>   There's nor night nor day,
> nor reward nor punishment, nor heaven nor hell,
>   where all is done and our mortality at last
> made evident--we are in earnest and have left the play   (M 19)

but also a dis-closure, possibly, of all such boundedness. Thus, from the
final poem in _Dante_:

> Open out like a rose
> that can no longer keep its center closed
> but practising for Death lets go,
> lets go, littering the ground
> with petals of its rime

And in the variations on Jonson's _Hymenai_ one sees that this opening out
anticipates and participates in an epochal as well as individual apocalypse
(etymologically, "to uncover"):

> Slow, slow, even as time alone erodes the matter,
>   I turn and turn upon my life.
> Tho I resist the learning, the drive to study it out
>   returns
>
> * * *
>
>   In the old stories, the protagonist learns
> what Time has to do with him. And in his true
>   identity burns within the learning.
>   He serves the years.
>   There comes an overturning of his Age. (M 31-32)

Predecessors from Duncan's earlier work exist for these two passages
as well. The first recalls the second half of "Sonnet 4."

> sure as the rose scattering its petals to prepare is sure
> for the ripeness near to the perfection of the rose.
>
> I would know the red _thee_ of the enclosure
> where thought too curls about, opens
> out from, what's hid,
>
> until it falls away, all the profuse allusion let go   (BB 3)

The second recalls instances throughout "The H. D. Book" where Duncan writes
of the impact of World War II on the poetry of H.D., Williams and Pound.
The suggestion is that a Geist of crisis made manifest by the war acquires
a particularly personal relevance for the three of them because of their
advancing age. In "Nights and Days," Duncan writes:

> Was it that the war--the bombardment for H.D., the imprisonment
> and exposure to the elements for Ezra Pound, the divorce in the
> speech for Williams--touched a spring of passionate feeling in
> the poet that was not the war but was his age, his ripeness in
> life. They were almost "old"; under fire to come "to a new
> distinction."
>   Where the fullness of their age was also the fullness of an
> historical age, as if the Second World War were a trouble of
> the times, unprepared or prepared for its old age? (H.D. II, 1,
> 111)

Very clearly, Duncan in A Seventeenth Century Suite is reading his own life,
work and times in a manner identical to that in which he reads those of H.D.,
Williams and Pound. What I'm calling the Uroboric impulse in these recent
works is in fact (again, Uroborically enough) something which has char-
acterized Duncan's writings from the very start: a need or desire to root
his experience, artistic and otherwise, in an assurance of precedent pro-
vided by those who have gone before.

II

Guyanese novelist Wilson Harris has written an essay entitled "The
Phenomenal Legacy,"[4] a piece whose foremost concerns are in many ways the
same as those which hold our attention here: community, inheritance, col-
lapse, revelation. In his consideration of tradition and the concept of
"phenomenal legacy" Harris implicates the past in an order of inevitabil-
ity whose character is one of deferred and, by way of this deferral, orac-
ular applicability to the present. "Phenomenal legacy" assumes as one of
its forms a certain obduracy whose manifestation is a function of crisis,
an obduracy which appears, in fact, to invite ordeal. ("I profit/by every
calamity," H.D. writes in "The Walls Do Not Fall.") Making a claim for some-
thing of an "apprehension by means of the potential intellect," Harris
posits the notion of wholeness--of which the relevance of the past to the
present is his prime illustration--as the issue of some such wooing of cat-
astrophe. This way of approaching the idea of unity invests it with an un-
customary aura, as of something ominous, sinister and threatening, to be
greeted as much with dread as with celebration:

> In the medium of art and science one becomes susceptible to a
> species of unpredictable arousal, one virtually becomes a species
> of nature which subsists on both mystery and phenomenon, partic-
> ipating in an otherness akin to the terrifying and protean reality
> of the gods. It is within this instant of arousal that abolishes
> the "given" world that one's confession of weakness really begun:
> a confession that because of mortality, the mortality of all as-
> sumptions, there is and must be an inherent device of conscious-
> ness which looks beyond the fortress of self-created things to-
> wards a paradoxical womb through which we are being cautioned
> that a fantastic originality exists as the omen of unity.

In light of this, I think, one can begin to get inklings of why Dante and
A Seventeenth Century Suite should be at once among the most derivative and
among the most confessional of Duncan's works. It is within this instant of
arousal that abolishes the "given" world that one's confession of weakness
has really begun.

But the confessionality with which all this has to do is not restrict-
ed, as Rosenthal's sense of confessional is, to the autobiographic. As it
relates to Dante and A Seventeenth Century Suite confessionality is also
mediumistic. The derivative nature of the work, that is, in itself consti-
tutes a confession. Hence the aura of "subjectivity" generally attendant
upon the use of the term confessional might perhaps be replaced by a sense
of susceptibility or of being subject to. The "species of unpredictable
arousal" upon which Harris remarks would have such notions of self as "sub-
jectivity" implies called into question if not dismissed outright. In
Dante Duncan speaks, accordingly, of a "restitution/of my self from every
loss of me," going on in poem X of Book Two (having acknowledged the poem's
indebtedness to Robert Adamson, Pound, Whitman, Shelley, Rossetti and Wil-
liam Morris) to interrogate the bounds of identity and authorship:

> Go, my songs, then in zealous
>   liberality, no longer mine,
> but now the friendship of the
>   reader's heart and mind
> divine; find out,
> as if *for* me, in every soul
> its excellence, as if *from* me
>   set free. ¿ "my" songs--?
> the words were ever ours each thot
> his own . . .

Though there's also the more familiar confessional tone:

> In my youth, not unstaind
> and in much ignoble; in manhood,
> struggling to ring true yet
> knowing often my defection from
> these graces Dante lists
> proper to Man: temperance, courage,
> love, courtesy,
> and loyalty . . .

This mix of the autobiographic and the mediumistic makes for the con-
nection between the arrogance or insensitivity of which Duncan accuses him-
self at points and the otherness of which the poems claim to be a transmis-
sion. In this regard several lines quoted earlier come to mind:

> . . . There's that in me as fiercely beyond
>   the remorse that eats me in its drive
> as Evolution is in
>   working out the courses of what will last. (M 30)

The sense expressed here of a larger identity "fiercely beyond" the claims
of personhood clearly poses a threat to whatever senses of fellow-feeling
those claims promote. The communal or communionist thrust of Dante and A
Seventeenth Century Suite is consistently haunted by the possibility that
what Uroboros symbolizes amounts to no more than an inflated solipsism--
communion not with others but with an Other which is simply a trope for the
self (lower-case, non-Jungian self) or the clan. In thinking about the com-
munality of these works one bears in mind a dialectical unity posed against
but also inclusive of the bounded, self-embracing unity of Uroboros. The
Uroboric circle will thus be broken at points by a disclosed and, ideally,
dis-closed solipsism, as when in Dante Duncan quotes his own accuser:

> ". . . and you, I know from other occasions, are apt to get
> caught up in one of your talking jags when you don't listen to
> anyone else and it becomes exhausting to listen to you . . ."

But not so "simply" a trope. No matter how nonchalantly stated, the
fact is that life enigmatically turns upon an absence. Duncan's friend

and fellow poet Robin Blaser, writing of what he calls "the practice of
outside" in Jack Spicer's work, comes again and again to speak of a duplic-
ity, a doubling or folding back, a tropicality or reversibility which,
bearing the brunt of an irreducible mystique, composes the world:

> Jack used an Orphic methodology, as if the cosmos or love had
> fallen into hell. The experience is tropic--in the turn, hell
> is discovered and the true and the false begin to play. And,
> unfortunately, as Jack says, the dictation will be true and
> false . . . because as a proposition of an ultimate duplicity in
> the real itself, the dictation will be wild and playful, a dis-
> appearance and an appearance, an invisibility and a visibility
> exchanging their powers in the heart.

This disappearance or invisibility, "manifested" in language's ability to
negate, is the also literal phenomenon of death:

> . . . death is an interrogation close to the world because it is
> not ourselves. Death and ghostliness in this work must be seen,
> not as a choice against life or even a helplessness within it,
> but as a literal pole, where life is present to a point and then
> suddenly absent from an articulation. The curious thing about
> language and experience, which haunts Jack's work, is that they
> are so immediately reversible. And as a friend said, discussing
> this essay with me, if you don't have knowledge of that rever-
> sal, then you don't have the heart of it.[5]

As the apparently literal intrusion of an all too figurative Other ("ap-
parently" because death itself attests to a duplicity as the crux of figur-
ation), death, at a number of points in these two Duncan works, becomes a
wished-for reassurance that otherness isn't merely a manner of speaking.
("The grave's a comfort if we come to that.") But the truth of duplicity
is that nothing is ever _merely_ what it is; that the literal itself is al-
ready figurative as well as prefigured and that among the evidences of
this all-pervading figurativity is the translatability between language and
experience suggested by the synonymy of _literal_ with _actual_ or _factual_.

In both _Dante_ and _A Seventeenth Century Suite_ Duncan is concerned with
the relevance of texts from the past to present-day occurrences, partic-
ularly to those of a catastrophic or disastrous nature, such as the Vietnam

war. A prime example of this occurs in <u>A</u> <u>Seventeenth</u> <u>Century</u> <u>Suite</u> where,
as does Denise Levertov in "Advent 1966," he sees the napalmed children of
Vietnam prefigured in Southwell's "The Burning Babe":

> "*A pretty Babe*"   that burning Babe
>   the poet Southwell saw,
> a scorching, a crying, that made his cold heart glow,
>   a fuel of passion in which
> the thought of wounds delites the soul
>
> . . . .
>
> I cannot imagine, gazing upon photographs
>   of these young girls, the mind
> transcending what's been done to them.
>   From the broil flesh of these heretics,
> by napalm monstrously baptised
>   in a new name,   every delicate and
> sensitive curve of lip and eyelid
>   blasted away,   surviving. . .
>   eyes. . Can this horror be calld their
> *fate*? . . .   (M 22-23)

Here, as throughout both works, "bookishness" and "worldliness" pervade one
another, arguing by implication the impossibility of any such Adamic, un-
indebted or fully-constituted presence as Rich would want. As in the fol-
lowing poem from <u>Dante</u>, Book III, the poems attest to a marriage, less for
better than for worse it seems, between the present and the past:

> out of the side-lesions of Congress,
>   the bills and appropriations breeding their trade,
>   the mounting flow of guns, tanks, planes, fires,
>   poisons, gasses, fragments of metal tearing flesh
>   from flesh, thermonuclear storings, outpourings of
>   terror   even into Zion
>
> that now swells and bursts asunder,
>
> the remnants of the old Jehovah, Lord of Hosts, of that
>   rule of Jealousy and Wrath the Father proclaimd,
>   advance, divided against Itself,
>   the two identities
>   Yahweh and Allah in one conflagration,
>   America's industries feeding the abscess.

This marriage, having both a world and a poetic text in which to announce itself, serves as a metaphor for the susceptibility of the present to an absence or an Other for which the past constitutes a trope. Small wonder, then, that intimations of apocalyptic change ("othering") or annihilation ("absenting") pervade the poems.

The so-called "double science" of French philosopher Jacques Derrida designates the coinherence of "worldly" and "bookish" by the term textuality. As Alan Bass explains:

> Derrida proposes to elaborate a "double science," a "science" in which each concept, each term carries within it the principle of its own death. Once one has determined the totality of what is as "having been" made possible by the institution of the trace, "textuality," the system of traces, becomes the most global term, encompassing all that is and that which exceeds it.[6]

The most global term. As do Dante and A Seventeenth Century Suite in a more implicit way, this "double science" eschews the notion of absolute origin or originality. As Bass again explains, Derrida substitutes for it a "notion of an origin other than itself, here called 'trace,' [which] makes it impossible to locate any origin, ever to constitute a full presence." The "double science" attributes the persistence of this insufficiency or non-original originality (corresponding, I think, to Duncan's "the burden of our spectral need, the/debt, the mounting dues" in A Seventeenth Century Suite) to the trace, "a kind of writing before writing as we know it," as Bass calls it, an inscription prior to or "fiercely beyond" presence as well ("writing as we know it" being that which locates and thus loses the trace, relinquishing the absence of an otherness it also is, an absence it can at best report--thus also not, in a sense, relinquishing it). What I've been calling the Uroboric impulse--the iterative nature of "originality" ("the river has returned to its beginnings")--can also be discussed in this regard:

> The disappearance of an origin implied in this enlarged conception of writing (writing as différance, the word invented by Derrida to connote production of spatial and temporal difference), also entails an enlarging of the concept of repetition.

> . . . the thing itself, in its identical presence, is
> "duplicitous" (true and not-true), is doubled, doubles itself,
> as soon as it appears, or rather it appears as the possibility
> of its own duplication: it _repeats_ itself, its origin is its
> repetition. (VC, 347-348)

We begin to see that the derivative character of _Dante_ and _A Seventeenth_
Century Suite, their reliance on earlier work--that of Duncan himself as
well as others--symptomatizes in an unusually self-conscious way the
"onticity" of dependence, the indebtedness of being to an otherwise absent,
oddly iterative Source.

NOTES

[1] _Stony Brook_, 3/4 (Fall 1969), 360-363.

[2] Olson, _Causal Mythology_ (San Francisco: Four Seasons Foundation, 1969),
p. 4.

[3] _A Caterpillar Anthology_, ed. Clayton Eshleman (Garden City, N.Y.: Double-
day, 1971), p. 62.

[4] _The Literary Half-Yearly_, Vol. XI, No. 2 (July 1970), 1-6.

[5] "The Practice of Outside," in _The Collected Books of Jack Spicer_, ed.
Robin Blaser (Los Angeles: Black Sparrow Press, 1975), p. 285 and p. 277,
respectively.

[6] Bass, "'Literature'/Literature," _Velocities of Change_, ed. Richard Macksey
(Baltimore: Johns Hopkins University Press, 1974), p. 349. Hereafter refer-
red to as _VC_.

ROBERT DUNCAN AND THE POWER TO COHERE

Gerrit Lansing

Some poets are <u>careful</u>. Not all are. Robert Duncan is a careful poet.
He minds this, i.e. lives in a constant knowledge of his own armamentarium.
At times he may even resent his scruples. But I hope not often, as this
attention is lovable. He from the beginning has held the hammer that could
strike my bell, but that wasn't the only reason I came to love as I do his
writing. It was too that I saw how it mattered to him to matter to me.
Care for the tool.

A poet's care for his tool is not a matter of depth, nor of interest
(value), but of typology. Without doubt, of <u>intelligence</u>, in a proper Fic-
inian sense, including adventure, a quality. Of careful poets of these
States, Poe and Whitman are exemplary, and Crane and Dickinson, and Spicer,
Ashbery, Stickney, and H.D. Not especially Olson, Emerson, Pound, Eliot, or
Stein, to name some poets whose work is thought to be so by care distin-
guished.

This care is of ear, and attends the unchosen weather of the paradig-
matic and syntagmatic forces of present language. The warm air that ripen-
ed the grain is also motive of the work.

Robert Duncan's process is a mill that grinds what is given, out, and,
in, bright particulars that include ideas. A mill of dreams. The acres he
draws on are even more ample than those of Beatrix Potter, and, unlike her,
he never says to trespassing children "get outa my hayfield!" He joins Wal-
lace Stevens and Friedrich Schlegel in the conviction that all poetry is
romantic poetry, and romance is didascalion in conditions below the godly.
But the distinction of <u>La realidad y el deseo</u> so wistfully sharpened by
Luis Cernuda melts in dream when it sways into the semblance of another
dream of open form, a real estate of commons, unenclosed, "an eternal past-

ure folded in all thought" ("Often I Am Permitted To Return To A Meadow,"
OF 7).

The open form is never absolutely open, but in Duncan's desire that
idea operates, hangs on the boughs of the tree of gifts. The notion of open
form, Butor's mobility, teases us now, and rightly. It leads a mind of
Duncan's height to the likes of semiology, music, children's tales, the
propositions of evocation. So mathematick lore was drawing Spicer at his
death, and Olson's mind was driving to a new perception of the Rational,
the heave of logos from its eerie heaven, present in existence as dogmatic
figuration. So to speak is to discriminate.

And so to speak, for such a careful maker the dance turns in contem-
plation of the act of écriture, opening the field of grammatology, as
Jacques Derrida, say, shows it prime. And then cosmography, as the el-
ements relate to testify (so that Robert Duncan functions as a contemporary
Bernard Silvester, who made all ordonnance his province) that fiction is the
truth of creation, no covering but the soul itself. It cannot but cohere,
since the power to be powerless is of this armamentarium, to work a passage
over (from "At the Loom, Passages 2"),

> And the shuttle carrying the woof I find
>   was *skutill*   *"harpoon"*   --a dart, an arrow
>   or a little ship,
>
>   *navicula*   *weberschiff,*
>   crossing and recrossing from shore to shore --
>
>   (BB 12)

This is the loom on which the web is woven, the old coherences of night
and day in the emerging rimes made by novelty's grand continuing incursion.
The power to cohere in the yield of, and to, the things that make it so.

A NOTE ABOUT ROBERT DUNCAN AND MUSIC

Lou Harrison

"A/volition./To seize from the air its forms." This marvelous notation
from Robert Duncan's "Light Song" is one of the exceedingly few statements
about music that a musician himself may rejoice in. It is indeed so close
to the mark that one marvels that a technically **nontrained musician could**
have written it. And in the same song, as a composer of music himself, he
has just said—"a music,/with set conjugations, notes, the light-/est
estimations of ravished ear/naturally contrived. The contrivance/vanishes
into itself" (D 107).

A stanza or so later I found myself immortalized by mention from this
superb poet. At several times in our lives Robert Duncan and I have been
close together in attitudes and work, and it is an honor to me that he has
well approved at least one of my settings of his work. I should add here
that it is generally not my custom to compose to verse of my contemporaries,
or even friends, for I've always been afraid of offending the poet by my
musical shenanigans.

Still, the temptation here was too great. I am myself a "Sunday poet"
and found that I enjoyed other composers' settings of my own verse, and by
analogy decided to broach the matter to Robert—with the result that two of
my larger works are settings of his work, the most successful one being my
"Peace Piece II" (1968), an "all out" exposition of his astonishing "Up
Rising Passages 25," that long great, exasperated single sentence of pro-
test against the Vietnamese war. It occurs to me to wonder who else, beside
Wilfrid Mellors and myself, have worked to Duncan's lines.

200

But I want only to speak of two matters: his own musical compositions, and the larger meaning of music in his work. He first frankly sang his own melody in 1947 as the central section of his "Sleeping All Night." Not until 1954 did he again regard overt melody as a part of his work, and he has recorded those sections of _Faust Foutu_ which are concerned. The beautiful "A Song of the Old Order" and others are also recorded by Robert Duncan on two tapes made in Aptos about four or five years ago.

All those melodies share a diatonic simplicity, both major and minor, and have a kind of "fitting" with the words which is of rich rhythmic variety. Changing meters are common, and bring a fascinating phrasing and balance to the larger sections, which are themselves clearly defined. They have some resemblance to the rhythmical Vedic chants or to some more complex modern recitative. Still, they make melodies, and lean to the air. These are not like the complex structural stage work of Ezra Pound, whose "Le Testament" is among the important twentieth-century operas, nor of the same poet's sonata for violin or his work for string orchestra.

Duncan has no formal musical training that I know of, but this has not prevented in him an astonishing knowledge of the whole art of music, including an understanding of much of its lovely esoterica. It would be a huge labor, I think, to extract some compendium of the innumerable musical references in his work, both the direct and the symbolic ones, for they seem a very part of the work of his verse and are everywhere to be found in it. Indeed, music is a sign, or the sound of Order, "the music that's the heart of all things." The whole universe we know he seems to know as music: "First there is the power, and in the power/is the tone or tune,/so that all of creation moves with a music, the sound having its open/doors in the mind" (T 2); "the scale of five, eight, or twelve tones/performs a judgment/ previous to music. The music restores/health to the land" (OF 10); "The actual stars moving are music in the real world. This is the meaning of the music of the spheres" (OF 13). We begin to hear the great Dryden diapason and see the planets align over kettledrums.

But this all implodes too, "the drift of sand/at the edge of the sea's eternal roar/where my dry hands impetuous for sound/unlock from keys/inventions from inventions of the world's music/upon a breaking harpsicord" (OF

57); "it's to win particular hearts,/to stir an abiding affection for this music,/as if a host of readers will join the Beloved/ready to dance with me" (OF 61). The melodies are in the earth-roots, the web of hearts, and in the sensuous syllables which string his verse as well.

If one is a musician, it is hard not to be swept up in his transport, the field and the lines of it, for he is among the most lyric of poets, and his mastering of measure is great, and the on-going sound of him, the rich baritone of his actual voice, calls and hums and sings.

[UNTITLED]

R. B. Kitaj

From far away, and for most of twenty years I have been far away
from America, there are secret pleasures which are tasted in the mind. My
America dwells there. It doesn't hurt so much anymore, the distancing
from American talk, the long voyage home. There is another American geog-
raphy where those silent pleasures are turned when they are most needed.
Over the water from London and across the west, I always want to be sure,
in a way, that incredible lives are stirring and pulsing in half-lit inte-
riors Vuillard might have painted if it were not the case that they belong
to another geography. No "Revue Blanche" can explain those interiors at
21st Street but I would not be surprised if Duncan had a few copies tucked
away in one of his libraries.

It's so good and warming for these cold London bones, so secret--the
invention of owning deep vignettes, unlikely pictures into most precious
lives . . . "under bluer skies than are generally seen over the Thames," as
Maugham put it.

Duncan the whirlwind came down from the skies to stay with me only dur-
ing one great month a few years back. That's why my daydreaming has him
mostly in his own lair . . . and beloved Jess--always there and no place
else.

I had read much of Pound and Eliot before I was twenty. Indeed, I
sometimes think Poundism was the ruin of me as a painter. (Many others are
sure of it.) For too many years I tried to carry over the spirit and the
American letter of that transcendent modernist into painting and onto prin-
ted sheets, down blind paths of ambition for picture-making . . . after the
grandness of Pound's kind of running maze in our time.

Since I passed forty, I am not so sure that the Pound thing has done me in. To a brink maybe, but I feel good about that kind of past now. There are many reasons for me to be more generous about the ways I spent my earlier days. Foremost in my mind's eye looms the figure of Robert Duncan, who, with Creeley and some other reading and living, has cleared my path onto a field-mesa of living poetry as source, bearing at once on "right" painting instincts for me. What higher calling can a poet achieve than to light a fire by which someone else can learn living a life? Duncan makes that fire for me every day in my head where he dwells when I am not there with him and Jess in the Mission.

In the very early sixties, as a student at the Royal College of Art, I lived at Dulwich Village in south London. I knew very little about living poetry. Before that, when I was in the army, I used to get into Paris on weekends from Fontainebleau and had bought copies of Black Mountain Review there as they came out. They were left in the boot of my car when I sold it and now I am happy to pay Peter Howard $15 each to regain them. To tell the truth, I don't remember how I reacted to the Duncan, Creeley, Olson things in those little journals. The only lingering memory was of pretty crappy art . . . vestigial gesturing art . . . no?

Dulwich Village, 1960 or 61? One night I walked over to our local, a truly grand pub called Crown and Greyhound which tried to compete with and serve the lovely Georgian buildings all around it. I never drink. I have survived the Merchant Marine, the U. S. Army and the art world without drinking. I used to go to the Crown and Greyhound because my friend and neighbor Alisdair Aston and some other English poets arranged readings upstairs at the pub every month or so. That memorable night, a few people read their poems—John Wain, the novelist, was one, and then a tall American (Southern gent) who changed the course of my unlettered life somewhat. First there had been Pound-Eliot; then from that night, Jonathan Williams was to introduce me to an astonishing new-language, American poetry.

This little essay is not about Jonathan or Pound but I wanted to tell how I came to Duncan. Over the next years, Joanthan laid it all on for me.

Duncan's poems are very, very difficult for me. I hardly ever fear the difficulty of poetry anymore. The circumstance of poetry is in many ways such an inverse from the talk we are used to that I feed on the tit (poem) as if the difficult turn of words was the very milk I want. I think

the fashionable Barthes says that the pleasures of the text are extracted
by readers who show no shame in the various contradictions they encounter
(in themselves?). I want to take this to explain in newer words the busi-
ness of "understanding" a poem to come later, after other business, other
pleasures are conducted. Anyway, when I feel the need and we are in the
mood, I can ask Robert, the town explainer. My own pictures are said to be
difficult and they are because everywhere I am and whatever I take in seems
to me in a natural state of complex unspeakableness. The poem arranges the
unspeakableness into yet another version and so can a picture. Some of us
choose to dwell at a poet's forest pool where he has collected his versions,
his reflections of half a lifetime or more of living difficult lives and
taking versions of them which readers might learn and pleasure. Some of us
will take in a great range of versions . . . more than most people. Duncan
takes in the shares of many lions. I loved listening to him and the dying
Etonian wunderkind Cyril Connolly going over their Latin poets together at
my table. Duncan is a high-pitched answer to Pound's question, what would
America be like if the Classics had a wide circulation . . . I think Con-
nolly found that out and I hope it pleased him, coming to Duncan at the end
of his trail leading from the Mediterranean.

Art now drinks at many wells. Degas said of Parisian art life:
"There is too much going on" . . . and that was a long, long time ago . . .
so be it.

Duncan the impure was bound to water where I would go. Ashbery's gor-
geous impurities are of another essential order for me and the pictures I
want to make. Creeley in his lines seems untainted, saint-like. The lines
in John of the Cross and Creeley come to me from places I love and fear to
tread.

I hardly needed Robert in the flesh. Medieval Scenes, Roots and Bran-
ches, Jonathan's beautiful edition of the Letters . . . all that helped feed
my pictures and store in my mind. Then, when he appeared at my studio door
at Berkeley in 1967, a phase was to begin which will remain not only to ses-
sions of sweet silent thought but to the pictures ever.

His household was just terrific for me. I'm tempted to say really
well-hung . . . after the sort of dark museum houses you encounter in back-
street Europe which used to be the households of the painters who left them
. . . Moreau's house in Pigalle and many lesser known places. The Duncan/

Jess house is a retreat in which to re-live some of the life of that town.
The really large collage pictures as you begin to climb upstairs have their
birthplace up beyond where Jess Collins keeps his archives . . . their
place is among the few masters of that arcane practice. When I first saw
the beautiful Ed Corbett black abstraction at a stair landing I was re-
minded of the stupid disposition of reputation. Corbett died in agony, may-
be greater than Rothko's. He is hardly known in America and unknown here
in the rest of the world. He was, in these stunning charcoals, among the
most wonderful abstractionists and I am no great protagonist of abstraction.
Pictures and libraries fill the old place. I wonder if Kenneth Anger's
collection of M. P. Shiel still rests at the top of the house where I dis-
covered The Purple Cloud and Shiel and the fabulous G. Stein things? Frank
Baum in the master's bedroom? Down every alleyway, pictures, out of post-
war, westcoast, Balearic, neo-surrealist, early and more heroic modernist
days and years and ever on . . . leading to more libraries and more un-
orthodox art.

So much depends on what you want to do with your days, with your life.
Some comrades are built in such different ways from yourself that the alien
chemistries are charmed into a link. But Duncan chooses to live some of
the lives I would live. He gets them together in his texts in visions
which shock me into recognition. I devour his sense of past, of heroism,
his syntax, his wasp-talmudic take in an arcane myth-dredging tradition, the
way his lines and life burn on his own townism . . . its late sunlight and
westernamericaness, the expectation and surprise as so much value is given
out of the mouths of libraries! Lines, poems, poetry, like coloured pic-
tures, even drawing . . . in some of the possible quality of those pursuits
. . . in their impurities, can arise, do arise in households, behind closed
doors . . . out of the mouths of libraries.

One day in Duncan's kitchen, I was drawing his profile on a copper
etching plate while he read to me from Lady Gregory. It could seem so
wrong, as if there are newer things to do in an age when men fly faster than
sound. But they still pour out of their churches and kill each other in
the streets like they always did so I suppose it's something else, like
they say, to draw from the face and read aloud. Eliot said Pound was full
of "grand stuff." Duncan says in my own grand copy of Heavenly City Earth-
ly City:

And we go on, borrowing and borrowing
from each other

R. B. Kitaj, "Etching of Robert Duncan"

DUNCAN'S CELTIC MODE

Séan V. Golden

<u>Ross</u>.   Where is Duncan's body?
<u>MacD</u>. Carried to Colmekill,
The sacred storehouse of his predecessors,
And guardian of their bones.
                    <u>MacBeth</u> II, iv, 33-36

("*So foule and faire a day I have not seene,*" another
  murderous heart declares, who from Medusa's head
  expects that Burning Would--to echo Joyce's pun--
  will never come to Dance Inane . . .
                    "Stage Directions, Passages 30")

  For a burning would is come to dance inane.
  Glamours hath moidered's lieb and herefore Coldours
  must leap no more. Lack breath must leap no more.
                    <u>Finnegans Wake</u> 250.16-18

        Colmcill, the Dove of the Church, was born an Irish prince. He receiv-
ed his training as a poet, became an abbot and a missionary, waged a bloody
war over a book, was exiled in consequence, saved the bardic order from
extermination, and founded on the island of Iona one of the most famous
monasteries of western Christendom. Iona's sacred precincts housed the
bones of Scotland's kings and may have been the birthplace of the <u>Book of</u>
<u>Kells</u>. Iona's complex orders of associations interweave into a pattern
which can provide an entry into Robert Duncan's Celtic Mode. The three au-
thors I have linked here by allusion share in common an understanding of the
verbal wizardy of Celtic verse. Though many of Shakespeare's greatest plays
derive their themes and forms from Celtic sources, only <u>MacBeth</u> utilizes
fully the power of puns and paradoxes which animates the structure of Irish
and Welsh verse. In <u>Finnegans Wake</u> James Joyce renewed the bard's inter-
weaving of many meanings into a single polysemous thread. Enchantment,

incantation, the casting of spells by the weaving of words--these are el-
ements inseparable from MacBeth and from Celtic verse, and they partially
explain the sense of "otherness" which distinguishes the Celtic world and
its art, the world of faerie, from what is conventional in English-American
verse. This Celtic Mode is integral to Duncan's poetry, and to his view of
Poetry, and so must be explored.

    "The name Duncan, my little Webster's Collegiate Dictionary tells me,
means brown warrior, from the Gaelic," Duncan writes in "Returning to Les
Chimères of Gérard de Nerval," and he makes the same point in As Testimony.
The Gaelic would be Donnchadh, brown (or possibly noble) warrior (it could
also plausibly be donnceann, brown or noble head). Duncan's characteristic-
ally etymological approach to words is bolstered by the circumstances of his
own name (friends called him "the unguarded Duncan") and family background
into providing a tangible link to the Celtic world. "My aunt's name--Fay or
fairy--had to do with illusions or enchantments, bewilderings of the mind
in which we saw another world behind or under things, and at the same time
with the enchanters themselves, the folk who lived under the hill. Fate,
faith, feign, and fair, we find, following the winding associations of fay,
fey, fairy, in the O.E.D., are related" (H.D. I, 5, 4). In his youth Duncan
learned to image the fairyworld as "the otherness or alien nearness of the
dead and of hidden elements, of illusion and delusion in our daily life, the
witchcraft of phantasy and the bewitched obsessions of madness, all the psy-
chological dangers, combined as if they were the heart's wish." Childhood
readings of Thomas the Rimer, reinforced later by Helen Adam's readings of
that ballad, and Robert Graves's evocations in The White Goddess, bear fruit
in Duncan's later work in "The Green Lady" and "Often I Am Permitted to Re-
turn To A Meadow" ("She it is Queen Under The Hill/ whose hosts are a dis-
turbance of words within words/ that is a field folded"). Fairies and the
world of faerie recur frequently throughout Duncan's work, as in "Nel Mezzo
Del Cammin Di Nostra Vita":

                            a fairy citadel,
                a fabulous construction out of
                    Christianity where Morgan le Fay
                carries the King to her enchanted Isle
                                (RB 23)

and in examples from Medieval Scenes I shall examine later. Duncan's fair-
ies are not the elves and goblins which fairy tales for children have dete-
riorated into, they represent a world which holds very potent power over
the world of men. "Fay from fata had to do with the dead. The fairies as
fates or norns were spinners of the threads from which life was woven, who
measured out man's span and cut the cord to deliver him into death as they
once had cut the first cord or chord when the music began." His Gaelic
name, his aunt's link to the world of faerie, these personal concerns may
have provided the inclination and the base from which Duncan began his ex-
ploration of the Celtic world which would figure prominently in his writing.

In high school this inclination was supplemented by the teacher whose
reading of a poem by H.D. set in motion the powerful poetic forces which
have been chronicled in "The H.D. Book." "Edna Keogh was Irish. She was
consciously Celtic. She found me out, tried me too, with Stephens' Crock
of Gold and Deirdre, with books of Fionn and the world of glamors and
wishes." Edna Keogh knew a writer from the generation of Yeats, an Irish
woman who had been badly treated by the State Department--"Ella Young, a
gaunt beautiful touched old woman, clairvoyant, whom I in turn as a young
student at Berkeley once heard speak of those poets who practiced magic,
those women who saw into what was beyond the common sense, that folk that
dwelt upon the margins of fairy" (H.D. I, 2, 30, 31). Later Duncan studied
the Celtic realm in a seminar on Germanic and Celtic art wherein his project
was the Gundestrup cauldron and his research led through catalogues of
Celtic remains to the ethnography of the Celts of the Danube. Archaeology
supplemented the world of faerie without replacing it. "The old Kelts of
the Danube, of the Gundestrup kettle, and of Roquepertuse and Entremont
loom large; but . . . I am addicted too to the aesthetically forbidden--to
Celtic twilight and the phantasmal predilections of theosophical reveries
and reverends."[1] These early experiences and studies of the Celtic world
were followed by literary masters who practiced in their work techniques
they had acquired outside the mainstream of English verse in their explora-
tion of the Celtic world--Robert Graves through The White Goddess; G. M.
Hopkins, Dylan Thomas, and J. M. Synge through their use of sound and rhythm;
and James Joyce. Finnegans Wake is the most essentially Celtic work of art

produced since the Middle Ages. Joyce's liberties with words, his confi-
dence in his own right and power to create and shape them, to weave them as
he would, were anathema to Ezra Pound and Charles Olson, two more of Duncan's
masters. Olson even banned the book at Black Mountain, but Duncan held
readings of it there anyway. He frequently lists Joyce among his masters,
and quotes from Finnegans Wake in several works--in "The H.D. Book" I, 6, "The
Dance," and "Stage Directions." In Faust Foutu he structures one of the
Nurse's speeches on one of Joyce's rhythms, that of Anna Livia Plurabelle--
"Aye, my incubator innocent deary, twould take the least idea crossing his
mind to betray the black of the way it travels and damnation he's always
pointing up and painting down, hard to please and limp to learn, chased by
impure thots from pole to pole" (FF 5). (The Nurse's speeches are also
structured on rhythms of Synge--"Sure, how could such a pure sweet thing,
a girl with all the dear cathedrals of the western world softening their
glory for her sake until their burning windows were no more than petals of
immortal flowers falling" [FF 7-8]). A summary outline of this Celtic
world and its art will provide a working analogy and entry into specific
examples of Duncan's Celtic Mode.

The Celts were outsiders to the Mediterranean world. The Celtic realm
stretched from Spain to Asia Minor and from Italy to Ireland. To the Med-
iterranean world they were dreaded warriors and barbarians who fought
naked, believing dead warriors entered the other world, who sacked Rome and
Delphi and were mercenaries for Alexander and the Egyptians. Geographical-
ly located on the outer fringes of the Greco-Roman world, outside the bound-
aries of history and the Empire, they were part of an "other" world, and
their culture differed greatly from the prevailing world's view. The Celts
were not materialistic and they left no monumental architecture or human
effigies. They believed in the interpenetrability of a physical and a spir-
itual world, and put their values in warfare, bravery, and art. The druids,
who were supplanted by Christian missionaries but lived on in the bardic
order, organized universities and structured society. Their mythology and
attitude toward life were totally alien to the humanism of the Greco-Roman
world which we have inherited. Women were equal in property rights and
fought beside the men in battle, ruled over tribes, and had equal access to
the druidic and bardic orders. The art forms developed by this nation whose

back Caesar broke in Gaul were abstract, anti-humanistic; naturalistic
forms were metamorphosed into symbolic patterns and form and structure were
often more important than content and sense. This Celtic realm survived in
Ireland and Wales past the Middle Ages and the art works of the early Mid-
dle Ages (which often figure in Duncan's poetry) present the best examples
of how the spirit and techniques of that earlier Celtic world have survived
into our own.

Illuminated manuscripts, the greatest examples of Celtic painting, typ-
ify Celtic art with their intricate abstract forms which reveal a simultan-
eous naturalism. Whole borders of manuscript pages are taken up by inter-
locked spirals and concentric circles which, distinguished at first glance
only by color, depict birds, hounds, or serpents whose elongated necks and
limbs entwine their neighbors. They clasp each other in their jaws and an-
cillary lines followed out to the sides reveal legs and claws, but the body
has been subjected to abstract patterning. Abstraction and naturalism as a
visual pun introduce an exuberant humor. An example from the Book of Kells
will illuminate this. One page is devoted entirely to the word Quoniam.
The Q dominates half the page, containing u and o within itself, while the
letters niam are relegated to a lower corner. A troop of human figures wind
their way among the letters. A translation of the Latin introduced by this
word explains why--"Forasmuch as many have taken in hand . . ."--it is a
verbivisual pun. The pun is the essence of Celtic art and literature, and
many passages cannot be adequately translated because they are, like Fin-
negans Wake, densely packed, multilayered sequences of puns whose meanings
are simultaneous and often contradictory. Verbal facility, the felicity of
puns, emphasis on individual words, particularly proper nouns, etymologies--
all of these form the content and structure of Celtic literature. The tend-
ency toward abstraction reveals itself through strict and intricate rules
for meter and sound. This insistence on a careful and intricate patterning
of sounds to which content is frequently subordinated parallels the abstract
quality of Celtic art. The Celtic mind took in everything whole. "It's of
the essence of the Celtic mind that the very letters in writing being engrosst
we have in turn to become engrossed to return to the mode of what is going
on, we have to read into the page . . . which word 'engrossed' I but
researcht recently to find it comes from working out the gross letter in an

illuminated manuscript."[2] Duncan has commented on illuminated manuscripts
as a paradigm for creation often, and sees the essential nature of their
process as a pun. "The artist is always addressing and engrossed in the
field of the whole page . . . the whole page is the immediate presentation
of the Book or the Creation. . . . We have the sensation of a pun, of a
human or "outrageous" co-incidence when any element strikes an immediate
rime in itself; rimes expanding into the patterns of resonance and of un-
likeness as they are distributed in time are (as in dreams) thematic puns."[3]
This understanding illuminates his work, even as his work illuminates this
proposition.

The central importance of sound-play in the structure of Celtic verse
is one technique which can be brought over into verse in English, and this
was done by some of Duncan's masters, as some examples will show. One of
the central devices of Welsh prosody is cynghanedd, the exact duplication
of an order of consonants. Robert Graves supplied an approximation in The
White Goddess:

> Billet spied,
> Bolt sped.
> Across fields
> Crows fled,
> Aloft, wounded,
> Left one dead.

The consonants are repeated while the vowels are varied. The one poet who
has truly brought the spirit of this form over into English is G.M. Hopkins,
who studied the meters and wrote in Welsh. Consider this extended use of
cynghanedd from "The Leaden Echo":

> How to kéep--is there any any, is there none such, nowhere
>   known some, bow or brooch or braid or brace, láce,
>   latch or catch or key to keep
> Back beauty . . .

The br alliteration which leads to brace, which rhymes with lace, which al-
literates with latch, which rhymes with catch, which alliterates with key
and keep, is deliberate and exact use of a specific rule of cynghanedd by
Hopkins, whose work is full of similar examples. In Little, Louis Zukofsky,
still another of Duncan's masters, reproduced Welsh verse forms exactly:

> O T'd aerie too hid *his* strad   Ottid eiry, tohid istrad,
> dear is 'nt rue cade weary cad   diuryssint vy kedair y cad,
> m' need awe ah gnaw nim(bl') gad   mi nid aw, anaw nim gad.
>
>   <u>Little</u>, 48   from <u>Caniad Cadwgan</u>

(Snow falls, it covers the valley;/ Warriors hasten to battle;/
I do not go, a wound does not allow me.)

Zukofsky's versions of Welsh verse in <u>Little</u> derive their meanings from a
complex composed of the sound value of the original as heard in English, the
English meanings of the words, their echoes of the Welsh meanings, and the
poem's context. His strict insistence on the sound value <u>per se</u> respects
the mode of his models.

Duncan chose not to follow strict conventions but to engage in open
process or "free invention," but his attention to sound, and to being en-
grossed in every and any given area of his work, follows the spirit of this
bardic attention to sound. He has written poems whose intricacy of sound
parallels the examples given:

> .   Arranging the rose in a white vase
>   the magician made it vanish.
>   He made where a cry arose a rose
>   a crow arise
>   and made it appear
>   in her fair hair.
>   "Eluard's Death" (BR 56)
>
>   The moon's up-riding makes a line
>   flowing out into lion's mane
>   of traffic, of speeding lights.
>
>   "Night Scenes" (RB 5)

In <u>A Play With Masks</u>, the words of the Bard Sublime, "full skull and rattl-
ing your bones," are heard by the Orphic Skold as, "foul scold and riddling
pure tones." A similar play on sounds occurs later--"Not since Orifice in-
vented the Liar . . . Not since Horrorface invented the Lure" (A/P 10, 11).
<u>Faust Foutu</u> is full of such play--"pointing up and painting down," "the lit-
tlest one, the least one," "For everv war we've won there's another war to
win," "that makes one war of the whole world and no more than a whore of the

mother of us all," and this excerpt from the quintet which closes the play
(the very idea of a quintet, several simultaneous utterances, partakes of
the nature of a pun, and of Celtic art):

```
4      A tidy mess      A mass      A tide
5                                          him.
                                              (FF 67)
```

Duncan's Celtic Mode is clearer in other ways than sound. The image
of Celtic art recurs in Duncan's writing as an image of his concerns and
intentions in writing. Early in "The H.D. Book" he recounts an incident at
Berkeley when, because he would not stop reading Joyce's poems aloud, he
missed military drill and ended his academic career. One particular poem
focuses his concerns at that moment, "I hear an army charging," and he
recognizes the Celtic background of the poem ("these horsemen of the surf
are an old Celtic idea"). The Celtic world and the Celtic poet were in-
strumental in forming his own notion of poetry. In "The H.D. Book" he cites
Taliesin, a Welsh bard and wizard, as an image of the poet, and describes
Celtic art as an extension of the philosophy of the Celtic world. "The co-
operation of fantasy and reality, the interchange of being, had a counter-
part in the old Celtic affinity for interweaving forms, shape-changings,
reincarnations, in an art where figure and ground may be exchanged" (H.D.
I, 2, 30-31). Celtic artwork becomes an image in his poetry. "The artist
breeds complications in order to enrich: the intertwining and doubled
images of marginal illuminations, the underpainting and mixing of tones in
the luxuriance of Titian, the elaborations of the poet worked in the inter-
changes of vowels and consonants, undermeanings and overmeanings. So
Joyce, presented with the largest gift of the century by his patroness
Harriet Weaver, developed and complicated his Finnegans Wake--a jeweled,
overworked texture that only the extravagantly endowed artist could venture"
(H.D. II, 2, 20). His image is of illuminated manuscripts. "Not only the
images of the poem arise from vision but the formal concept relates primar-
ily to illumination, painting or tapestry" (H.D. II, 3, 117). In "The
Continent" it is this image of the illuminated page which structures the
poem:

                          in margins

                  the writ illumined, wreathed round
                  with pomegranate
                  . . .
                  vine tendril into talon curls,
                  faces in the fruit occur.
                  The artist of the margin
                  works abundancies

                  and sees the theme is much too big
                  to cover all o'er, a decorative frieze
                  out of earthly proportion to the page
                                              (RB 172)

and:

                  There's only the one promise

                  and from its flame
                  the margins of the page flare forth.
                  There's only one page,

                  the rest remains
                  in ashes.
                                              (RB 176)

In his introduction to Jess Collins's _Translations_, Duncan speaks at
length on the nature of Celtic art and magic. His comments about the paint-
ings there are often applicable to his own work, as he himself points out in
concluding. One painting in particular, _Ex_. _3--Fionn's Finnegas_, centers
this discussion. In it the painter has "translated" a lathe grinding
machine from a print into a painting. A text accompanies the painting,
taken from _The Tangle-Coated Horse_ by Ella Young. "'What help is there in
words?' said Finnegas. 'You could not teach me how to snare the Salmon:
I could not teach you more woodcraft than you know already.' 'You could
teach me poetry,' said Fionn." Duncan sees this painting as illustrating
"the stage of the phantasmal or faerie world of images, the work of the
imagination to trick or amaze the mind, that the tradition of magic and
romance as powers of the artist in the Celtic civilization, typified by the
bardic poet Finnegas, proposes."[4] In a long description of the multiphasic
nature of Collins's work he touches upon a number of concerns common to
his own work and uses the image of Celtic art to provide an analogy.

> A pun is an element that sets into motion more than one possibil-
> ity of statement. This brush-stroke at once appears as a member
> of the painter's language of painting--we see it as a statement
> of the act of painting, or as a statement of paint--and as a mem-
> ber of the image of a foot. In Celtic design, ground is every-
> where possibly figure; figure, ground. In a field of interacting
> melodies a single note may belong to both ascending and descend-
> ing figures, and, yet again, to a sustaining chord or discord.
> A rhyme is a member in whose force of identity we remark--remem-
> ber or anticipate--the presence of another member. . . . The
> "completion" of the painting is the realization of its elements
> as "puns" or "rhymes." The painter works not to conclude the el-
> ements of the painting but to set them into motion, not to bind
> the colors but to free them, to release the force of their inter-
> relationships. [5]

This is precisely the nature of Celtic art, the recurring analogy by which

Duncan describes his own art. In Medieval Scenes Duncan uses the images of

tapestries and the process of weaving them to illuminate his vision of the

Celtic world. Puns and rhymes interweave with the images to create a multi-

phasic portrait, as in "The Banners":

> The Swan is the signet, heraldic joy.
> The Banners make animate the inanimate day.
> No longer mere, but night-mare changed.
> The Swan, the sign, displays its grace.
>
> The lion in the loin that slumbers
> shakes the sheath of sleep back from his claws
> and stretches. The poets
> weave upon that tapestry a spell
> of flowering, gold-threaded tendrils of a vine;
> make animate each animal form
> with conceit of loving. There
>
> as if washt up upon a wave of violet,
> of blue, vermillion and clear yellow,
> the poets animate a unicorn,
> animalization of the beckoning swan.
> This is the night-mare thread of their loom.
>
> (FD 54)

The poem continues in this vein, as do all the poems in Medieval Scenes,

weaving complicated pictures of the poet's vision. For in the weaving of

the tapestries there is a weaving of spells and magic is another fundamental

element of the Celtic Mode. In the third and fourth chapters of "The H.D.
Book" Duncan traces the growth of the spirit of romance in Provence, partly
out of the Arthurian legends which made their way there from the "hinter-
lands of Wales." This story of Arthur's world was shaped by Celtic art--
"The Celtic genius, a poetry that was not a rational melody but a weaving
of a spell, so intertwined and elaborated its figures that we now see the
one Eros, now the Other." And he concludes, "I too may be Celtic, and a
spell be necessary here; weaving is necessary to keep many threads and many
figures so that every thread is central and every figure central to threads
and figures." One further step transforms his concern from allusion to
something more central. "It is of the essence of Poetry that sexual rite,
fertility rite, Christian rite, and Celtic magic rite, may be confused,
transmuted in an alembic, until we cannot divide the magic from the divine"
(H.D. I, 3/4, 79, 81). In the Celtic world Poetry and the Poet are potent
elemental forces suffused with magic.

Calvert Watkins has drawn an etymological portrait of the poet and
poetry in the Celtic world.[6] Poets maintained history, mythology and the
law. The law was maintained in verse tracts, suspect unless it had "a
thread of poetry around it." The normal word for poet in Irish is fili,
originally meaning seer or wise man; it is cognate with a verb for sight.
Poetry was filidecht, what the poet said. Another verb applied to poetry
is canid, which is cognate with Latin canere, both meaning to sing, chant,
or recite, both terms of augural or magical language. An older Irish word
for poetry which is embodied in the Welsh word for poet (prydydd) is creth
which is associated etymologically with words for magic and bewitching.
Watkins sees it as likely "that the image underlying OIr. creth is one of
magically transforming something into something, rather than the simple no-
tion of craftsmanship in Greek [poiesis, poieo]." [7] The Irish word for
prophecy is fath, cognate with Latin vates, poet or seer. Poetic art in
Irish is signified by ai, in Welsh by awen, both cognate with words for wind,
the image being one of breath or blowing--in-spir-ation. In the Celtic
world the druid and the bard were inseparable, as were poetry and magic.
Duncan has recognized this. "If poiein, the concept of the poet fashioning
the poem, enters into my poetics, and it does; so also does the Celtic idea

of the poet as bard, the chant that enchants, the myth or tale as *spell* and words that cast images upon the mind," he writes in The Truth and Life of Myth (TLM 67). In "Orders, Passages 24" he writes:

<blockquote>
I put aside

whatever I once served of the poet, master
   of enchanting words and magics
                 (BB 77)
</blockquote>

in order to take a public political stance. In the preface to Caesar's Gate Duncan speaks of his apprehension at the moment of creation, derived no doubt from this sense of potency. "It is the grue, the sense of coming near to grief, that signifies in the lore of the Scotch folk, the weird of poetry" (CG xviii). In his introduction to The Years As Catches he reiterates this Celtic element of his poetics. "For when a rhythm began in my writing it would carry me on into a dimension in which fantasy, the glow and fusion of images that the Celtic world knew as the world of fairy, would take over" (YAC v).

While the world of fairy and his sense of the Celtic poetic mind inform Duncan's poetics, specific Celtic devices, allusions, and key plots structure particular poems. A final exploration of his practice will illustrate this. In the Celtic world metamorphoses and transpersonalizations animate myth and literature as well as art. Duncan's parents' theosophic-Hermetic teachings figured the world in the same way. Images of bear, owl, salmon, falcon, horse, fox, lion, are not totemic subscriptions in his work, but transpersonalizations. "My Mother Would Be A Falconress" is a major poem derived from the Celtic tradition of shape-shifting, and animals retain echoes of metamorphoses in many other poems as well.

Medieval Scenes takes its structure and imagery from medieval tapestries, and its force from the Celtic world where to weave is to weave a spell. In "The Dreamers," "Each sleepy bearish hero short of love/recounts his dreams" (FD 51). The image of Arthur is embodied here in a pun, the sleeping lord who will return to save his people, whose name means bear. The speaker of the poem has within his heart a "Hibernia of dreams" (FD 52). "The Banners"

combines both kinds of weaving ("The poets/weave upon that tapestry a spell
. . ."). [8] In "The Kingdom of Jerusalem" Duncan uses the image of the fairy
world--"The hosts of the glittering fay return" and "The palaces of the fay
appear."

> The people of the goddess Danu smile
> evasively and work their spell.
>
>   (FD 55)

To spell is to make words, to spell them. It is also to cast a spell. Our
language retains the primitive awe of literacy, the control of words. One
whole "Passages" poem is devoted to spelling. In "A Poem Slow Beginning"
Duncan writes, "the letters by which we spell words compel/magic refinements"
(OF 15). The people of the goddess Danu, the Tuatha De Danann, were one of
the mythic invading races of Ireland. They were wizards and craftsmen who
were subsequently defeated by the last invading race, the Milesians. In
defeat they were awarded the world beneath the ground and the sea. They are
the folk of the sidhe so prominent in W.B. Yeats's poetry, the fairy host of
Irish folklore. In The White Goddess Robert Graves links them to the daugh-
ters of Danaus and the Danaans, seeing in the myth of their migration a pos-
sible historical truth. Duncan's own research at the time The White Goddess
appeared (1948) cross-referenced Graves's findings. In "The Mirror" Duncan
uses the daughters of Danaus to image and structure his poem, constructing
a wide net of associations to support his wide-ranging use of the fairy
world as image. In "The Adoration of the Virgin" it is "druid wood" of
which the statue is made. The oak tree was sacred to the druids and their
name may be derived from it--another pun operating beneath the level of
consciousness to exercise magic on the mind. In "Huan of Bordeaux" Morgana
le Fay appears, exercising, like her mythic source the Morrigan of Irish
warlore, a deadly magic "like a sphinx of stone," who becomes "Our Lady of
the Lake." (In many of these poems Morgana le Fay, and that aspect of fae-
rie most associated with her, characterize lust and its power over men,
spellweaving as sexual power and magic.)

     The Arthurian world, the world of Malory, and the world of faerie
which lies behind the most fruitful element of medieval literature is

ultimately Celtic, and it has not lost its peculiar "otherness" despite the
multiplicity of non-Celtic cultures which have restructured and retold the
tales. The same dread, the same magic of pun and paradox and transformation
which informs MacBeth, informs Arthurian literature. This is the world of
faerie which lies behind so many of Duncan's poems. In Medea at Kolchis
Arthur is a major character. He has a sister Edna who has succumbed to the
fascination of the world of faerie. Fay, faerie, fairy, fairy hosts, the
lords of fairy, Avalon--these are all words which appear too frequently in
Duncan's work to be analyzed individually. Suffice it to say that they draw
their complex meanings from the complex of associations that underlies Dun-
can's understanding of the terms, which has been suggested here.

Arthurian material, the Matter of Britain, is the most readily available
(cf. "Parsifal" and "Saint Graal" and images of the Grail in poems like
"Shadows"), but hardly the sole Celtic source for his work. There is a purer
source of Celticism in the untarnished literature of Ireland and Wales. From
Irish tales of Cuchullain and Fionn mac Cumhal, Duncan has taken the image of
wisdom represented by the nuts of wisdom on the hazel tree which fall into a
pool to be eaten by a salmon which, if caught and eaten, will impart wisdom
to men. Both of these heroes accidentally succeed in acquiring this wisdom.
This is the incident quoted in Ex. 3--Fionn's Finnegas, and Duncan uses it
in two poems. In "Poetry, A Natural Thing," the image is of the

> salmon not in the well where the
>   hazelnut falls
> but at the falls battling, inarticulate,
>   blindly making it.
>   (OF 50)

In "Apprehensions" there is an extended use of the image, of "man like a
salmon" swimming, of "a pool, dark and steady mood," and of "a seed encased
in its shell" (RB 34). But his most Celtic poem, his most deliberately
Celtic work is "From The Mabinogion." In this poem Duncan has taken an
incident from "Branwen, Daughter of Llŷr," the second Branch of The Mabinog-
ion. Branwen's misfortunes as the wife of the King of Ireland provoke her
kinsmen in Britain to invade and wage a war in which only five pregnant

Irish women and seven Britons survive. Branwen dies lamenting the destruc-
tion she has caused, and the British leader, Bendigeidfran, has his head
severed, magically surviving and instructing his followers to proceed to
Harddlech where they will spend seven years feasting. Then they must pro-
ceed to Gwales in Penfro, where they will spend fourscore years of happiness
--as long as they do not open a door facing Cornwall. In that place "there
came to them no remembrance . . . of any sorrow in the world. And there
they passed the fourscore years so that they were not aware of having ever
spent a time more joyous and delightful than that." But there came a day
when Heilyn son of Gwyn broke the spell. "He opened the door and looked on
Cornwall and Aber Henfelen. And when he looked, they were as conscious of
every loss they had ever sustained, and of every kinsman and friend they had
missed, and of every ill that had come upon them, as if it were even then it
had befallen them."[9] They then completed the task set them by Bendigeidfran,
which was to bury his head in London where it would protect the land. Dun-
can's poem follows the plot strictly up to the opening of a window, where he
offers his own images of loss and desolation:

> we saw the land behind us--
>
> our wastes, our age, our hearts' loss
> --and I do not know what we saw:
>
>> this man a wreckt car,
>> this man a Lover turn away,
>> this man an empty glass upon the bar,
>> this man a parody of what he was,
>> because of our Lord.   (RB 117-18)

He concludes as the tale does--"That is what the tale says"--and reinforces
the archetype of experience the tale contains:

>> For I think we've been in
>> this joint before.
>>   (RB 118)

Duncan sees the heroes as "incarcerated in a grand illusion." "The poet-
hero Taliesin is one of the seven heroes, and this incarceration in the

marvelous palace . . . seems to me like a phase in Poetry."[10] The opening of
the window or the door he sees as a second phase in Poetry, the door of con-
sciousness, which turns into a third phase, a quest for truth, represented
by the burial of the magic head. This poem again demonstrates the import-
ance of the Celtic world for Duncan's poetry. Here he has embodied the
sense and significance of his poetics in a poem which draws its peculiar
power from his strict adherence to the Celtic source. He has translated into
contemporary American poetry an authentic instance of the Celtic Mode.

Duncan's poetry and poetics are too complex to be characterized by one
influence. In the context of his larger body of work the Celtic elements I
have outlined here might seem less significant than the Hermetic traditions
which inform his work. Celtic art and the spirit of Celtic civilization are
present in his work, though, and this essay takes its own relevance to his
work more as an image of a kind of poetry which both illumines and is il-
luminated by Duncan's poetry, a potentiality surfacing here and there in
the work of a few poets which strikes the reader as uncannily different, as
outside the realm of normal experience. In his epilogue to Caesar's Gate
Duncan writes of the kingdom of the Avars as standing "at the limits of
geographical reality as it fades into the irreal, even as the ancient Celtic
world stands at the limits of historical reality" (CG 62). He stands himself
on the outer fringes of the "real" world, in tune with that Other world, like
the people of "Passages 1," the Celts who stood and stand at the fringes of
the conventionally known world, disturbing the psyche with their witness to
another mode of being and doing.

NOTES

[1] Letter from Robert Duncan, 9 Feb 1977.

[2] Letter from Robert Duncan, 23 Feb 1977.

[3] Ibid.

[4] Translations by Jess (Los Angeles: Black Sparrow Press, 1971), p. ix.

[5] Ibid., p. iv.

[6] Calvert Watkins, "Indo-European Metrics and Archaic Irish Verse,"
Celtica, 6 (1963), 194-249.

[7]Ibid., 213-214.

[8]The Ancient Indo-European image of the poet, Calvert Watkins points out in his essay on etymology in <u>The American Heritage Dictionary</u>, is the "weaver" (or crafter) of words"--*<u>wekwom</u> <u>teks</u>.

[9]<u>The Mabinogion</u>, trans. Gwyn Jones and Thomas Jones (London: Everyman Library, 1949), pp. 39-40.

[10] Robert Duncan, "Shakespeare's <u>Romeo</u> <u>and</u> <u>Juliet</u> as it Appears in the Mysteries of a Late Twentieth Century Poetics," <u>Fathar</u> <u>For</u> (June 1972), pp. [56, 57].

"AN INHERITANCE OF SPIRIT":
ROBERT DUNCAN AND WALT WHITMAN

Mark Johnson and Robert DeMott

"Whitman is not diffuse."
Duncan to Charles Olson, 8 January 1958

It is a lifetime's task grounded in disciplined reading to trace the
generative presences in Robert Duncan's intellectual and poetic develop-
ment. His chrestomathy comprises dozens of predecessors because, like any
great poet, he has borrowed from sympathetic sources to enrich the field of
his own poetry. "My vision of poetry," he has recently said, "has been
drawn from Carlyle as well as from Whitman, from Dante, from Burckhardt,
from Pater and Symonds as well as from Pound or Olson—wherever another
man's vision leads my spirit towards a larger feeling" (H.D. II, 7, 60-61).
From among this constellation of masters, Robert Duncan has repeatedly sin-
gled out Dante, Shakespeare, and Whitman and their lasting influence on his
work, and of the three, he has written most eloquently on Whitman. In his
essay, "Changing Perspectives in Reading Whitman," Duncan cites the follow-
ing lines from the 1885 edition of Leaves of Grass while discussing Whit-
man's notion that poetry was "ever to be fruitfully incomplete":[1]

> Who learns my lesson complete?
> . . . .
> Draw nigh and commence,
> It is no lesson . . . . it lets down the bars to a good lesson,
> And then to another . . . . and every one to another still.

A similar principle of openness informs Duncan's work. Recalling his enthu-
siasm for Charles Olson's essay "Projective Verse" (1950), Duncan explains,
"and this seems to me the essential thing, that poetry is language that

becomes so excited that it is endlessly creative of message" (I [19]). <u>The Opening of the Field</u> is the book which announced Duncan's allegiances to open form. It should come as no surprise that in the course of its writing "<u>Leaves of Grass</u> was kept as a bedside book" (CPR 100), providing Duncan with a touchstone for his evolving conceptions of poetic theme and form, personal and collective identity, mythic awareness and spiritual kinship. In a resounding testimony, Duncan locates his own attraction to Whitman:

> Setting out in 1855, Whitman had to go on faith. He had
> the courage of a grand fidelity. But he had no alternative.
> The poem commanded him. Its reality and truth were imperative.
> It commands me reading today--the vision of what the Poem is,
> and within that, *Leaves of Grass* as it has been for me in my
> own creative life an incarnation of that <u>Presence of a Poetry</u>.
> This body of words the medium of this spirit. Writing or read-
> ing, where words pass into this commanding music, I found a pres-
> ence of person more commandingly real than what I thought to be
> my person before; Whitman or Shakespeare presenting more of
> what I was than I was. (CPR 89)

The music issuing from Whitman's poetry (and his prose) creates resonant harmonies in Duncan. Lines from "Answering" recall Whitman's "I Hear America Singing," with its emphasis on "varied carols" and "strong melodious songs":

> The men are working in the street.
> The sound
>
> of pick and pneumatic drill
>
> punctuates
> the chirrup a bird makes,
>
> a natural will
> who works the tossing dandelion head
>
> --a sheaf of poems.
>
> They are employd
> at making up a joyous

> possibility.
>
> They are making a living
> where I take my life. (RB 125)

Similarly, in section 4 of "The Propositions," Duncan explicitly calls
forth the image of Whitman's noiseless, patient spider and celebrates
"tremblings of the veil,/shakings of the center" caused by a fly caught in
its web (OF 36). The idea of the poet-spider, launching forth "filament,
filament, filament, out of itself," to connect disparate "spheres,"[2]
becomes for Duncan an ideogram of the poet's centrality in the world he
both enters and creates: "In Whitman," he writes, "there is no ambiguity
about the source of *meaning*. It flows from a 'Me myself' that exists in
the authenticity of the universe" (CPR 100). Like Whitman, Duncan is large
and contains multitudes. He fulfills the serious office of the Romantic
poet, searching out forms commensurate with the intrusion of disturbances
which enter the poem.

                                    I

    From the very first lines of the 1855 edition of Leaves of Grass, Whit-
man was concerned with the identity of the Self, later amplifying those
lines to strike the inclusive note characteristic of his democratic urge:
"One's-Self I sing, a simple separate person,/Yet utter the word Democratic,
the word En-Masse" (LG 1). Robert Duncan, too, is concerned with both the
individual and his place in the world, as he asserts in this statement:
"Our consciousness, and the poem as a supreme effort of consciousness, comes
in a dancing organization between personal and cosmic identity" (TOU 135).
Whitman phrased it similarly: his "Walt Whitman, a kosmos, of Manhattan
the son" (LG 52), fulfills both an individual and a typological role. Whit-
man's compulsion toward a fictive portrayal of the various aspects of his
personality was the basis for his prophetic, revolutionary poetry. At the
end of his career, in "A Backward Glance," he reiterated this conception of
the Self: "This was a feeling or ambition to articulate and faithfully ex-
press in literary or poetic form, and uncompromisingly, my own physical,

emotional, moral, intellectual, and aesthetic Personality. . ." (LG 561).

The creation and projection of this multiple Self, which Duncan calls the "grandly conceived personality Whitman created" (CPR 88), is one of the chief liberating features of Whitman's poetry, and one of his most significant legacies to twentieth-century poets.[3] The immediate presence of Whitman's poet-protagonist informs Leaves of Grass and its continual evolution justifies the growth of his book, not by additions, but by organic evolvement; each new edition is a possible statement of the whole, the ensemble. Duncan describes this expressive mode in his Whitman essay: "As we begin to see evolution as a field in which series of variations, visions and revisions, and mutations, impulses and inspirations anew, are at work, these Leaves of Grass are individual reincarnations of a single identity" (CPR 91-92). From this seminal idea, Duncan argues that Whitman's influence extends in several directions, and the unifying fictive "I" serves both formal and thematic functions in processual poetry. Elsewhere, Duncan has written that uncovering the ground of being necessary for poetry "involves an active and searching intellect at work to imagine the beginnings not only of person but of the larger 'I' in man and the largest consciousness we have of our 'I' in our belongings to the process of the Cosmos."[4] The two poets imagine identity and reality in similar terms, both drawing on a mystical awareness of latent presences. Whitman's notion of Personalism, expounded in Democratic Vistas, is the root from which Duncan's coincident belief grows. Personalism fuses the diverse properties of exemplary human and divine life. "This is the thought of identity," Whitman wrote,

> Miracle of miracles, beyond statement, most spiritual
> and vaguest of earth's dreams, yet hardest basic fact,
> and only entrance to all facts. . . . Under the luminous-
> ness of real vision, it alone takes possession, takes
> value.[5]

In his poetry and prose, Duncan grapples (much as Whitman did) with the meaning of America, not as political entity alone, but as the generative source for poetic and personal endeavor. It is undoubtedly the native American literary line to seek the basis of poetry in antipoetic or unpoetic material and to redeem the creative potentiality of mundane subjects.

Emerson had invited poetic expression equal to the qualities and character-
istics of the evolving nation. Whitman answered the invitation repeatedly.
In his essay, "Slang in America," he found an inherent piquancy in social-
ly nontraditional language which captured his imagination and provided
intimations of a mythic past:

> Such is Slang, or indirection, an attempt of common humanity
> to escape from bald literalism, and express itself illimitably,
> which in highest walks produces poets and poems, and doubtless
> in pre-historic times gave the start to, and perfected, the
> whole immense tangle of the old mythologies. For, curious as
> it may appear, it is strictly the same impulse-source, the same
> thing. Slang, too, is the wholesome fermentation or eructation
> of those processes eternally active in language, by which froth
> and specks are thrown up, mostly to pass away; though occasion-
> ally to settle and permanently chrystallize. (CP 420)

Thus an ideal of democracy, working through freedom of language and the
redemptive power of the writer as namer, provided Whitman with both a
processive basis for his poetic vision, and a revivification of primordial
concerns. "The poetic urge," Duncan says, "to make poetry out of the com-
mon language, is to make room for the existence of the poet, the artist of
free speech" (HD II, 5, 344). In Whitman's loving embrace of the partic-
ulars of American life, Duncan centers his affinity:

> In the very place where often contemporary individualism
> finds identity most lost, Whitman takes the ground of his
> identity and person: in the "particulars and details magnif-
> icently moving in vast masses." He saw Democracy not as an
> intellectual ideal but as an intuition of a grander and deeper
> reality potential in Man's evolution. . . . (CPR 100)

Reading Whitman, Duncan enters this line of felt presences, though in Dun-
can's cosmology evil is more prevalent than Whitman's transcendentalism
allowed. Whitman's projection in Democratic Vistas was toward a future,
ideal America envisioned as a conjunction of a "new earth and a new man"
(CP 230). Duncan, whose "Man's Fulfillment in Order and Strife" draws
heavily on Democratic Vistas, takes up the condition of the present. He
sees a basis for artistic order which participates in incarnate reality:

"So the poet searches out the actuality of the world into which he extends
what is now *his* world or Self--his search transformed into an art--in
order to realize in imagination the world. From the reality of this order,
an 'interior' feeling that has its heart in the apprehension of universe,
being and even self, more real than he is, speaks to him" (MF 239).

Like Whitman, Duncan is preoccupied with the place of the creative
individual in society, but with the nation's full entrance into Viet Nam
in the 1960's, the dualism inherent in the meaning of America asserts it-
self:

> In our poetic tradition, our conscience as poets, we inherit
> a vision not only of the potentialities for good latent in the
> entity of these States, but also of the profound potentialities
> for evil. I drew not only upon the current of my own feeling
> as my vision sprang into life for me, sensing deeply the threat
> of a terror to come beyond the terrors we know in what the Viet
> Namese suffered--I mean the terror we must have in so far as we
> remain "American" in America's crimes--but also upon my studies
> of how America had been seen by poets I recognized as inspired
> visionaries. Whitman's vision of America in his Eighteenth
> Presidency essay had come in earlier in the Passage series.
>   (MF 242)

In "The Fire, Passages 13," Duncan quotes from The Eighteenth Presidency
in which Whitman castigates the pro-slavery movement and the tumultuous
political situation during the 1856 presidential campaign.[6] The text and
spirit of Whitman's address enters Duncan's poem establishing a synchronous
field with twentieth-century politics. Whitman warned against candidates
Fillmore and Buchanan, "Two dead corpses . . . walking up and down the
earth," corrupting the spirit of party politics and federal covenant; Dun-
can's censure is directed at the unmitigated presence of demotic Evil
("glints of the evil that one sees in the power of this world") which
threatens to destroy the old and vital traditions like language, music and
nature:

> About Him, as if to drown sweet music out,
>
>   Satan looks forth from
>   men's faces:

> Eisenhower's idiot grin, Nixon's
> black jaw, the sly glare in Goldwater's eye, or
> the look of Stevenson lying in the U.N. that our
> Nation save face   (BB 43)

and later:

> faces of Princes, Popes, Prime Usurers, Presidents,
>   Gang Leaders of whatever Clubs, Nations, Legions meet
>
>   to conspire, to coerce, to cut down   . (BB 44)

The treatment becomes increasingly strident in later poems, most ev-
idently in the Passages dealing with Lyndon Johnson and the Viet Nam War.
"Up Rising, Passages 25" (the title itself an echo of Whitman's brief es-
say, "National Uprising and Volunteering," first collected in Specimen Days
in 1882), and "The Soldiers: Passages 26" are unrelenting in their con-
tempt for the Permanent War Economy. The latter evokes Whitman's words in
bitter irony:

> *"The United States themselves are essentially the greatest poem"?*
>
>   Then America, the secret union of all states of Man,
>
>   waits, hidden and challenging, in the hearts of the Viet Cong.
>   *"The Americans of all nations at any time upon the earth,"*
>
>   Whitman says--the libertarians of the spirit, the
>
>   devotées of Man's commonality. (BB 113)

Duncan holds a far less sanguine view of America than Whitman, but his
desire to call up its presence, despite inherent contradictions, is equally
imperative. At the political level Duncan can work less on faith than Whit-
man, and he is too honest to fool himself that Whitman's egalitarian optim-
ism remains viable for all men in the twentieth-century: "Totalism--
ensemblism--is haunted when we return to it today in the dark monstrosities
of socialistic and democratic totalitarianism" (CPR 79). Yet Man's poten-
tial for World Order sustains Duncan as it sustained Whitman:

Once we read the United States as belonging to the greatest
poem, the race of all races, and we hear Whitman speaking of
Americans throughout the population of Man--every place and
any place and time of Man--then, underlying these United States
and this America, comes a mystery of "America" that belongs to
dream and desire and the reawakening of earliest oneness with all
peoples--at last, the nation of Mankind at large. (CPR 81)

In _Democratic Vistas_, Whitman recognized that the world's "perverse

maleficence," which in "downcast hours the soul thinks . . . will always

be" (CP 222), could be transcended by a balance between democracy and per-

sonalism. In "Man's Fulfillment in Order and Strife," and in _Bending the_

Bow, Duncan takes up the disorders which moved Whitman, finding that male-

volence, a constant attribute of humanity, cannot be defeated, but must be

"acknowledged and understood" (MF 232). To recover a vision of wholeness

associated with communal presence is to reach back beyond the specific

agents of evil and to enter willingly the contradictory processes of the

universe, seeking the "unity in multiplicity of humanity" (MF 235). For

Duncan, "the word _God_," secularly considered as numen, Ideal or Real,

"becomes necessary where there is an intense feeling of presence and one-

ness in opposites" (MF 236). Duncan's belief in kinship, natural harmony,

and human potentiality remains a constant force in his poetic vision and

often rises to affirmation: "The cosmos will not/dissolve its orders at

man's evil," he announces in "Orders, Passages 24" (BB 79). In "The

Multiversity, Passages 21," he sees through the faces of corrupt men who

have perverted the natural good and he claims that the basis for community

still resides in "the freedom of/individual volition" (BB 73). Here he

is echoing Whitman's statement in _Democratic Vistas_ that the "problem . . .

presented to the New World, is, under permanent law and order, and after

preserving cohesion, (ensemble-Individuality,) at all hazards, to vitalize

man's free play of special Personalism, recognizing in it something that

calls ever more to be consider'd, fed and adopted as the substratum for the

best that belongs to us. . ." (CP 234-235). Seeking the essential expe-

rience which could inform the temporal world, Duncan wants to redeem the

past through the intuition of a Primal Scene, paralleling Whitman's con-

cept of Eidolons. In both cases the presence of the Real occasionally

flashes forth, providing the poet with apprehensions of a larger and older
design. "The poet labors to unite the Ideal," Duncan writes, "--and
Whitman sees the Ideal not as belonging to the world of the high-minded
paradigms but to the world of primordial latencies--and the Real, even as
his mission is to present a path between the Real and the individual soul"
(CPR 96).

The difficulty for the contemporary poet is generated by the creative
contradiction between Whitman's sense of political and personal fulfillment,
and Duncan's realization that he comes too late in history merely to re-
capitulate the older poet's stance. "How far from Whitman's sense of what
it means, of filling and fullness, my own poetic apocalyptic sense of signs
and meanings fulfilled is" (CPR 90). He expresses this loss in "Poem
Beginning With A Line By Pindar":

> In time we see a tragedy, a loss of beauty
>   the glittering youth
> of the god retains--but from this threshold
>   it is age
> that is beautiful. It is toward the old poets
>   we go, to their faltering,
> their unalterable wrongness that has style,
>   their variable truth,
>   the old faces,
> words shed like tears from
> a plenitude of powers time stores. (OF 63)

He asks, "What/if lilacs last in *this* dooryard bloomd?" and sees "Harding,
Wilson, Taft, Roosevelt,/idiots fumbling at the bride's door. . . ." The
harshness of the imposed structures of political systems can be antithetical
to the openness of poetic processes, and can break the tradition of the
spirit of romance: "Where among these did the spirit reside/that restores
the land to productive order?" Chanting the declension of presidents since
Lincoln, Duncan laments,

> How sad "amid lanes and through old woods"
>   echoes Whitman's love for Lincoln!
>
> There is no continuity then.

Despite the "smokes of continual ravage," the music of spiritual kinship
can occasionally be heard by the poet:

> It is across great scars of wrong
> I reach toward the song of kindred men
> and strike again the naked string
> old Whitman sang from. Glorious mistake!
> that cried:
>
> "The theme is creative and has vista."
> "He is the president of regulation." (OF 64)

Whitman's words from the 1855 Preface to Leaves of Grass are mistaken
in the specific light of historical realities, but the mistake is glorious
in the sense Duncan speaks of, the spirit of the proposition creating a
compelling moment which can inspire later poets. Whitman had argued that
poetry is generated in the painful throes of "doubts, suspense . . . sur-
rounding war and revolution" (CP 230). Duncan accedes in this, finding
that poetry issues from and entertains repeated patterns of "order and dis-
order" (MF 249), necessary for the imagination's health. In "The Pindar
Poem," he continues:

> I see always the under side turning,
> fumes that injure the tender landscape.
> From which up break
> lilac blossoms of courage in daily act
> striving to meet a natural measure. (OF 64)

The natural measure is the signature of the visionary poet who balances his
and the world's mutations with glimpses of nature's processes, primal pres-
ences, or first forms; these in turn command him to find a structure that
can contain "the variety of man's experience of what is real" (TLM 12).
Composing a "true epithalamium" where discordant opposites enter (and re-
define) the boundaries of the poem and "dance together" (TLM 38), remains
for Duncan the high task of Romantic poets, a company he willingly enters
with Whitman.

II

Whitman revolutionized poetry, discovering an expansive form to express his unconventional subjects, themes and ideas. Leaves of Grass is the archetypal organic poem, its open and processual method as much a part of the subject matter as its content.[7] In Duncan's apt description, Leaves was "not a blueprint but an evolution of spirit in terms of variety and a thicket of potentialities." He continues:

> His own work in poetry he sees so, moved by generative urgencies toward the fulfillment of a multitude of latent possibilities. And so we are actually in the throes, the throes in which the ideal and the reality are at work . . . not recollections in tranquillity, nor summations of study, but, to be in the throes of a poetry in which the poet seeks to keep alive as a generative possibility a force and intent hidden in the very beginning of things, long before the beginning of the poem, the *Leaves of Grass* having its form not, as the *Divina Commedia* had, as the paradigm of an existing eternal form, but as the ever flowing, ever Self-creative ground of a process in which forces of awareness, Self-awareness, of declaration and of longing work and rework in the evolution of what they are, the evolution of a creative intention that moves not toward the satisfaction of some prescribed form but towards the fulfillment of a multitude of possibilities out of its seed. Whitman begins to see as we do, the flow of some prescribed form but toward the fulfillment of a multitude of as a field of being, not toward progress and improvement but toward variety and an awareness of variety. (CPR 76–77)

We can take Duncan's appraisal here as self-revelatory. Significantly, his adoption of the poem as a field of composition in which the poet becomes a unifying register of perceptions parallels Whitman's fictive strategy. Whitman realized that he could not fully capture an evolving reality: "The word I myself put primarily for the description of [my poems] as they stand at last, is the word Suggestiveness. I round and finish little, if anything; and could not, consistently with my scheme. The reader will always have his or her part to do, just as much as I have had mine" (LG 570).

To testify and embody the ceaseless variety of life, both poets seek an open form where disturbances and interruptions can freely enter the fabric of the poem. "For all these new and evolutionary facts, meanings, new poetic messages," Whitman stated, "new forms and expressions, are inevitable" (LG 565). Duncan concurs: "In the work itself the multiplicity of

wonderings makes for impulse after impulse toward larger form, broken by
other apprehended forms. It is in the departures from what is forming
that the poetic of the rug appears--a form disturbed thruout by the direc-
tive of many forms" (HD II, 7, 59). The basis for open form resides in
organic growth, and the poet's willingness to follow "the primary processes
of thought and feeling, the immediate impulse of the psychic life" (TOU
136) which occur as the poem is in composition. In "Food for Fire, Food
for Thought," Duncan says, "This is what I wanted for the last poem,/a
loosening of conventions and a return to open form" (OF 95). Duncan, who
abhors the strictures of conventional form, would fully approve of Whitman's
rejection:

> The poetic quality is not marshalled in rhyme or uniformity
> or abstract addresses to things nor in melancholy complaints
> or good precepts, but is the life of these and much else and is
> in the soul. The profit of rhyme is that it drops seeds of a
> sweeter and more luxuriant rhyme, and of uniformity that it
> conveys itself into its own roots in the ground out of sight.
> The rhyme and uniformity of perfect poems show the free growth
> of metrical laws and bud from them as unerringly and loosely
> as lilacs or roses on a bush, and takes shapes as compact as
> the shapes of chestnuts and oranges and melons and pears, and
> shed the perfume impalpable to form. (LG 714)

Compare Duncan's "Yes, As a Look Springs to Its Face":

> Poems come up from a ground so
> to illustrate the ground, approximate
> a lingering of eternal image, a need
> known only in its being found ready.
>
> The force that words obey in song
> the rose and artichoke obey
> in their unfolding towards their form. (OF 60)

The large form each poet works toward is the result of a mutual, organic
coinherence of all the parts of the poem.

Where Whitman turned to the "ensemble" (LG 23) as the only structure
large enough to suggest the comprehensiveness of his vision, Duncan has
spoken of his poetry as a collage where a number of elements enter the poem

to create new complexes of meaning. The importance of the collage tech-
nique is evident in "The Collage, Passages 6":

> [I mean to force up emblems again into these passages of a
> poetry, passages made conglomerate, the pyramid that dense, a
> mountain, immovable; cut ways in it then and trick the walls
> with images establishing space and time for more than the maker
> knows he acknowledges, in it]   (BB 19)

In a revealing passage in "Changing Perspective," Duncan joins several
significant aspects in his intellectual heritage:

> Democracy was the politics of ensemble, as Hegel's was the
> philosophy of ensemble, and Whitman saw his *Leaves of Grass*
> as belonging to the poetics of the ensemblist. The word
> "ensemblist" he italicizes. Dreaming of the ensemble of
> created and creating forms, Whitman was the poet of primary
> intuitions, ancestor of Whitehead's *Process and Reality* and
> of our own vision of creation where now we see all of life
> as unfoldings, the revelations of a field of potentialities
> and latencies toward species and individuals hidden in the
> DNA, a field of generations larger than our humanity. Back
> of our own contemporary arts of the collagist, the assembler
> of forms, is the ancestral, protean concept, wider and deeper,
> of the poet as devotée of the ensemble. Back of the field as
> it appears in Olson's proposition of composition by field
> is the concept of the cosmos as a field of fields. Our field
> in which we see the form of the poem happening belongs ul-
> timately to, is an immediate apprehension of or sense of
> locality in "the infinite variety, the past, the surroundings
> of to-day, or what may happen in the future," the grand ensem-
> ble Whitman evokes. (CPR 78)

The Passages and the Structures of Rime are so expansive and receptive that
they welcome the varied intrusions of the poet's consciousness, laying out
before him a polysemous correspondence of elements (BB x) both known and
hinted, which force each reader to reassess what unity means.

The "oracular" voice sustains energy for this extended structure
because fresh beginnings (CPR 85) are necessary to approach the seminal
source of meaning, and to "read the hidden presences in things" (MF 239).
Duncan considers Whitman's sexual metaphors as the potent "basis of his
poetic understanding--where it arises in the course of the climax of a

love-grip or of a poetic seizure, has the authenticity of a primal intui-
tion." Like the psychoanalyst, the true poet, accepting the bardic role,
searches for "a return into present feeling, into consciousness, of the
origins, the return of a life . . . going back beyond the boundaries of
species, to the Primal Scene of Creation. . ." (CPR 95-96). Thus, for
example, "Starting from Paumanok" sings of "A world primal again, vistas
of glory incessant and branching (LG 26), and in "Final Confessions-Lit-
erary Tests," Whitman says, "I cannot divest my appetite of literature, yet
I find myself eventually trying it all by nature--first premises . . . the
crowning results of all, laws, tallies and proofs" (CP 197). In "Another
Animadversion," an "old lady . . ./turning over the pages of *Leaves of
Grass*" (OF 85) presents one version of the possible return "to roots of
first feeling" which the poem enacts. Every poet, Duncan writes, "seeks to
commune with creation [in Democratic Vistas, Whitman said "commune with the
unutterable"], with the divine world [Whitman: "reach the divine levels"];
that is to say, he seeks the most real form in language. "But this most
real is something we apprehend; the poem, the creation of the poem, is it-
self our primary experience of it" (TOU 135-136). Attainment of mythic
origins is possible when the poet assumes the visionary role, and enters a
form where mystery is alive. In "The Architecture, Passages 9," Duncan
incorporates a quotation which provides a reflexive comment on the entire
series:

> ". . . it must have recesses. There is a great charm in a
> room broken up in plan, where that slight feeling of mystery is
> given to it which arises when you cannot see the whole room from
> any one place . . when there is always something around the
> corner"   (BB 26)

As glosses here, we should recall Whitman's note to himself, dated pre-1855:
"Something behind or afterward--Leave the impression that no matter what is
said, there is something greater to say--something behind still more marvel-
lous and beautiful,"[8] or his conviction that at its best, "poetic lore is
like what may be heard of conversation in the dusk, from speakers far or
hid, of which we get only a few broken murmurs. What is not gather'd is
far more--perhaps the main thing" (CP 196). Poetry as a fictive engagement

of the potency ascribed to first forms can only be approximate because it
is impossible for the poet to attain a lasting habitation with primordial
design.   In "Passages 33," Duncan laments:

                                                        no one

                         nor poet
                         nor writer of words

              can contrive to do justice to the beauty of that
                 design he designs from

                    we pretend to speak   the language is not ours
              and we move upward beyond our own powers into
                    words again beyond us unsure measures   (T 11)

The threat of the waning clarity or efficacy of the sacramental presence
remains for Duncan the greatest disaster for the imagination. Again, in
"Passages 33," he concludes with Whitman's celebrated hieroglyph of hope,
presented as an urgent prescription for salvation in our time:

                    A million reapers come to cut down
                    the leaves of grass we hope to live by

                       except we give ourselves over to the

                       end of things. (T 13)

    Whitman is as much a formative influence on Duncan's work as Dante or
Blake, providing him with a special legacy that answers Duncan's imagina-
tive needs: "Whitman nowhere presents the architectural ordering of the
universe and spirit that Dante presents. . . . He is the grand proposer of
questions not to be settled, the poet of unsettling propositions" (CPR 75).
Duncan has called the Romantic movement in poetry "the intellectual adven-
ture of not knowing" (TLM 62), and he is firmly grounded in that tradition.
Striving to extend the thematic and formal boundaries of the poem, Duncan
goes beyond a concern for the poem itself into a total and often mystical
participation in the rites of the "evolving and continuing work of poetry

[he] could never complete--a poetry that had begun long before [he] was
born and that extended beyond [his] own work in it" (MF 230). His most
characteristic poem in this vein, Passages, can end only with his life--
the process of the entire venture more important than the product. Again
we hear Whitman, this time from the 1872 Preface to Leaves of Grass: "But
what is life but an experiment? and mortality but an exercise? with refer-
ence to results beyond. And so shall my poems be. If incomplete here,
and superfluous there, n'importe--the earnest trial and persistent explora-
tion shall at least be mine, and other success failing, shall be success
enough" (LG·740). The premise of incompleteness, the weight of the "never
achiev'd poem" (CP 194), is a heavy burden indeed, but one which Robert
Duncan, of all our contemporary poets, is best able to carry to fruition.

NOTES

[1]Robert Duncan, "Changing Perspectives in Reading Whitman," in Edwin Havi-
land Miller, ed., The Artistic Legacy of Walt Whitman: A Tribute to Gay
Wilson Allen (New York: New York Univ. Press, 1970, p. 86. Hereafter
cited as CPR.

[2]Walt Whitman, Leaves of Grass, Comprehensive Reader's Edition, ed. Harold
W. Blodgett and Sculley Bradley (New York: W. W. Norton, 1968), p. 450
Hereafter cited as LG.

[3]Robert Bertholf, "The Fictive Voice in the Poem: Chapter I, Part I," Cred-
ences, I (1974), 84. See Diane Middlebrook, Walt Whitman and Wallace Stev-
Stevens (Ithaca: Cornell Univ. Press, 1974), pp. 18-19.

[4]Robert Duncan, "Man's Fulfillment in Order and Strife," Caterpillar, 8/9
(October, 1969), 237. Hereafter cited as MF.

[5]The Works of Walt Whitman, Vol. II. The Collected Prose, ed. Malcolm
Cowley (New York: Minerva Press, 1969), p. 232. Hereafter cited as CP.

[6]Walt Whitman, The Eighteenth Presidency!, ed. Edward Grier (Lawrence:
Univ. of Kansas Press, 1956). Whitman's essay was never published in his
lifetime. Grier's edition is based on sets of extant proof sheet with
corrections by Whitman. The section Duncan incorporates in "The Fire"
appears on pp. 22-23 of Grier's edition.

[7]See Albert Gelpi, The Tenth Muse: The Psyche of the American Poet (Cam-
bridge: Harvard Univ. Press, 1975), pp. 174-179, for a collaborative judg-
ment on Whitman's importance to open-form poetry.

[8]Quoted by Harold Blodgett, "Teaching 'Song of Myself,'" ESQ, #22 (1961),2.

ROBERT DUNCAN: A SELECTED CHECKLIST

HEAVENLY CITY EARTHLY CITY. Berkeley: Bern Porter, 1947.

POEMS 1948-49. Berkeley: Berkeley Miscellany Editions, 1949.

MEDIEVAL SCENES. San Francisco: Centaur Press, 1950; reprinted as MEDIEVAL SCENES 1950 and 1959 (with a preface by the author and an afterword by Robert Bertholf) Kent, Ohio: The Kent State University Libraries, 1978.

FRAGMENTS OF A DISORDERED DEVOTION. San Francisco: privately printed, 1952; reprinted, San Francisco: Gnomon Press; Toronto: Island Press, 1966.

THE SONG OF THE BORDER-GUARD. Black Mountain, N.C.: Nicola Cernovich, 1952. Broadside.

CAESAR'S GATE POEMS 1949-1950 WITH COLLAGES BY JESS COLLINS. Palma de Mallorca: Divers Press, 1955; reprinted as CAESAR'S GATE POEMS 1949-1950 WITH PASTE-UPS BY JESS. Berkeley: Sand Dollar, 1972.

LETTERS POEMS MCMLIII-MCMLVI. Highlands, N.C.: Jargon, 1958.

FAUST FOUTU AN ENTERTAINMENT IN FOUR PARTS. Stinson Beach, Calif.: Enkidu Surrogate, 1959.

SELECTED POEMS. San Francisco: City Lights Books, 1959.

THE OPENING OF THE FIELD. New York: Grove Press, 1960; reprinted, London: Jonathan Cape, 1969; and New York: New Directions, 1973.

UNKINGD BY AFFECTION. San Francisco: San Francisco Arts Festival Commission, 1963. Broadside.

AS TESTIMONY: THE POEM & THE SCENE. San Francisco, White Rabbit Press, 1964.

WRITING WRITING A COMPOSITION BOOK STEIN IMITATIONS. Albuquerque, N.M.: Sumbooks, 1964.

ROOTS AND BRANCHES. New York: Scribners, 1964; reprinted, New York: New Directions, 1968; and London: Jonathan Cape, 1970.

WINE. Berekely: Oyez, 1964. Broadside.

MEDEA AT KOLCHIS THE MAIDENHEAD. Berkeley: Oyez, 1965.

THE SWEETNESS AND GREATNESS OF DANTE'S DIVINE COMEDY. San Francisco: Open Space, 1965.

UP RISING. Oyez: Berkeley, 1965. Broadside.

PASSAGES 22-27 OF THE WAR. Berkeley: Oyez, 1966.

THE YEARS AS CATCHES FIRST POEMS (1939-1946). Berkeley: Oyez, 1966.

SIX PROSE PIECES. Mt. Horeb, Wis.: Perishable Press, M.CM.LXVI.

A BOOK OF RESEMBLANCES: POEMS 1950-1953. New Haven: Henry Wenning, 1966.

THE CAT AND THE BLACKBIRD. San Francisco: White Rabbit Press, 1967.

CHRISTMAS PRESENT, CHRISTMAS PRESENCE. Los Angeles: Black Sparrow Press,
     1967.

EPILOGS. Los Angeles: Black Sparrow Press, 1967.

THE TRUTH & LIFE OF MYTH AN ESSAY IN ESSENTIAL AUTOBIOGRAPHY. New York:
     House of Books, Ltd., 1968; reprinted, Fremont, Michigan: The
     Sumac Press (in cooperation with Soma Books), 1973.

NAMES OF PEOPLE. Los Angeles: Black Sparrow Press, 1968.

BENDING THE BOW. New York: New Directions, 1968.

MY MOTHER WOULD BE A FALCONRESS. Berkeley: Oyez, 1968. Broadside.

THE FIRST DECADE SELECTED POEMS 1940-1950. London: Fulcrum Press, 1969.

DERIVATIONS SELECTED FROM 1950-1956. London: Fulcrum Press, 1969.

ACHILLES' SONG. New York: Phoenix Book Shop, 1969.

PLAY TIME PSEUDO STEIN. New York: The Poet's Press, 1969; reprinted, San
     Francisco: The Tenth Muse, 1969.

POETIC DISTURBANCES. Berkeley: Maya Quarto, 1970.

BRING IT UP FROM THE DARK. Berkeley: Cody's Books, 1970. Broadside.

A SELECTION OF 65 DRAWINGS FROM ONE DRAWING-BOOK 1952-1956. Los Angeles:
     Black Sparrow Press, 1970.

TRIBUNALS PASSAGES 31-35. Los Angeles: Black Sparrow Press, 1970.

ROBERT DUNCAN AN INTERVIEW BY GEORGE BOWERING & ROBERT HOGG. Toronto:
     The Coach House Press, 1971.

GROUND WORK. San Francisco, privately printed, 1971.

THE MUSEUM. Brooklyn, Australia: Beyond Poetry, 1972.

IN MEMORIAM WALLACE STEVENS. Storrs: The University of Connecticut, 1972.

POEMS FROM THE MARGINS OF THOM GUNN'S MOLY. San Francisco: privately
     printed, 1972.

A SEVENTEENTH CENTURY SUITE IN HOMAGE TO THE METAPHYSICAL GENIUS IN ENGLISH
     POETRY 1590/1690: BEING IMITATIONS, DERIVATIONS & VARIATIONS UPON
     CERTAIN CONCEITS AND FINDINGS MADE AMONG STRONG LINES. San Francisco:
     privately printed, 1973.

FEB 22, 1973. Berkeley: Arif Press, 1973. Broadside.

AN ODE AND ARCADIA (with Jack Spicer). Berkeley: Ark Press, 1974.

DANTE. Canton, N.Y.: Institute of Further Studies, 1974.

THE VENICE POEM. Sydney, Australia: Prism, 1975.

A SONG FROM THE STRUCTURES OF TIME RINGING AS THE POET PAUL CELAN SINGS:
     Malakoff, France: Orange Export Ltd., 1977.

THE SENTINALS. Kent, Ohio: The Costmary Press, 1979. Broadside.

Others:

Donald Allen, ed. THE NEW AMERICAN POETRY. New York: Grove Press, 1960.

Howard Nemerov, ed. POETS ON POETRY. New York and London: Basic Books,
     Inc., 1966. (RD's essay, "Towards An Open Universe," pp. 133-146.)

Audit/Poetry (featuring Robert Duncan), IV, 3 (1967).

Donald Allen and Warren Tallman, eds., THE POETICS OF THE NEW AMERICAN
     POETRY. New York: Grove Press, 1973.

MAPS, 6 (1974) [special issue on Robert Duncan].

"The H.D. Book"

Part I: Beginnings.

Chapter 1: Coyote's Journal, 5/6 (1966), 8-31.

Chapter 2: Coyote's Journal, 8 (1967) 27-35.

Chapter 3: Tri-Quarterly, 12 (Spring 1968), 67-82.

Chapter 4: Tri-Quarterly, 12 (Spring 1968), 82-98.

Chapter 5: "Occult Matters," Stony Brook, 1/2 (Fall 1968), 4-19.

Chapter 6: "Rites of Participation, Part I," Caterpillar 1 (October 1967),
           6-29.

Chapter 6: "Rites of Participation, Part II," Caterpillar 2 (January
           1968), 125-54.

Part II: Nights and Days

"From the Day Book,--excerpts from an extended study of H.D.'s poetry"
     Origin 10, first series (July 1963), 1-47.

Chapter 1: Sumac, I, 1 (Fall 1968), 101-46.

Chapter 2: Caterpillar, 6 (January 1969), 16-38.

Chapter 3: Io, 6 (Summer 1969), 117-40.

Chapter 4: Caterpillar, 7 (April 1969), 27-60.

Chapter 5: section one, Stony Brook, 3/4 (Fall 1969), 336-47.

Chapter 6: from chapter 11, IO, 10 (1971), 212-15.

Chapter 6: section two, Credences, 2 (August 1975), 50-52.

Chapter 7: Credences, 2 (August 1975), 53-67.

Chapter 8: Credences, 2 (August 1975), 68-94.

Chapter 9: Chicago Review, 30, 3 (Winter 1979), 37-88.

NOTES ON CONTRIBUTORS

HELEN ADAM is a ballad writer born in Scotland in 1909, who now lives and
writes in America. Her most recent books are Turn Again To Me (N.Y.:
Kulchur Press, 1977), and Ghosts and Grinning Shadows (Brooklyn:
Hanging Loose Press, 1979), with collage illustrations by the author.
Her interest in both poetry and prose is chiefly with the weird and
the uncanny, and his mastery of this realm of beautiful and hidden
mysteries is what she most admires in Duncan's work.

ROBERT J. BERTHOLF is Curator, Poetry and Rare Books Collection at SUNY
Buffalo.

DON BYRD is Associate Professor of English at SUNY Albany. He is the au-
thor of a book of poems, Aesop's Garden (1976) and a critical study
of Charles Olson, Charles Olson and the Writing of the Republic,
forthcoming from the University of Illinois Press.

JESS COLLINS is now at work on a large canvas entitled "Narkissos" which
culminates three series of work, Translations, Salvages and Paste-Ups.

MICHAEL DAVIDSON is Director of The Archive for New Poetry, and a member of
the Literature Department at The University of California San Diego,
La Jolla. He is the author of numerous articles on contemporary
poetry, and a book of poems, The Mutabilities & The Foul Papers (1976).

ROBERT DEMOTT is a Full Professor of English at Ohio University, where he
teaches American literature. His essays, articles, reviews and poetry
have appeared in Journal of Modern Literature, Paideuma, Modern Fiction
Studies, Steinbeck Quarterly, Western Humanities Review, Quarterly
West, Ohio Review and elsewhere.

SEÁN GOLDEN is Assistant Professor of English at the University of Notre
Dame, and is presently preparing a collection of Irish literature.

THOM GUNN was born in England in 1929. He has spent half his life in
Northern California, most of it in San Francisco. His recent books of
poetry are Jack Straw's Castle (1976), Poems 1950-1966: A Selection
(1969) and Games of Chance.

LOU HARRISON, the distinguished American composer and conductor, has, among
the hosts of his writing and recordings, set Duncan's poem "Uprising"
to music. He presently lives in Aptos, California.

MARK JOHNSON is Assistant Professor of English at Central Missouri State
University. His most recent publications have been on Walter Percy,
and contemporary poetry.

R. B. KITAJ is a painter who lives in London and Catalonia.

GERRIT LANSING is a poet who published a little magazine Set (2 issues, 1961-1963) from Gloucester, Mass. His principal book of poems is The Heavenly Tree Grows Downward (Plainfield, Vt.: North Atlantic Books, 1977). He presently lives in Annapolis, Maryland.

DENISE LEVERTOV's most recent books are Life in the Forest (1978), and Collected Earlier Poems, 1940-1960 (1979), both published by New Directions. Awaiting publication is Pig's Dreams: Scenes from the Life of Sylvia, with pictures by Liebe Holton. She is active in the anti-nuclear movement.

MICHAEL and JOANNA McCLURE still live and work in San Francisco. His most recent books of poems is Antechamber & Other Poems (N.Y.: New Directions, 1978) and her most recent book is Wolf Eyes (San Francisco: Bearthm Press, 1974).

NATHANIEL MACKEY is the author of numerous articles and poems, and now teaches on the Board of Studies in Literature at The University of California at Santa Cruz.

ERIC MOTTRAM is now Reader in American Literature at The University of London, and Lecturer in American Studies, Institute of United States Studies, The University of London. He is the author of twelve books of poetry, a critical book, William Burroughs: The Algebra of Need (1977), and The Kenneth Rexroth Reader (1974).

IAN W. REID is Professor of Literature at Deakin University, Victoria, Australia, and Associate Editor of Meanjin Quarterly. In addition to numerous articles and translations, he has published several books, both of criticism (including The Short Story and Fiction and the Great Depression in Australia and New Zealand) and of poetry (including Undercover Agent).

HAMILTON and MARY TYLER still live in rural Sonoma Co., California. Mary taught classes in English, emphasizing poetry, until her recent retirement. Hamilton has authored these books: Pueblo Gods and Myths (1964), Pueblo Animals and Myths (1975), and Pueblo Birds and Myths (1979), all from the University of Oklahoma Press. Organic Gardening Without Poisons (1970) and Gourmet Gardening, from Van Nostrand Reinhold. The Swallowtail Butterflies of North America (1975) and Owls by Day and Night (1978), both from Naturegraph Publishers.

JAYNE L. WALKER is Assistant Professor of English and Comparative Literature at The University of California, Berkeley. She is presently at work on a full length study of Gertrude Stein.